KU-263-660

Cardiff Libraries
www.cardiff.gov.uk/libraries

Llyfrgelloedd Caerdydd
www.caerdydd.gov.uk/llyfrgelloedd

ACC. No: 03201828

Cecily Neville

Thou shalt, where thou livest, year by year
The most part of thy time spend
In making of a glorious legend
Of good women, maidens and wives
That were true in loving all their lives.

Chaucer, *The Legend of Good Women*

Cecily Neville

Mother of Kings

AMY LICENCE

AMBERLEY

941.04

For Tom, Rufus and Robin

First published 2014

Amberley Publishing
The Hill, Stroud
Gloucestershire, GL5 4EP

www.amberley-books.com

Copyright © Amy Licence 2014

The right of Amy Licence to be identified as the Author
of this work has been asserted in accordance with the
Copyrights, Designs and Patents Act 1988.

All rights reserved. No part of this book may be reprinted
or reproduced or utilised in any form or by any electronic,
mechanical or other means, now known or hereafter invented,
including photocopying and recording, or in any information
storage or retrieval system, without the permission in writing
from the Publishers.

British Library Cataloguing in Publication Data.
A catalogue record for this book is available from the British Library.

ISBN 978 1 4456 2123 4 (hardback)
ISBN 978 1 4456 2132 6 (ebook)

Typeset in 10pt on 12pt Sabon.
Typesetting and Origination by Amberley Publishing.
Printed in the UK.

Contents

	Genealogical Tables	6
	Introduction	9
	Prologue, 1495	13
1	A Significant Year, 1415	17
2	'Rose of Raby', 1415–1429	25
3	Duke of York, 1411–1429	37
4	His Young Duchess, 1429–1437	51
5	Becoming a Mother, 1438–1442	65
6	The Question of Edward, 1442–1445	77
7	Loss of Focus, 1446–1452	85
8	The Lord Protector's Wife, 1453–1455	101
9	Fortunes of War, 1455–1459	115
10	Fickle Fortune, 1459–1460	131
11	In the Name of the Father, 1461–1464	145
12	A Family at Love and War, 1465–1471	163
13	The King's Mother, 1472–1483	179
14	Slanders, 1483–1485	191
15	Old Age, 1485–1495	203
	Epilogue	213
	Notes	219
	Bibliography	235
	List of Illustrations	241
	Acknowledgements	243
	Index	251

Cecily Neville's immediate family.

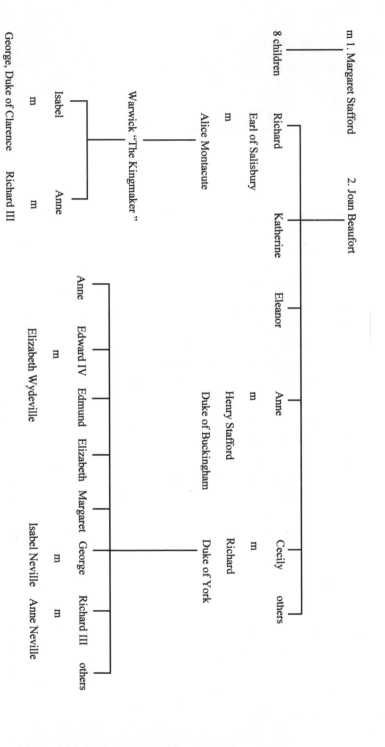

Descendants of Cecily Neville and Richard, Duke of York.

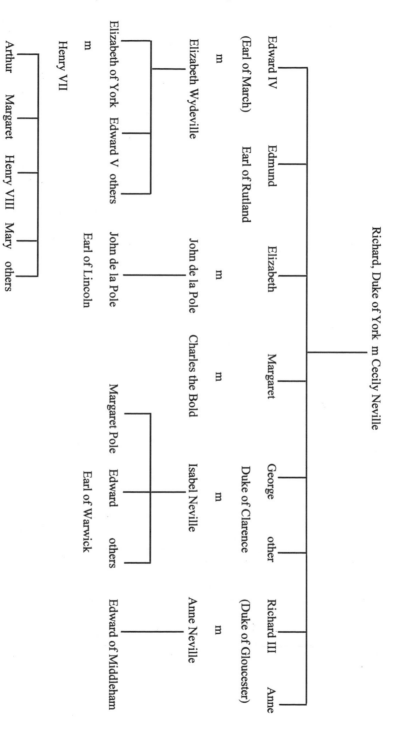

The descent of Cecily Neville and Richard, Duke of York, from Edward III.

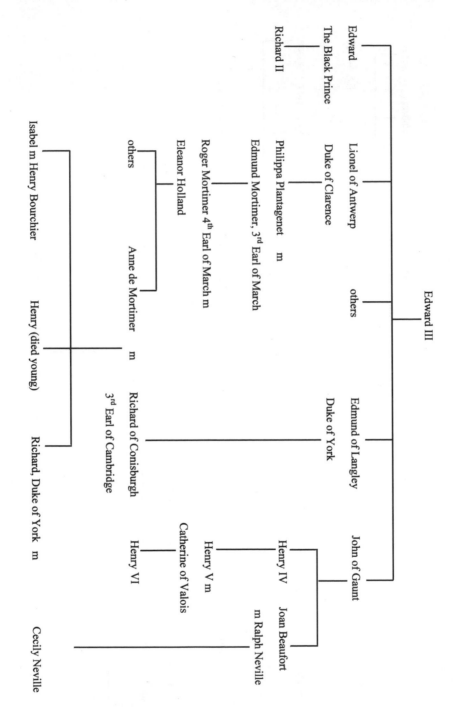

Introduction

But the mother of Richard III was no common character. Although her actions are not absolutely interwoven with the public records of the land as were those of her husband, she was nevertheless fully as remarkable for the varied fortunes that marked her troubled life, and for the vicissitudes to which she was exposed in consequence of her political connection. She is therefore entitled to a distinct and especial notice, not merely as one of the most eminent women in the age in which she flourished, but because Cecily, Duchess of York, will be found a most important personage, and to have occupied a very prominent position in the eventful life of her youngest son Richard III ... She ... evinced a greatness of mind during periods of unexampled trial, and displayed a zeal and rectitude of purpose in the active performance of conjugal and maternal duties of no ordinary description, that render her even more an object of admiration, than of sympathy for the poignant sorrows which marked her sad and eventful career.[1]

Writing a biography of Cecily Neville has been rather like striking a series of matches in the dark. There are moments when she steps forward and claims the historical limelight, when rumours question the paternity of her son Edward, or the moment she learns of his victory following the Battle of Towton. But her voice is muted. A couple of her letters survive and her household ordinances outline her routine in old age; more faintly still, she can be glimpsed inside the Great Hall at Raby Castle, or among the ruins at Fotheringhay or Berkhamsted. Most often, though, she is omitted altogether from the records, even at times when she must have been suffering or celebrating the most. A large proportion of her life lies amid the darkness of lost records and burned letters, the rubble of the houses in which she feasted and bore her children, and the formality of official documentation that marks what she was doing but not how she was feeling.

Between the words of Caroline Halstead in 1844, in italics above, and the publication of Sarah Gristwood's *Blood Sisters* in 2012, there has been little critical attention devoted to Cecily Neville, Duchess of York. Scholarly essays have focused on her patterns of reading or the religious bequests she made at the end of her life. Whole swathes of her existence, including the early years of her marriage, have remained something of a historical black hole. This is down to the paucity of material that survives. It is not a reflection of Cecily's long and fascinating life, which has captured the attention of novelists and dramatists, happily unrestricted by the rules that govern non-fiction and therefore able to create a vivid and memorable portrayal of 'Proud Cis' or the 'Rose of Raby', as Cecily is known to legend.

Some may question the wisdom of attempting to write a biography which, of necessity, must impose a degree of conjecture over the bare scaffold of facts. Yet, the further and wider the researcher digs, the more can be discovered regarding the circumstances of Cecily's life, her family, her homes and experiences. In attempting to write the first full-length non-fiction study of the duchess, I have searched through the primary sources of the day – the Parliamentary Records, Patent Rolls, Fine Rolls, surviving letters, chroniclers and accounts – for any snippet that adds to the wider picture of her life. Sometimes a single reference has allowed me to place her in a particular location, which has considerably altered the fabric of the story. By the same means, I have been able to determine the locations of friends and family members, to weave their stories in with hers. For, above all, Cecily's life is a blend of the political and personal, perhaps to a greater extent than many of her contemporaries, given that she bore at least thirteen children, some of whom would play leading roles in the history of England, France and Burgundy. There are also a surprising number of satirical verses surviving from the fifteenth century that deal, overtly or covertly, with the themes and events of the day. A few refer specifically to Cecily's family, while others relate their activities or comment upon events in which they were involved. Many of these have been overlooked in traditional accounts of the Yorkist dynasty, although they are just as valuable as the more popularly cited prose sources and chronicles in their reflection of contemporary feeling.

When I planned this book, in the summer of 2013, the time was right to recreate Cecily's story. Her image had become distorted by popular culture to the extent that her portrayal was somewhat one-dimensional, simply because this was the only dimension known or required. She struck me as a sufficiently interesting figure to stand alone, instead of being a foil in another woman's story. With imagination and a thorough collation of all the scattered jigsaw pieces, no matter how small, it was possible to compose a narrative of her life that made sense and allowed her to breathe a little. In some cases it has been necessary to imagine how she felt, to extend empathy across the divide of centuries, which has been achieved by comparing the lives of her contemporaries or understanding the expectations of her era. The medieval mind, though, remains something of a closed world, determined by belief systems that appear alien to the modern world, and subtleties that have been entirely lost. In many cases, therefore, it has been more sensible to suggest possible responses and interpretations rather than to impose them.

Cecily was clearly a strong, determined and proud woman, the centre of an extensive family network that reached far across the dynasties of York and Lancaster. It was the closed nature of this small genetic pool that provoked the conflicts of the mid-fifteenth century and set her children, nephews and grandchildren against each other. The implications of their infighting would continue for generations after Cecily's own death, well into the reigns of her Tudor descendants. Remarkably, she reached her eightieth year shortly before she died and outlived the majority of those with whom she shared the most important years of her life. In many ways she was typical of a medieval noblewoman, with her arranged marriage, large family and piety, but she was also extraordinary because of the position she occupied in the shadow of the throne. Descended from Edward III through her mother, she became the wife of a man whose ancestral line should have made him England's king. Shortly before his birth, that right was derailed and, with his wife at his side, he spent decades attempting to restore his position. Then, just as this dream was becoming a reality, fate dealt Cecily a terrible blow. She would go on to become the mother of kings but perhaps Cecily Neville, Duchess of York, was the best queen England never had. This is her story.

Prologue
1495

A man joyeth sumtyme in gold and sylver, and in gret substaunce of erdly goods, in bewte of women, but this joy is not perfyght, but this joy is not stabill, but it is mutabill as a shadow; for he that this joyth in the bewte of his wyffe, it may fortune to morwyn he shall folwyn her to chirch upon a bere.[1]

On 31 May 1495, an old lady was putting the finishing touches to her will. It had been a long and difficult process. In fact, a full two months had passed since the first words were inscribed on the page, and, since then, several different hands had added a line here or there, giving the document a hurried air. Over that time, the many rooms of Berkhamsted Castle had disgorged a lifetime's possessions, the cupboards and coffers opened, the gold boxes bestowed. Outside the windows, spring had slowly turned to summer, bursting out greenly in the Hertfordshire countryside. She had watched the days lengthen as she lay propped up alone on a feather bed hung with embroidered panels.

Cecily, Duchess of York, had once been a famous beauty of her age. She was a beloved wife, a proud, 'noble princesse',[2] a matriarch dressed in jewels, at the centre of political events in England, France and Ireland. For a few weeks, she had even come breathlessly close to becoming queen. At the age of eighty, she had outlived many of her thirteen children, her twenty-two legitimate grandchildren and thirty-one great-grandchildren. Two of her sons had sat on the English throne and three of them had met with violent deaths. Her family had been irrevocably shaken by personal and political scandals over which she had little control. The will she dictated in 1495 made proud mention of the fact that she was the mother of the late King Edward IV, but there was no reference to her younger son, who became Richard III. This was probably an example of the pragmatism she had learned through life; after all, the man who killed Richard now sat on England's throne and had taken Cecily's granddaughter as his wife. To him, she left some money and two gold cups.[3]

But gold cups meant little to her now, they were easily given away. In recent years, she had lived as a vowess or lay sister, running her household like a religious establishment, with prayers and devotional readings, business and contemplation.[4] The largest portion of her bequests was made up of religious items, such as altar candles, cloths and crosses. In the past, she had revelled in possessions such as the cloth of estate, the gold spoons set with diamonds and cushions made from purple cloth of gold. Hanging in her wardrobe were blue satin gowns furred with ermine; a short gown of crimson velvet lined with black; a gold girdle with a diamond-studded flower, a sapphire, an amethyst and eight pearls; a double string of white amber beads, set between large golden ones; a kirtle of purple silk decorated with silver gilt; and a gold enamelled pomander.[5] It was a wardrobe fit for a queen. To her grandson, Prince Arthur, she bequeathed the most poignant bequest of all: a set of bed hangings decorated with the image of the Wheel of Fortune. It was an image that could be taken as an apt comment on her own life.

In her chamber at Berkhamsted Castle, on 31 May, she dictated her final wishes to her secretary. In the deepening silence, his pen scratched out her words across the paper. Her confessor, Sir William Grant, was close by, waiting to hear her final words and administer the Catholic rite of extreme unction. Her witnesses were Master Richard Lessy, the dean of her chapel, the clerk of her kitchen, Richard Brocas, and Gervays Cressy. She was well enough to reach her crabbed hand forward and write her name, her 'signemanuell',[6] before pressing her oval-shaped personal seal in to the hot wax and making the document official.

Cecily committed her soul to God and her body to lie beside 'my moost entirely best beloved Lord and housbond' Richard, 'in his tumbe within the collegiate church at Fotheringhay'.[7] Thirty-five years had passed since his death and she had had plenty of time to anticipate their reunion in the afterlife; there were many other loved ones also waiting to receive her there. She died soon after adding her signature to the document. It may have been later that same day or, as the *Chronicle of London* suggests, early in June. In accordance with her wishes, she was buried in the church of St Mary and All Saints, beside the Northamptonshire home she had shared with her husband and children, miles from the scene of her death.

That August, Cecily's will was proved at Lamberhithe, the London palace of the archbishops of Canterbury. The commission was granted to Richard Lessy to execute her many bequests, and the business of clearing Berkhamsted began. By then, her body had been transported 70 miles north and placed beside that of her husband, Richard, Duke of York, in the chancel of the choir at Fotheringhay church. As a widow in 1476, she had witnessed the creation of the magnificent tomb their sons had chosen in his honour, when they removed York's mortal remains from a post-battle grave and reinterred him close to home. Now she lay beside him, having outlived them all.

However, the duke and duchess were not to remain in peace for long. According to an account of 1634, the chancel was destroyed during the Reformation, 'that fury of knocking churches and sacred monuments in the head'[8] instigated by their great-grandson, Henry VIII. Their bodies were then moved outside, in to the graveyard, until Elizabeth I visited the site. Dismayed at the state of the memorial to her ancestors, she ordered their tomb to be rebuilt. In 1566, the grave was opened and the bodies of the duke and duchess 'appeared very plainly to be discerned'. Around her neck, Duchess Cecily was wearing a silk ribbon, from which hung a papal indulgence, a remission for earthly sins, 'penned in a very fine Romane hand ... as faire and fresh to be read, as it had been written but yesterday'.[9] The bodies were encased in lead and reinterred seven years later, under the monument that remains in the church to this day. But for an accident of birth, they might be lying in Westminster Abbey.

I

A Significant Year
1415

I liken a kingdom in good estate
To stalwart man, mighty in hele [health]
While none of his limbs the other hate
He is mighty, with another to deal[1]

Cecily Neville was born on 3 May 1415. It was a year that would go down in the annals of English history and literature as a byword for patriotism, valour and national glory. As she lay in her cradle at Raby Castle that summer, alternately rocked and suckled by her nursemaids, a fleet of wooden ships filled with soldiers crossed the Channel and landed on the coast of Normandy. They were not prepared to leave without a fight.

The Lancastrian dynasty was still in its infancy. In 1399, the grandchildren of Edward III had clashed over the throne, rupturing the line of inheritance and replacing the senior branch of the family with a junior line. Richard II had succeeded his grandfather and ruled since he was a child of ten but, after his behaviour had grown increasingly despotic, he had been deposed by his cousin, Henry Bolingbroke, who then became Henry IV. With the country still embroiled in the Hundred Years' War with France, the new Lancastrian king had to defend his own title in England as well as abroad. On his death in 1413, the crown passed to his son Henry V, an energetic and ambitious military man, determined to enforce his Plantagenet claims in France. War was in the air again.

In fact, it had already been decided upon before Cecily was born. Negotiations with the French king, Charles VI, had broken down, and the Great Council had approved Henry's request to invade France on 19

April. It was going to prove costly, though – too costly, even for a King of England. Henry had to ask for help but he had the Royal Treasury to fall back on, with its beautiful and historical pieces of jewellery, plate and symbolic items. In June, the City of London loaned him 10,000 marks to fund the campaign and in return, in security, he gave them a gold collar, decorated with his heraldic symbol of the antelope in white enamel, green garnets, diamonds and pearls, weighing 56 ounces. It was clearly a precious item, 'made of workmanship in crowns and beasts',[2] personal to Henry and symbolic of his family and kingship. Bound to redeem it by New Year's Day, he was anticipating returning home.

When Cecily was three months old, Henry led a crushing defeat of Charles's forces around 40 miles south of Calais. This encounter has gone down in history as the Battle of Agincourt, still a meme of national culture thanks to Shakespeare's version of events. The stirring St Crispin's Day speech is frequently cited as the epitome of patriotism, an inspirational rallying cry memorably delivered by Sir Laurence Olivier or Kenneth Branagh. According to *Henry V*, those who fought would be recalled in 'flowing cups', raised in their memory as 'the happy few, we band of brothers'. Their king tells them their exploits will be taught by good men to their sons; they will show their wounds with pride and become household names across the realm. Conversely, those who would not fight, whose fear led them now to desert their king, should 'hold their manhoods cheap', and Henry would not deign to fight in the company of those who 'feared his fellowship to die with us'.[3] Such were the sentiments of kingship and masculinity, loyalty and bravery by which Cecily and her family would live and die.

The battle was a milestone in English culture long before Shakespeare was writing. 'The Agincourt Carol', composed soon after the events of October 1415, recorded how Henry fought with 'grace and myght of chyvalry', with God on his side, causing 'affray' that France would 'rewe tyl domesday'. Typical of the medieval chivalric code, the 'manly' king achieved his victory 'marvelsuly'.[4] A second contemporary song, 'King Henry V's Conquest of France', has the thickets and swamps of the battlefield 'choked with knights dead in their armour', with archers 'face down as if sleeping'.[5] Henry himself received an axe blow to the head, striking off the decorative 'crown' of his helmet, yet survived to seize the moment and name the battle after the nearby castle of Agincourt. Welsh chronicler Adam of Usk describes Henry 'as a very lion', committing 'himself to God and the fortunes of the sword'. In these accounts, the victory over the annihilated French seems absolute, easily won, with the English king emerging as something akin to a medieval superhero, striding across swathes of his victims, surviving a rain of mortal blows.

The reality was less glamorous. The chronicler Enguerrand de Monstrelet estimated the French numbers to be around six times those of their opponents, but that Henry's secret deployment of 200 archers to the rear of the enemy forces was a significant factor in their defeat. More English archers, totalling 13,000, advanced with the king. Their arrows hit the French horses, sending them 'smarting with pain' into a 'universal panic'.[6] George Chastellain's *Chronicle of Normandy* echoes this account, with a thick 'shower of arrows' forcing the French to retreat 'amongst their own people'. This broke the line of their waiting troops, who foundered in the soft ground, allowing the English to wade in with their swords, mallets, hatchets and billhooks. The French were 'more and more defeated' and soon the place was scarred by the 'pitiful sight' of the 'dead and wounded who covered the field'.[7] *Gregory's Chronicle* for 1415 has Henry making 'hys way thoroughe the thyckyste of alle the batayle' and listed the English dead at no more than eighteen 'personys', in comparison with considerable French losses.[8] The imbalance in numbers was partly due to the order, recounted by Monstrelet, that Henry gave his men to 'massacre' all their prisoners. When Henry found himself 'master of the field', he 'made a circuit of the plain' and announced that it was not him but God who had made this 'great slaughter ... as punishment for the sins of the French'.[9] Then, he and his armies returned to London where he was received both 'worthily and ryally'.[10] His return, and the news it brought, would have great significance for Cecily's future.

The London to which a victorious king returned would have been almost unrecognisable as today's city. In 1415 it was home to around 50,000 people.[11] Thus it was almost 160 times smaller, in population terms, than the 8 million recorded as being resident in the census of 2011. Of course, it was also physically much smaller in the fifteenth century. Surviving maps from before and after Cecily's time show a squat, uneven semicircle, enclosed by thick walls, roughly centred on the modern square mile. Practically the entire city sat on the north bank of the river, stretching as far as Cripplegate in the north, although Moorfields and Spitalfields, or St Mary Spital, lay outside its thick walls. A few houses clustered on the south, including the Tabard Inn, frequented by Chaucer's pilgrims, but most of the land there was still open countryside and marshes. The Thames was wider than in the twenty-first century, at least twice as wide, maybe more. It was the reason that the Romans had founded the city where they did, providing an essential thoroughfare, salmon and oyster to grace the table and water for cooking and washing.

Fifteenth-century London was also a centre of international trade. Towards the east, just past the solid stone bastion of the Tower, sailing ships unloaded their cargoes. Spices, bolts of cloth and precious gems came from as far afield as Oslo, Constantinople and Kiev, Alexandria, Algiers and Cadiz. There was only one bridge, London Bridge, top-heavy with buildings and frequently under repair. Rental accounts from 1420 list a fishmonger and butchers among its residents as well as the tolls paid by carts crossing from one side to another. A sum of 2 shillings and 8 pence was paid weekly to feed 'the bridge dogs'.[12] In the middle of the bridge perched a chapel, dedicated to St Thomas Becket. A new key was bought for the vestry door that year, at a price of 3 pence.[13] Travellers would kneel there to give thanks on their safe arrival in the city or ask protection for their imminent departure.

Below London Bridge, life was less harmonious. Small craft were sucked dangerously through the bridge's arches, briefly losing control in the rushing white water. Many must have been damaged or lost vital equipment. In 1420, the bridge accounts show two new pairs of sculls, or oars, were purchased for a boat named *Thomas*, as well as two new chains, shavehooks and a bead hook.[14] Beyond the bridge lay the calmer stretch of river, flowing west past Blackfriars, the location where Cecily's future London home, Baynard's Castle, would soon be rebuilt from an existing medieval town house. From there, the river ran on to Bridewell, Whitefriars and the ruins of the Savoy Palace. Once the grandest of all London's fine houses, it had been owned by Henry V's grandfather, John of Gaunt; his employee Geoffrey Chaucer had worked there before it was destroyed in the Peasants' Revolt of 1381. At that point, the Thames turned south, past York Place, which would later become Whitehall, and on to the royal region of Westminster. Over half a century after Henry V's victorious return, Cecily would visit it as the queen mother.

At the dawn of the fifteenth century, London was a mosaic of greys, browns and greens, a tableau of steep roofs, muddy thoroughfares and the leafy oases of gardens, fields and orchards. Within the walls, rich and poor lived closely together. Some houses were large and grand, built of red brick, with windows of glass and gates of iron. These sat amid acres of garden, surprisingly large for an urban setting, with lawns running down to the riverfront or spreading out to the walls. Other homes spilled out in complex units, like jigsaw pieces, with new rooms and courtyards added one by one, over time. Poorer dwellings, dark and unstable, rose up shoulder to shoulder down dark alleyways. Made from wood and straw, they were the constant fodder of rapacious fires and deadly epidemics. Almost every year there were new cases of plague. Inside there was little to steal, but the wild pigs that roamed the city might nose their way in, smelling the broth or cabbage boiling in a pot on the hearth. No one could touch them, as they were owned and protected by the Hospitallers of St Anthony. All a mother could do was be vigilant and chase them away if they approached the makeshift cradle where her child was sleeping.

The physical city, like its people and their businesses, underwent a constant process of reinvention. Walls fell down and boundaries were disputed. Drains got blocked and waste found its way into the many little tributaries of the Thames, which ran through and under the streets like veins. In the 1360s, Edward III had complained that when travelling downriver he 'beheld dung and ... stools and other filth accumulated in divers places'.[15] Yet the city was as varied and complex as it was dangerous. The contemporary poem 'London Lickpenny' (or 'Lackpenny') describes marketplaces that offer velvet and silks, felt hats and spectacles for sale, while stolen goods are resold at the Cornhill. Drinkers in East Chepe clatter their pewter pots to the accompaniment of street songs such as 'Julian and Jenkin'.[16] The air may have been acrid with smoke and the stench of latrines and tanneries, but it resonated with the peals of bells from dozens of churches too, summoning the pious to prayer. Henry V's capital was also a place where a man could be burned alive for commissioning a heretical religious text. Only that August, Lollard John Cleydone, an illiterate leather worker, lost his life for owning a copy of the anti-Papist tract 'The Lanterne of Light'.

Life and death sat close together in fifteenth-century London. King Henry left France during the season of killing, the old blood month from the Anglo-Saxon calendar. The date 11 November marked Martinmas Day, the feast of St Martin, when animals were traditionally slaughtered to prepare for the winter ahead. This had been such a problem in the past, with carcasses mounting in the streets, even in the shadow of Old St Paul's Cathedral, that since 1369 it had been illegal to butcher them within the City walls. Anyone dumping rubbish in the street could expect a hefty fine. By 1415, the main meat market was at Smithfields, or the smooth field, which also acted as a site of execution and an arena for jousting. The busy thoroughfares leading to and from it were witness to sickness, dirt and disease, as well as human and animal waste. When word arrived of the king's imminent arrival, his route was swept and washed, lined with sand or rushes and the crowds kept at bay.

The victorious Henry V landed at Dover on 23 November amid stormy weather. When news reached the city, its representatives set out en masse to meet him at Blackheath. They formed themselves into a reception committee, ordered by spiritual and temporal hierarchy, waiting for the first lookout to bring news. The king was coming home; the King of England, Henry V, drenched in the glory of his victory at Agincourt, was on his way back to his capital. They made a colourful procession, with the city's mayor and aldermen in 'orient-grained scarlet'[17] followed by 400 citizens dressed in clothing dyed with murrey, a purplish-red, mounted on 'well-trimmed' horses.[18] Adam of Usk puts the number closer to 10,000, adding that they also wore striking particoloured hoods, half white and half black, and were 'exulting in heart'. With them was a mass of England's clergy, dressed in their 'sumptuous copes'[19] and carrying heavy, shining crosses. Some carried censers that trailed the rich scent of religion in their wake.

But the king himself scorned celebration. Riding slowly towards them, Henry appeared 'grave and sombre', displaying little regard for the 'vain pomp and shows', or the preparations ahead, designed to honour his arrival in the city.[20] In 1415, he was a tall, slim young man of twenty-nine, reputed to stand at 6 feet 3 inches, with dark hair cropped in the French style above his ears. His face was lean and his nose thin and long, with eyes flashing 'from the mildness of a dove to the brilliance of a lion'.[21] Modest and pious, he requested that his helmet, with its 'blows and dints' from battle, should not be carried with him for the common people to see, nor should any songs be sung about the victory, because 'the praise and thanks should altogether be given to God'.[22] According to the poet Lydgate, the king was 'truli a gracious man' known for his military prowess, who had done 'godly' work 'through God's hand' in France.[23] Adam of Usk related how the king was keen to pass through the secular celebrations and make 'much reverence and giving of alms' at the tomb of St Erkenwald in St Paul's. Later, Henry would arrange solemn funerals for the slain and go on pilgrimage on foot from Shrewsbury to St Winefride's Well in North Wales, where he gave thanks for his victory.[24]

Yet Henry could not avoid the pageants made in his honour by his grateful subjects. They were recorded in Latin by the scribes of the Lord Mayor of London and have survived in the Cottonian Collection, now in the British Library. Approaching London Bridge, the procession drew to a stop. Across the towers of the bridge, banners of the royal arms had been hung and a placard bore the legend 'the City of the King of Righteousness'. Trumpets played along with other wind instruments, perhaps the shawm, crumhorn, pipe and recorder, cutting through the November air. Ahead of them, on the bridge's tower, was mounted a 'gigantic figure' holding the keys to the city, beside an equally tall female, 'intended for his wife'. On either side, towers were erected, made from wood covered in linen. One was decorated with a marbled effect, the other painted to look like green jasper, and on top sat the king's heraldic beasts, the antelope and lion.[25] Across it hung a banner bearing the words 'glorious things are spoken of thee, O city of God'.[26] Further along, a pavilion had been built with battlements and turrets, housing a figure of St George, which *Gregory's Chronicle* describes as being 'royally armed'. His head was adorned with a laurel crown studded with jewels, and his coat of arms featured on a crimson tapestry that hung behind. Little boys dressed in white, with angelic wings, sang from the windows of a house, representing the heavenly host extending God's blessing to the victorious English king. The crowds cheered triumphantly as he paused to hear them sing.

Then the procession reached the Cornhill, where the conduit was draped in crimson and emerald silk and hung with coats of arms. White-haired prophets in golden coats released sparrows and small birds on the king's approach, some of which flew and settled upon him.[27] There were also actors dressed as the Twelve Apostles, kings of England, martyrs and confessors, who chanted sweetly on the king's approach. Wine and wafers borne on silver leaves refreshed the party. From there, the progress was slow. At the famous cross of Chepe a temporary castle had been built, of timber covered with linen, also painted to depict blocks of white marble, with red and green jasper. Before it, on a stage, 'was moche solempnyte of angelys and virgenys syngyng' merrily.[28] More boys showered down gold coins and laurel leaves upon the king's head as he passed beneath them and virgins blew gold leaves from 'cups in their hands'.[29] A canopy, painted to represent the sky and clouds, with each corner supported by an angel, fluttered above a magnificent throne. It was occupied by a glittering figure representing the sun, over two centuries before the birth of Louis XIV of France, the most famous monarch in history to employ that device. The sun in splendour had been used as a heraldic device by Richard II but now, returning to his capital, fresh from the legendary field of Agincourt, Henry V was England's new sun king.

Yet not everyone who had fought in 1415 returned triumphantly. Very few Englishmen fell on St Crispin's Day, but one of them was Edward of Norwich, 2nd Duke of York, another grandson of Edward III. *Gregory's Chronicle* recorded that 'thorowe Goddys grace the kynge made hys way thoroughe the thyckyste of alle the batayle; and ther was slayne on the kyngys syde the Duke of Yorke'. Some sources cite that he was killed by a head wound, while others claim he was crushed to death amid the press of bodies. York was the highest-ranking English nobleman to die that day, and his death raised the question of where his title would pass. Despite being married twice, he had not fathered an heir. He had first been wed at the age of eight and his second wife was twenty years his senior. His childless life, and the manner of his death, would secure Cecily's future.

York's brother, the Earl of Cambridge, had predeceased him by two months. Yet he had not died a hero's death; quite the opposite. He had been a traitor, seeking to reverse the line of succession back to a senior royal line. Only that August he had been beheaded for his part in the Southampton Plot, which aimed to replace Henry V with his cousin, the Earl of March. Yet he left a son, a four-year-old, still under the jurisdiction of women in the nursery. The boy's mother had died in the process of giving him life, so now he was an orphan. Perhaps the king was moved by his plight. The child was judged incapable of being tainted by his treasonous activities; in fact, he was considered to have been betrayed by his father. After Agincourt, the young Richard Plantagenet was permitted to take his uncle's title and become Duke of York. It was by this small boy's new status that Cecily and her children would come to be known.

2

'Rose of Raby'
1415–1429

Off birth she was hihest of degree
To whom alle aungelis did obedience[1]

Raby Castle stands amid a large deer park about 18 miles to the south-west of Durham. On summer afternoons, the gates of this family home are thrown wide to admit the public who come to see its walled gardens and medieval rooms, and to sip tea amid the old stables of the coach house. But the castle had been attracting admiration from visiting historians and artists long before the horses were retired and their former stalls filled with the aroma of freshly baked scones.

In 1817, the Romantic landscapist J. M. W. Turner perched on the surrounding hills and sketched Raby's fortifications and feathery trees. His drawings show a panorama of towers, façades and turrets with a little blue wisp of smoke escaping to the sky. For it is indeed a romantic landscape, steeped in legend and history. With its solid stone walls topped with impressive crenellations, Raby seems to fit the image of a fairy-tale castle, sheltering fair maidens and repelling intruders. And, like any building with a significant past, it has undergone stages of development, making it a jigsaw of its different owners and influences, something of an historical hybrid, marked by the ghostly imprints of past owners. Visitors might peer across its landscape and call, hesitantly, like Margaret Schlegel in E. M. Forster's *Howard's End*, 'Saxon or Celt?'

The castle was very popular with Victorian visitors. They swished through the rooms in their crinolines and frock coats clutching a brand-new hardback guidebook. Published in 1857 by Whittaker & Co. of London, it was written by an anonymous author known only by the initials 'F. M. L.' Its job was to steer the mid-Victorian couple through centuries of life inside the grey stone walls. There was much to cater for the plush, heavy tastes of the day, with descriptions of furnishings, the library, engravings and portraits. The writer was also interested in the passage of time his generation had witnessed. He understood that progress was inevitable and that the past should not be lamented; in his lifetime, the stagecoach had vanished and horse-drawn carts were being replaced by the 'iron mammoth', the spreading railway which had such an impact on Victorian England. 'We must not regret them,' the preface prompts the reader, 'they have had their day.'[2]

The Victorian lady and gentleman approached the castle in their barouche, driving through the park towards the 'noble pile',[3] a 'baronial manor of former times'.[4] The building appeared on 'elevated ground', with nine towers glimpsed 'from between the waters', crenelated and imposing.[5] Above the shimmering lake, a typical fairy-tale castle appeared, perhaps already familiar to the nineteenth-century eye from the extensive sketches made by J. M. W. Turner in 1817. Entrance was through an impressive gatehouse flanked by two towers, each with its own stone guardian staring out across a moat that had been dry for a century. But, by the time the barouche rattled across the causeway, the days of siege and civil war were over, so the iron portcullis and drawbridge were no longer needed. They drove on to the Neville Gateway, the main entrance, where one door still bore the insistent marks of an ancient battering ram, a reminder of the family that occupied the castle during the turbulent medieval period.[6]

The nineteenth-century visitors were conducted through well-disposed rooms, to admire expressive portraits described by the guidebook in a suitably Great Exhibition register: Panini, Vermeer and Vernet, Lely, Lorraine and Vandyke were all 'worthy of notice' or 'as fresh as if but just finished'. New additions to the building 'harmonise[d] perfectly' and all were alliteratively appreciated, being 'elaborate, exquisite and elegant'. Then, amid the draperies of lion's skins and 'chaste' gold-and-white ceiling, the castle's past, the 'olden times', according to F. M. L., began to emerge. The Baron's Hall once entertained 700 knights plus their retainers and, below the Victorian lady's Balmoral boot, lay the cellars, complete with huge oven. Once, the fires blazed, down in the bowels of the castle, roasting the meat turning on spits and heating the vats of wine, boiled with spices. Raby was self-sufficient, with all its provisions stored within the thick walls. This was, of course, 'a very essential arrangement for the subsistence of those in feudal times when, at any time, they were subject to the attacks of their neighbours'.[7]

It was during those 'feudal times' that Cecily Neville was born at Raby Castle. The location of her arrival, and the family into which she was born, immediately marked her above the majority of her fifteenth-century contemporaries. The impressive towers and setting of Raby, its very size and scale, were a suitable location for the birth of a woman who would come to consider herself 'queen by rights', whose family would come to conquer and rule the land. It was a bloodline that derived from Norman France, where significant years of Cecily's life would be passed, as the duchess of the realm's lieutenant. The connection went back at least six centuries.

Cecily was the youngest child of a very significant dynasty. Her ancestors had been based at Neuville-sur-Touques, just over 100 miles to the immediate west of Paris,[8] while other sources cite a village named Calle de Neu Ville as their home. They derived their surname from the place of their birth as far back as the ninth century.[9] Nevilles were among those thousands of men who crossed the Channel to England in 1066, dressed in their chain-mail hauberks and now iconic helmets, with the bar descending to protect the nose. Occupying a heavily wooded site, with marshland surrounding them, they fought from morning until dusk until the English King Harold was killed. William the Conqueror rewarded his men; many received lands and titles, so they settled and married into local families. Cecily's ancestors came from one such eleventh-century success story, starting with a Richard de Novavilla,[10] whose mother was a cousin of the Conqueror and whose uncle, Foulk d'Anjou, provided forty ships for the fleet of 1066. Richard's four sons are likely to have fought for him but only two of these, Ralph and Gilbert, may have survived. Ralph is recorded as fathering a son at Scotton, Lincolnshire, around 1072, while Gilbert went on to found the line from which Cecily was descended.

Gilbert's son, Geoffrey de Neville, arrived around 1080 at Walcot in Lincolnshire, and in turn fathered a son of his own in 1115. It was around this time that Neville connections to Raby Castle are recorded, with this generation's heir possibly dying there in 1168.[11] By this point the Nevilles were also in possession of Brancepeth Castle, a Norman fortification built by the Anglo-Saxon Bulmer family near Durham, which probably came to the family through the marriage of Geoffrey's son to Emma de Bulmer. She bore two children, a son who died without issue and a daughter, Isabel de Neville, born around 1174. For a while it looked as if this branch of the Neville name might die out, but Isabel married into another local family with connections to the area dating back to pre-Conquest times. She and her husband were Cecily's six-times-great-grandparents. Her son, Geoffrey, took his mother's maiden name, and the direct Neville line continued.

Isabel's marriage brought fresh Anglo-Saxon blood into Cecily's family tree. The Raby estate had existed long before the Nevilles arrived there, long before the Conquest, while her ancestors were still in Normandy. The local area, centred on Staindrop, or Stainthorp, 'stony ground' parish, was an important centre for smelting lead ore and there is also evidence for Roman activity in the area. The north-east coast of England was particularly vulnerable to Viking invasion and, by the early eleventh century, the Danes had the upper hand and were settling in the area. F. M. L.'s guidebook claims that Raby and the surrounding area belonged to King Canute, who built a 'mansion' on the site, part of which was incorporated into the present castle's Bulmer's Tower. Its name – Ra (boundary) and Bi or Bry (settlement) – derives from Old Norse and was probably coined around this time. While resident there, Canute returned the parish to the monastery of Durham, its previous owner, perhaps as a gesture of goodwill to the local people.

After Canute, but before the Norman Nevilles made their way north, Raby was inhabited by the descendants of Scottish royalty. The connection goes back to King Duncan I of Scotland, immortalised by Shakespeare for having been slain in his bed by ambitious Macbeth. He was in fact not killed in his sleep, but the idea of treason and treachery was accurate enough – he was slain in battle, betrayed by his own men when leading an army into the lands traditionally associated with Macbeth. Duncan's brother Maldred became King of Cumberland and his son, Uchtred FitzMaldred, was born at Raby in 1120. His son Dolfin, or Dolphin, was granted the Staindrop and Raby estate by the Prior of Durham in 1131. Two generations later it belonged to Dolfin's grandson, Robert FitzMaldred, who married Isabel de Neville and fathered the Geoffrey who adopted his mother's surname.

Through the next six generations, the Nevilles lived at Raby. They governed castles, heard pleas, gathered taxes, kept the peace, fought against the Welsh and Scots and became sheriffs, barons and, ultimately, earls. Along the way they married into some of the leading families of northern England, including the Bertrams, FitzRanulfs, Claverings, Audleys, Percys, Latimers and Staffords. By the mid-fourteenth century the family was multiplying, with Cecily's grandfather John fathering nine children by two wives, in between serving in Scotland and France, acting as Admiral of the North, Steward of the King's Household and Knight of the Garter. His eldest son, Ralph, was born in 1364. He had begun his career under Richard II and served in Brittany during the Hundred Years' War. On the death of his father, Ralph inherited the title of 4th Baron of Raby and then, for his defence of the king in 1397, was awarded the earldom of Westmorland. The political scene was set to change, though. Dissent was brewing between royal cousins. Challenges were made to Richard's rule by the eldest son of John of Gaunt, Henry Bolingbroke, with whom Ralph was now allied by marriage. When Bolingbroke was banished in 1398 and his estates confiscated following his father's death the next year, Ralph switched sides. He was among those who received Richard's abdication in the Tower of London and then bore a sceptre when Bolingbroke was crowned as Henry IV. The earl was well compensated for supporting the regime, receiving grants and wardships and becoming Earl Marshall and a Knight of the Garter. Most of his children were born under the first Lancastrian king but, by the time Cecily arrived, Henry IV's son was on the throne.

Cecily's father, Ralph Neville, 1st Earl of Westmorland, appears in a colourful miniature by Pol de Limbourg in the book of hours of the Neville family, kneeling in prayer, dressed in long blue-and-gold robes, his hair fashionably cropped. Behind him are twelve of his children, eight of whom were borne by his first wife, Margaret Stafford, who died in 1396. Within six months Ralph had married again and a second panel in the book of hours depicts his next bride, the widowed Joan Beaufort, the legitimised daughter of John of Gaunt, son of Edward III. Behind her stand six daughters, dressed in elaborate gowns of gold, pink and green, with their hair caught up under the U-shaped 'hennins' (headdresses), studded with jewels and draped with white veils. One of them is Cecily, although it is not clear which. She might be at the back, being the youngest, or at the front, being the most senior in terms of marriage; it scarcely matters, though, as all the young women are depicted with interchangeable features – the high foreheads, pale complexions and regular features of conventional medieval beauties.

Her mother Joan, Countess of Westmorland, appears to have been a religious woman who makes an appearance in one of the most controversial texts of her times. *The Book of Margery Kempe*, perhaps the first autobiography in the English language, detailed the life and mystical experiences of an extraordinary woman who was Joan's contemporary. Sometime between 1408 and 1413, at Easter, Joan summoned Margery to visit her, as she was interested to hear her talk: 'My Lady herself was well pleased with you and liked your talk.'[12] In 1413, after fourteen pregnancies, Margery had asked her husband to live a celibate life. It was later claimed that, during her visit to the countess, she tried to persuade Joan's eldest daughter, Elizabeth, Lady Greystoke, to leave her husband. This was a radical move for the wife of a baron, who had already borne three children by 1412 and clearly did not heed Kempe's advice as she went on to have several more. Kempe was later cross-questioned about this, as it was 'enough to be burned for' but she claimed she had merely told them 'a good tale of a lady who was damned because she would not love her enemies'.[13] It was decided that Kempe would be imprisoned while a letter was sent to the countess to ascertain the truth. Joan must have written favourably about Margery, as she was not burned, but went on to live until after 1438.

When Cecily was born on 3 May 1415, her mother, Joan, was thirty-six. Married for the first time at the age of twelve, she had borne her first child two years later and gone on to deliver fifteen more over the next twenty-two years. She spent over half of her adult life carrying children, pregnant for the equivalent of twelve years in addition to the months spent in post-partum recovery. This was a fairly punishing regime, even for a medieval aristocratic mother, when any pregnancy ran the risk of maternal and infant mortality. Yet it was also her social, marital and religious duty, the defining act of a medieval woman; to the Nevilles and their contemporaries, Joan's high rate of fertility implied a divine blessing on the match and the clan. By the time she was expecting her final daughter, she knew what to expect. As an experienced mother, she was likely to have had a swifter labour but this was by no means guaranteed. Any complications that occurred during the birth, or infections that set in afterwards, could prove fatal in an era where the intercessions of unregulated midwives could prove equally as harmful as they were helpful. It took just one unwashed pair of hands or a single injury inflicted on the mother during birth for fatalities to occur. Each successive pregnancy intensified the risk but Joan must have been strong. She was lucky to survive and to lose only four babies during the process.

Joan Beaufort's high fertility rate was probably as much a function of her genetic make-up as any benefits her status could confer. Large families were the norm among her class. She was one of seven children born out of wedlock by her mother, Katherine Swynford, four of whom survived. Katherine also had at least three others as a result of her first marriage, and her second husband fathered at least ten more by three other women.

Cecily's father, Ralph, was aged around fifty at the time of his youngest child's conception, which took place in the summer of 1414. He was one of nine children and his father had been one of thirteen. While some noble families experienced unexplained difficulties producing heirs, or lost them as a result of illness, Cecily's ancestors through the Neville, Beaufort, Gaunt, Percy, Clifford and de Clare lines had been more than successful in multiplying their numbers.

The baby girl arrived into a sprawling family, a network of children multiplied by second marriages. She had ten half-brothers and sisters, eight of whom were Nevilles and two Ferrers. All of these were married by 1415 and had produced offspring of their own, except one, Elizabeth, who became a nun. In addition, Cecily had nine surviving full siblings. The eldest girls, Eleanor and Katherine, were seventeen and fifteen years her senior and had already been married, Eleanor to Richard le Despenser and Katherine for three years to John Mowbray, 2nd Duke of Norfolk. Katherine was five months pregnant at the time of her youngest sister's arrival and would deliver Cecily's nephew, John, that September. The infant Cecily may briefly have had the company of one sister in the Raby nursery, Anne, closest to her in age, although Anne was married in 1424 and bore a child in 1425, and may have been as many as a couple of years her elder. Her brothers George and Edward also appear to be close to her in age, as their marriages did not take place until the 1430s. A governess and wet nurse would have been appointed to care for the younger children while their mother recovered and returned to her duties as lady of the manor.

Soon after her birth, Cecily was baptised, either in the castle chapel or perhaps in St Mary's church, Staindrop, where the bones of her ancestors lay. With the site used for worship since the eighth century, the present church is first recorded as being given by King Canute to the newly founded Priory of Durham. The church had initially been dedicated to St Gregory, referred to by a 1343 grant made by Cecily's great-grandfather, but in 1408 her father founded a collegiate church in nearby Staindrop village in honour of the Virgin Mary. Countess Joan may have also had a hand in the work, or completed it after her husband's death a decade later, as Leland claimed that 'Johan erected the very house self of the college'.[14] It was a considerable establishment, with provision made for dozens of men, and revenue recorded at the Dissolution of the Monasteries in the 1530s of over £170. In 1412, William Horne was appointed as the church's first vicar and may well have been responsible for the baptism of Cecily.[15] Joan was certainly a pious lady, receiving permission from the Pope in 1422 to 'enter, with eight honest women, any monasteries of nuns, even enclosed, and stay there with the nuns, eating, drinking and talking with them, and stay the night'.[16]

At Raby, Joan's women would have prepared her newborn by dressing her in a white linen shift or chrisom. Carried by her godparents, the infant Cecily would have been met at the church door by a priest who placed salt in her mouth to drive away demons and represent the absorption of wisdom. Inside the church, she was anointed at the font and named, before prayers and promises were made at the altar. Some sort of feast would have followed at Raby to honour the occasion, before the earl's youngest daughter was returned to her mother.

With the Raby nursery run as part of the countess's household, the family came together on key occasions such as feast days, or for ceremonies and entertainment. Cecily and her siblings would have been familiar with the Great Hall, or Baron's Hall, described by the Victorian guidebook writer F. M. L. as 'noble'. By the nineteenth century it was much smaller than in its medieval heyday, as the author reminds us, citing Leland's comment that 'long before his age it was fals-rofid'.[17] The hall was lit by a three-sectioned window at the south and five along the western flank. A stone minstrel's galley was located on the north side. Off this was situated the private chapel that Cecily knew, perhaps, as a small child, gazing up at the stained glass 'of very early date', which the Victorian author claimed was brought from the Continent and depicted 'ecclesiastics in all the pomp of their most elaborate costume'.[18]

Otherwise, the younger children's lives would have been fairly sequestered and regimented. Surviving accounts from the household of the Percy family, great rivals of the Nevilles, described the nursery ('nurcy') as comprising a lady 'chamberer' and two rockers, plus the 'child of the nurcy'. On fasting or 'scamlynge' days in Lent, which the ordinance lists as Monday and Saturday, they were to receive white manchet bread and beer, plus four white herring, a piece of fried salt fish and a dish of fresh ling or a salt turbot. On non-fasting days their menu varied to include butter. Their entitlement to three dishes placed them above the gentlemen and yeomen ushers of the chamber, who received two, and below their brothers, who were allowed four, and their parents, who had six. Those children who were employed in the household, in the wardrobe, bakehouse and scullery, had the standard bread and beer plus only one dish of either herring or stockfish. The Percy accounts also reveal that the rocker of the cradle received wages of 20s and that the nursery was allocated two 'peks' of coal, the same as the master of grammar in the 'scolehous'.[19] The author F. M. L. describes the kitchen at Raby Castle, with a parallel gallery concealed within the wall, accessed by five windows. Blocked up by the nineteenth century, it was probably a service tunnel, a reminder of the constant movement between hall and kitchen, as armies of liveried servants hurried food to the table before it could cool.[20]

Soon after the birth of his last daughter, national conflict drew Ralph away from Raby Castle. Yet this was not at Agincourt, the most famous battle recorded by history for that year. In Henry V's absence, a fresh threat in the north had arisen. The Scots had crossed the border and were heading south, hoping to take advantage of a kingdom without its king. Since the 1380s, the earl had been involved in Scottish affairs, surveying the English defences, negotiating peace and receiving ransom money. He had experience as a Warden of the Marches, responsible for defending the Scottish border against attacks, a position that had been conferred upon his grandfather and held in the family ever since. Furthermore, that April, he had also been appointed a member of the Council of Regency under the king's brother, John of Lancaster, deputised to defend the northern borders of the realm while Henry fought across the channel. On 22 July 1415, Cecily's father headed an army that met the invaders at the Battle of Yeavering. At the head of a small force of around 450 English archers, he repelled almost 4,000 Scots at a site near the small Northumberland hamlet, today marked by an ancient stone. His tiny newborn daughter would have been unaware of the danger and his success.

The education of aristocratic girls in the fifteenth century was designed to prepare them for their future lives as the wives of great magnates. Thus, as outlined by contemporary writers such as Christine de Pisan, the *Ménagier de Paris* and many anonymous poets, girls should be decorous, polite, submissive and pious. In order to prepare girls for the running of their own households, they were taught practical matters such the use of medicinal herbs, spinning and sewing, as well as courtesy and deportment, music, dancing, how to handle servants and reading from the Bible and other religious texts. The medieval poem 'What the Goodwife Taught Her Daughter' was composed around 1430 and advocates the usual lessons about attending church, giving to the poor, not gossiping too much and being respectful to elders. It contains advice about manners and decorum, such as 'laugh thou not too loud nor yawn thy mouth too wide' alongside warnings about the behaviour of men: 'By him do not stand but let him his way depart, Lest he by his villainy should tempt thy heart.' Girls were taught to be modest and hard-working, to be a good wife, mistress of the house and neighbour, 'and to do to them as thou wouldst be done to'. The poem survives in four manuscript versions but only one of them contains an extra verse that would prove especially pertinent to Cecily's life:

> And if it thus thee betide
> That friends fail thee on every side
> And God from thee thy child take
> Thy wreak [revenge] on God thou must not take
> For thyself it will undo
> And all virtues that thee belongs to
> Many a one for her own folly
> Spills [ruins] themselves unthriftily[21]

But in the 1420s, these misfortunes lay far ahead. Cecily's future as the daughter of the house of Neville would have appeared as a glittering prospect, as the wife of a great magnate and mother of many powerful children. Before she was very old, she could see the destiny that was mapped out for her unfolding through the lives of her siblings.

During Cecily's early years, some significant births, deaths and marriages took place. In 1420, her eldest brother, Richard, married the fourteen-year-old Alice Montacute or Montagu, heiress of the Earl of Salisbury. They are recorded in *Gregory's Chronicle* as appearing as a couple at the coronation of Henry V's queen, Catherine of Valois, in February 1421. Together they would have witnessed the crowning, followed by the three-course banquet in the Great Hall, where Alice was listed last in precedence out of the ladies, simply as 'the wyffe of Rycharde Nevyle, doughter to the erle of Salusbury'. The feast included such delicacies as brawn with mustard, great crabs, roasted porpoise, powdered whelks, motley or coloured cream and marzipan subtleties, or carvings, in the shape of a pelican, a panther and St George leading a tiger.[22]

Richard and Anne's first surviving child was born two years later and named Joan, after his mother, but their second daughter, arriving in 1424, was named Cecily after her young aunt. Their firstborn son, also named Richard, would inherit his future wife's title and become known to history as Warwick 'the Kingmaker'. Another important baby arrived at this time, when Cecily was six years old, whose future was to be entwined with hers and those of her children. Soon after her coronation Queen Catherine fell pregnant, and on 6 December 1421 she gave birth to a son at Windsor Castle. Nine months later, when the king died of dysentery, the little boy became Henry VI.

Cousin Joan also made a very impressive match. Eleven years older than Cecily, Joan was probably named after her aunt, and was the child of John Beaufort and Margaret Holland, a half-niece of Henry IV. The King of Scotland, James I, reputedly fell in love with her while a prisoner in England. According to legend, he glimpsed her from a window as she was walking in the garden and was inspired to write the poem *The Kingis Quair* in her honour. In the absence of any surviving verifiable contemporary descriptions or portraits of Cecily, James's description of her cousin might shed some light on both girls' reputations for beauty. This princess of Cupid had 'goldin haire' and white throat but her attraction was concentrated in her air of 'bountee, richesse and womanly facture … wisedome, largesse, estate and connyng'. 'Hir faire fresche face, as quhite[white] as any ony snawe [snow] … in word, in dede, in schap, in contenance, that nature might no more hir childe avance … I not wher she be womman or goddesse.'[23] In 1424, James was released and the pair were married at Southwark Cathedral, then Southwark Priory, followed by feasting at Winchester Palace. It was a prestigious match for the bride. She went on to bear James eight children, and ruled Scotland as regent after his death. No doubt the romance of their unusual meeting filtered through to the Raby household; perhaps Cecily's mother told her stories about the beautiful, golden-haired lady who had married a king. It would have been the sort of tale to capture the imagination of a nine-year-old girl, hungry for her own life to begin. Cecily would not have long to wait.

3

Duke of York
1411–1429

Lo! On that mound in days of feudal pride
Thy tow'ring castle frowned above the tide
Flung wide her gates, where troops of vassals met
With awe the brow of high Plantagenet[1]

Richard Plantagenet, Duke of York, was thirteen in 1424. With his family, title and lands, he was an important English magnate in the making and a significant match for Ralph Neville's daughter. Like the ruling house of Lancaster, he could trace his descent directly from Edward III. Edward, though, had sired a large family, and it was the order of his children's births that complicated the nature of later royal inheritance. He had five surviving sons, all of whom fathered children who went on to compete for the English throne over the course of the next century, sowing the seeds for the Wars of the Roses.

Richard of York was Edward's descendant twice over, from both his second and his fourth son. He was the great-great-grandson of Lionel of Antwerp, and the grandson of Edmund of Langley. Edward died in 1377. His eldest son, the Black Prince, had died the year before, but he had fathered a son of his own, named Richard. This Richard now became Richard II. He fathered no children of his own, so named the offspring of his next brother as his heirs. This was the Mortimer family, the line from which Richard of York's mother came.

However, everything changed in 1399. Richard II had become increasingly despotic. After several years of conflict, he was deposed by the children of Edward III's third son, which began a new line of Lancastrian kings under Henry IV. His Mortimer heirs were incarcerated and the male line died out. However, there was a Mortimer sister, Anne, who married the Earl of Cambridge and died while giving birth to Richard Plantagenet in 1411. Four years later, Cambridge decided to fight to restore his wife's claim to the throne but was arrested and convicted of treason in what became known as the Southampton Plot. Sentenced along with him was his future wife's brother-in-law, Sir Thomas Grey. Rymer's *Foedera* records that, on 5 August, the commission was given to Thomas, Duke of Clarence, to carry out the execution.[2] It also records the confession made by Richard's father shortly before his death:

> My most dreadful and sovereign liege Lord, like to your Highness, touching the purpose cast against your high estate, having the Earl of March by his own assent and by the assent of myself (whereof I most me repent of all worldly things) ... to have had the foresaid Earl into the land of Wales without your licence, taking upon him the sovereignty of this land ... for the which point I put me wholly in your grace ... Beseeching to you, my liege Lord, for his love that suffered passion on the Good Friday, so have thee compassion on me your liege man.

He pleaded for mercy, explaining that 'other folk egged (him) thereunto', by which he had 'highly offended' the king, pleading 'for the Love of our Lady and of the blissful Holy Ghost'.[3]

His pleading did not save him, and the future of his four-year-old son, Richard, looked uncertain. However, the wheel of fortune swiftly restored the young boy to favour. For this, he had to thank his uncle, Edward of York, who was among those knights who sailed to France with Henry V in 1415. By being one of the few English men of noble blood to die on that day, he redeemed his nephew in the eyes of the Crown and secured his own reputation. Edward of York's death at the Battle of Agincourt went a long way to offset the execution of his brother for treason. An entry in the Calendar of the Fine Rolls for December that year records that the four-year-old boy was not to be penalised for his father's crime. Listed as 'Richard, son of Richard late Earl of Cambridge, his kinsman and heir',[4] he was allowed to inherit his uncle's dukedom of York and potentially to receive the title of Earl of March, with its extensive inheritance, so long as his maternal uncle, Edmund, did not produce children of his own. The Calendar of Fine Rolls for April 1416 lists the expenses in black cloth for Edward of York's funeral, held at St Paul's Cathedral. By the king's commandment, it was draped 'within and outside', made into banners, curtains and a standard. Henry and 'his brethren and other Lords' made offerings and kept a vigil. Medieval protocol made it unlikely that the young Richard would have attended, even if he was aware of the significance of the day.[5]

On 10 October 1417, Henry V entrusted the young Richard to Sir Robert Waterton. In the meantime, his possessions were carved up between loyal Lancastrians, until such time as the boy came of age. His new guardian was granted the boy's 'manor and lordship of Sowreby' in the Fine Rolls, until he was 'of full age' or 'so from heir to heir until one of them shall have attained lawful age'.[6] Richard's Essex manors at estates at Reylegh (Rayleigh), Racheford (Rochford), Tunderle (Thundersley), Estwode (Eastwood), Lovedene (Lovedown, near Hockley)[7] and others nearby and across the border into Suffolk were granted to Joan de Bohun, Countess of Essex and Hertford and Henry V's grandmother, 'by reason of the minority of Richard, son of Richard late Earl of Cambridge'.[8] His estates in Buckinghamshire, Hertfordshire and Herefordshire were equally distributed until his minority should come to an end.[9] This was in line with standard practice.

Richard's new custodian, Robert Waterton, had a history of custodianship. He had been made constable of Pontefract Castle from 1399 and had responsibility for King Richard II after his deposition that year and during the period when he is reputed to have died, early in 1400. Today it is still not clear exactly what happened to the king, or how he met his end, but Sir Robert was well placed to know the truth: in 1404, he denied charges raised in Parliament that Richard might have escaped or was still alive. In 1405, he was imprisoned by the Duke of Northumberland in a failed attempt to discover the truth. Later, Waterton was the gaoler of James I, King of Scots, before his marriage to Cecily's cousin Joan. He was also given responsibility for an important prisoner from the Agincourt battlefield, the Duc d'Orléans, who was incarcerated at Pontefract – although he was treated according to his rank and allowed out in order to visit the Waterton family home at Methley.

Richard's new guardian was a man in his fifties or sixties; wide-ranging estimates place his birthdate somewhere between 1350 and 1365 and, by the time he took on his charge, he already had a long and distinguished career serving two Lancastrian kings. He had been esquire to the body of Henry Bolingbroke, the future Henry IV, with whom he had gone on pilgrimage to the Holy Lands and, according to chronicler Adam of

Usk, had been the first man to greet Bolingbroke on the quayside when he returned from exile in 1399.[10] The new king appointed him as his Master of the Horse, sent him on embassies to France, Germany and Denmark and relied upon his support to crush the threat of rebellion by the Percy family. He was also Chief Steward, Sheriff of Lincolnshire and an executor of Henry VI's will.

The Waterton family came from Lincolnshire, probably from the medieval village of that name situated on the River Trent. During the fourteenth century, a John de Waterton married into the de Methley family and moved into the area. However, the seat at Methley Hall, between Pontefract and Leeds, was not conferred upon the family until 1410, when it was granted to Robert's brother John by the master of the hospital of Pontefract. It was an impressive, solid, castellated building, mostly ranging over three storeys, but rising to four in the turrets that flanked its entrance. One eighteenth-century watercolour depicts a great hall with huge carved wooden minstrels' gallery and staircase, embossed ceiling and floor-to-ceiling oriel window. The house was featured in a 1907 edition of *Country Life*, and a few surviving photographs give a sense of its grandeur but, after opencast mining was begun in the 1940s, it quickly became unstable and was demolished in 1964. Methley Hall was Sir Robert's chief residence, which he rebuilt considerably and extended with grants from the king; it was also the location of his death and his body now lies in the Waterton Chapel in nearby St Oswald's church. Methley Hall and the Manor of Woodhall at Methley, which was actually in Mickletown, are the most likely locations where the young Richard Plantagenet lived from the ages of four to twelve.

As a child, Richard would have lived with Waterton's family, as part of their household. At some point before 1408, Sir Robert had lost his first wife and married again, to a Cicely Fleming, heir to the nearby estate of Woodhall at Stanley. She bore him a son, Robert, and a daughter, Joan. The date suggests these two children would have been of a similar age to Richard, who then joined the young Robert both in the schoolroom for his formal education and out in the surrounding countryside, learning to ride, fight and joust. Joan was married on 15 August 1417[11] at St Oswald's church, Methley, so the young Richard would have been a guest at her wedding to Lionel de Welles, 6th Baron Welles. Lionel later became stepfather to Lady Margaret Beaufort.

Cicely Waterton would have been the closest maternal figure that the growing boy would have known in his early years at Methley, and he would have joined the household in mourning her death, which occurred sometime before he reached the age of eleven. She was laid to rest in an alabaster tomb in St Oswald's church, where her effigy reclines on a pillow, dressed in an elaborately decorated 'hennin', or headdress, with the long, draping sleeves fashionable at the time and her hips encircled with a narrow girdle. In 1422, Sir Robert married again. His new wife was Margaret Clarell, who had been widowed the previous year and had two sons and a daughter of her own. It is likely that William, John and Eleanor came to live at Methley with their mother, or were at least visitors there. Given that the eldest boy, William, lived until 1471, and that Margaret would go on to bear nine more children after Sir Robert's death, these three were probably still quite young at the time of the Waterton marriage. Robert also had at least one illegitimate child, Thomas, to whom the Manor of Woodhall passed on his death; he may also have been raised as part of the household. Richard would have shared a roof with them until the end of 1423, when national events meant the current terms of his wardship were reassessed.

Soon Henry V was at war again. In the summer of 1421 he had returned to France, capturing the city of Meaux after a five-month siege, although dysentery had decimated the English troops. Ultimately, though, it would prove to be a Pyrrhic victory, as Henry himself was unaware that he too had contracted the disease. Five months later, while at the Château de Vincennes, near Paris, he was suddenly taken ill and died between two and three in the morning of 31 August. He had reigned for less than ten years and was only thirty-five; his heir, an infant son, was not yet a year old. This unexpected loss was lamented by the poet John Lydgate, who called him the 'lode star of chivalry', with the chroniclers John Strecche, Chatelain and Monstrelet following suit. Hardyng claimed later that Henry's reputation was so powerful that, even while he was away in France, his England was a safe and peaceful place.[12] His death brought many changes, including the reassessment of the wardships belonging to the Crown; such valuable assets could be expected to change hands.

Ralph Neville, Earl of Westmorland, was now sold the custody and marriage of Richard, Duke of York, for 3,000 marks.[13] His service to the Lancastrian regime had already been recognised, with an entry in the Court Rolls for 1423 conferring upon him the grant of certain castles for his 'good and praiseworth service'.[14] That July, Neville's clerk, William Glenne, was granted the right to levy taxes from the local area to the value of 1,000 marks, as was his knight, Nicholas Bowet, that August. Richard was transferred to his keeping in the same year, when he would have left the only real family he had known at Methley and travelled up to Raby Castle. This was a significant moment for the young duke, then aged twelve, marking a milestone in his progression from childhood to adulthood. He had little choice about the decision but may well have considered it equable with the stages of social maturation his contemporaries were experiencing; twelve was the age of consent for girls and the time when boys might begin an apprenticeship or join a noble household as a henchman, to be trained in the chivalric arts. Soon after coming under Neville's guardianship, he underwent another significant rite of passage. In 1424, around the age of thirteen, Richard was betrothed to the earl's youngest daughter, the nine-year-old Cecily.

What the young couple thought of each other in 1424 is not recorded. It probably was not considered important. Even at such a tender age, they would have understood the union as being a career move, rather than driven by affection, with the aim to secure the most advantageous partner possible from among a fairly small aristocratic milieu. Under common and church law, the minimum age was twelve for girls and fourteen for boys, although in practice, many matches were arranged earlier than this in anticipation of later consummation. Engagements could be drafted between children as young as seven, which was considered a 'meaningful' age, although the clause was often built in to allow them to reject the match once they came of age. An example of this survives in a 1466 contract between the Stonor and Rokes families, when the children were permitted to annul the match upon reaching thirteen and fourteen; the young Henry VIII also repudiated his betrothal to Catherine of Aragon at fourteen, although he later went ahead and married her. Neither Richard nor Cecily appeared to object to the marriage and there would be no later calls for them to separate. Legends that Cecily was kept in a room with bars to prevent her from escaping to meet a suitor of whom her father disapproved are belied by her age and stem from works of fiction.

It seems most likely that Richard travelled up to Raby Castle at the end of 1423. He may also have spent some time at the court of the infant Henry VI. If he had not actually reached County Durham by 1424, there is a chance he may not have even met Cecily before the engagement was mooted, or even enacted. The contract could be drawn up and sworn by proxy but, although it is likely that they were introduced at some point, the legends of them growing up in the same household are misleading.

A letter in the Paston collection describes how the first meeting of a betrothed couple had gone well, as the girl 'made him gentle cheer in gentle wise', so there was probably no need for a 'great treaty between them'. During 1424, they would have had a little time to get to know one another at Raby, or the nearby Brancepeth Castle, which was also in Neville hands.

The year 1425 was to prove significant for Richard in more ways than one. On 17 January, his old guardian, Robert Waterton, died at Methley. Waterton was probably ill and aware that his end was in sight, as he had made his will seven days before this; perhaps increasing old age and incapacity had caused him to withdraw in his final years, and this might underpin the transference of Richard to the custody of the Nevilles. The news probably had not reached Raby before another important death occurred. On the following day, 18 January, Richard's uncle, Edmund Mortimer, died of plague after having been sent to Ireland. This meant that the boy assumed the titles of Earl of March and Ulster, as well as the Mortimer lands in Wales and on the border, although he would not be able to fully enjoy them yet. The Calendar of Close Rolls for 26 November 1425 and 20 July 1426 record that his lands were held in trust by March's widow Anne Stafford, Richard's aunt, 'by reason of the nonage [juvenility] of Richard, Duke of York'.[15] His value as a marital commodity rose as a result but his new guardian, and potential future father-in-law, was also ailing.

On the Sunday after Midsummer 1425, Ralph Neville witnessed an indenture granting lands in Watlous to Thomas de Neville and his wife Cecily. It was one of his last legal acts. On 12 October, he died at Raby Castle, at around the age of sixty. He was buried in Staindrop church under a stone effigy flanked by images of both his wives, although their bodies are actually buried elsewhere. The alabaster used was dug from a quarry owned by his father-in-law, John of Gaunt.

Ralph's title passed to his eldest surviving grandson, but the majority of his estates were left to his widow. The Calendar Rolls for May 1426 record an order 'to assign dower to Joan who was the earl's wife, of whom the king hath taken an oath'. That November, she was awarded arrears of 10 marks a year following an inquisition into the state of the earl's finances, which discovered she was owed it by the Sheriff of Westmorland.[16] Joan was already mother-in-law to the new earl before she became his stepmother. For around fifteen years he had been married to her daughter, Margaret, from her first husband. This made it awkward when Joan's stepchildren contested the split between their title and estates and applied for the restitution of their inheritance. Over the coming years, the dispute became acrimonious. In 1431, a recognisance was issued for the new earl to raise taxes on condition that he would not 'order or consent, do or procure no hurt or harm, to Joan Countess of Westmorland' or her eldest son by her Neville marriage, Richard, Earl of Salisbury, or enter 'unlawfully contrary to the law of England ... any lands or possessions of Ralph, late Earl ... in the possession of the said Countess'. A similar condition was extended to Joan and Richard, pending their appearance before the King's Council, and other such statements would appear in the royal accounts over the coming years. The situation would not be settled during Joan's lifetime.[17] Ultimately, Cecily's mother was protected by her royal inheritance, a further reminder to her children of the significance of their descent.

Joan's proximity to the throne now dictated the next stage in Richard of York's life. Before his death, Ralph had transferred the wardship to Joan, and she was now on the move. In 1425, she took Richard to London, to live at the Lancastrian court.[18] Cecily probably went too. She was then aged ten, a point at which she was not yet considered a 'maiden' but thought to be beyond the dependency of early childhood. In the absence of evidence, there is a slight possibility that she was left behind at Raby, continuing her education under the watchful eye of a governess, but it is more likely that she also made the journey south, especially given the circumstances of mourning and the disputed inheritance. The majority of Joan's surviving children were already married and Cecily was the youngest, so she probably accompanied her mother and fiancé to Westminster. They may have stayed at the court of the young Henry VI or with family or friends. A letter written by Cecily's older sister, Katherine, in 1434 gives a sense of the arrangements made for accommodation in the city. Writing from Lincolnshire to John Paston, she confirmed that she would be taking up his offer to stay in one of his properties: 'We pray you that your place there may be ready for us ... for we will send our stuff thither before our coming.'[19] When Cecily was in London in 1460, she borrowed the Southwark house of Sir John Fastolf, kinsman of the Pastons, who would soon serve with Richard in France. Equally, Joan and Cecily might have been found a place in the household of the widowed Queen Catherine of Valois, while Richard joined the young men clustering round the throne at the start of a new regime.

Born in December 1421, Henry VI had been nine months old when his father had died in France. Before his first birthday, he also became titular King of France, on the death of his maternal grandfather, Charles

VI. Henry V's shoes would have been difficult for his son to fill, even if he had been a fully grown adult. As an infant, he was governed by his uncles John, Duke of Bedford, and Humphrey, Duke of Gloucester, at the head of a regency council. On his deathbed, Henry V had also named Thomas Beaufort, Duke of Exeter, a son of John of Gaunt, as the boy's guardian. Obviously, in his early years, Henry was confined to the sphere of the nursery, and his care was treated separately from the government of the realm. His mother, the young Queen Catherine, was also resident at court and was permitted a degree of influence over his early years, playing a 'direct and immediate ... important role in bringing up her son'.[20] Initially, his nurse, Joan Asteley, was in charge of the nursery along with day nurses and chamber women; their salaries were doubled in 1424 and 1427 as their charge grew older.[21] From 1426, John, Lord Tiptoft, was steward of his household, and from 1427 his doctor was John Somerset. Later, Dame Alice Botiller taught him 'courtesy and nurture', and by the time the countess arrived at court, he was developing well; in 1428, he was considered to be very promising in 'wit and understanding'.[22] This was the world into which Joan Beaufort arrived, with Richard of York and her youngest daughter. There was a clear divide between generations, with older, experienced figures holding power until such time as young Henry and his peers came into their own. It must have been a place where glittering futures were anticipated.

The court remained close to London during this time, regularly moving between the favourite locations of Westminster, Windsor and Eltham, although Henry did venture further to his mother's residences and to sittings of Parliament at Leicester and Kenilworth. Joan and her charges accompanied him; it was at Leicester in May 1426 that Richard of York was knighted by John, Duke of Bedford. Also ennobled alongside him was one of Cecily's brothers, William, already married to the Yorkshire heiress Joan Fauconberg, who was described as an 'idiot' from birth. Watching them, carefully schooled by her mother in terms of her status, the young Cecily absorbed the ceremony and ritual that were her social dues.

Court life for Cecily would have been peripatetic and exciting after her years at Raby. Westminster at that time was a large complex of many buildings, including the palace, with its great hall, painted chamber and royal apartments overlooking the river, as well as the abbey and the multitude of buildings that the government of the realm and upkeep of the king's household required. It would have been a vibrant and busy place, where the most important people of the realm gathered, with the nobles and churchmen attending regular council meetings, ceremonial and religious occasions marked and the reception of ambassadors and visitors from all around the known world. Cecily would have attended the feasts, jousts and worship of a grand European court, with its patronage of the arts and notions of chivalry modelled by the king's uncles and leading men of the day. Hundreds of servants were employed, in duties that encompassed the domestic, administrative, defence and more: controllers, cofferers, almoners and clerks; officers, ministers, minstrels and workmen; from the archers to the vintners, the apothecary to the wardrobe, all had a part to play in the huge, unwieldy machinery of the court. Under Edward III, a duke of the royal blood had been entitled to an income of over £15, of which £13 and 4*d* was for his daily diet and the rest to fund his retinue of 300 men and their horses.[23] Yet by the 1420s, Cecily and Richard found themselves at a court in transition, in embryo; much had changed between the ordinances that survive detailing the running of Edward III's household and those that would be laid down for the adult Henry VI in 1455.

From 1428, the king's tutor was Richard de Beauchamp, Earl of Warwick. He appointed a number of young men to wait on the young Henry, whose future would be entwined with his. Among them were many other Nevilles or those connected to Cecily by marriage. For the young girl, watching her fiancé and family advance, the court would have been full of familiar faces: brothers, sisters, cousins, uncles and aunts, along with their children. First there was Anne Neville, Cecily's sister. In 1424, she had also been married to a royal ward, Humphrey Stafford, Duke of Buckingham, who had been knighted in 1421 and became a Privy Councillor three years later. There were Cecily's brothers: Robert Neville, who became Bishop of Salisbury on 26 October 1427, and Richard Neville, who inherited the title of Earl of Salisbury. This was also the year in which Richard Neville's eldest son, Joan's grandchild, was born. The baby would go on to become the famous 'Kingmaker' Earl of Warwick. Another key figure at court was Joan's son-in-law Henry Percy, son of the Henry 'Hotspur' of Shakespearian legend, who had been appointed to the Great Council during the king's minority. Percy had married Cecily's elder sister Eleanor Neville and by this point they already had eight children. They may also have encountered the newly restored Duke of Norfolk, John de Mowbray. He was the husband of Cecily's eldest sister, Katherine, which might have proved uncomfortable for young Richard, as Mowbray had sat in judgement on his father back in 1415. No wonder Joan took Richard and Cecily to court, with so many of her family close by; no doubt they joined in the young couple's wedding celebrations.

A marriage settlement would have been drawn up for Richard and Cecily. It no longer survives, but another from 1429, between William Haute and Joan Wydeville, can serve as a model of the conventions that Ralph Neville would have followed. The bride's dowry was listed as £40 per year, with an additional £400 marriage portion, and her father would bear the costs of the wedding at Calais. He would also provide her with a 'chamber as a gentlewoman aight for to have', like a trousseau, although this extended beyond clothing to personal jewellery and furniture. If the conditions were met, 'the said William shall have and with the grace of God wedde to wyff Jahn Wydeville'.[24] As the daughter of an earl and future wife of a duke, Cecily could have anticipated her own impressive 'chamber', with clothes, jewels and pieces of furniture to equip her for her life to come.

Richard and Cecily were definitely married by October 1429, when a papal indult was issued to them jointly, concerning their choice of confessor.[25] Sarah Gristwood suggests the ceremony took place soon after May 1427, when Cecily had reached her twelfth birthday, and this would be in accordance with contemporary practice. The location remains a mystery but they were probably either in London or County Durham. When Cecily's sister Katherine was married in 1412, the wedding took place in the chapel at Raby Castle, so there is a chance that Cecily and Richard were united there too. However, their location in London may suggest it was in one of the chapels at Westminster Palace, perhaps even in the queen's closet, in the presence of the king. The most likely location was St Stephen's Chapel, which had been, and would continue to be, used for royal marriages.[26] It was an important marriage, even without the benefit of hindsight, but it was not standard practice to record the details of the event. Over a century would pass before churches began to keep registers of birth, marriages and deaths; if Richard and Cecily's nuptials made it onto paper, that record has not survived. On her marriage, Cecily's heraldic coat of arms, which had been a Neville white saltire, or diagonal cross, on a red background, was impaled by that of her husband, with its French fleur-de-lys and English lions.

On 6 November 1429, Richard, Duke of York, attended Henry VI's coronation in Westminster Abbey, wearing clothing provided by the royal household. As his duchess and wife, Cecily would have been with him, along with several other members of her family who performed ceremonial roles. According to *Gregory's Chronicle*, the young king, just a month short of his seventh birthday, was borne into the abbey, in a scarlet cloth, by Richard Beauchamp, Earl of Warwick. Cecily's brother-in-law John de Mowbray, Duke of Norfolk, rode after them as Marshall of England, and her brother Richard, Earl Salisbury, rode with them as a Constable of England. Gregory describes the boy being 'a-rayde lyke a kynge in a ryche clothe of golde, with a crowne sette on hys hedde',[27] then led through the Palace of Westminster to the hall.

There, Richard and Cecily would have taken their places at the table. Seated on the right of the king were the barons of the Cinque Ports and the clerks of chancery, and on his left were London's mayor, William Estfeld, and his aldermen, along with other 'worthy commoners of the city'. The duke and duchess were probably on one of the two tables in the centre of the hall with the 'bishops, justices and worthy knights'.[28] It would have been the young couple's first taste of the type of celebrations that were apposite for medieval royalty, for a bloodline they shared. Later in life, they would gain a reputation for ostentation, for living 'like kings'. As an impressionable young pair, aged fourteen and eighteen, they participated in the entertainments and sampled the three courses designed to emphasise the claim of a Lancastrian child, which was technically a weaker claim than Richard's. As the first course was being served, the king's champion, Sir Philip Dymoke, rode in, armed as St George. He proclaimed to the four corners of the hall that Henry VI was the rightful heir to the crown and that if anyone disputed this 'he was redy for to defende hyt as hys knyghte and hys champyon'. Richard of York held his tongue, for now.[29]

Up from the kitchens came a boar's head, 'enarmoured in a castle royal', frumenty with venison, gilded meat, swan, stewed capon, heron, pike, red cream with 'a whyte lyon crownyde therein', custard royal decorated with a golden fleur-de-lys and fritters 'like a sun'.[30] It was followed by a subtlety of carved marzipan, depicting St Edward and St Lewis bringing Henry his coat of arms, which bore celebration verses. The second course included white meats, jelly decorated with *Te Deums*, pork, crane, rabbit, chickens, peacock, bream, fritters, custard and cream with an 'anteloppe crownyde therein and schynynge as golde'.[31] The food was decorated with powdered gold fleur-de-lys and white feathers. The second subtlety depicted the Emperor and Henry V, offering the young king the mantle of the Garter. Finally, they dined on quince compote, more roast venison, crabs and a selection of roast birds, including egrets, curlews, woodcock, plovers, quails and larks. There were baked meats, crisp fritters and pies powdered with lozenges, gilded white and decorated with borage flowers. The cream was coloured violet and the subtlety was of 'owre Lady syttynge, and hyr Chylde in hyr lappe, holdyng in everyhonde a crowne, Synt Gorge knelyng on that one syde and Synt Denys in that othyr syde'.[32]

The coronation and banquet must have been a memorable occasion for the young Cecily. It set a standard for the lifestyle suitable to one of royal estate that she would later try to emulate. However, on that November day, she probably did not imagine that her husband would ever challenge Henry VI's right to rule.

4

His Young Duchess
1429–1437

A womman of right famous governaunce
And wele cherisshed, I sey yow for certeyne;
Hir felawship shal do yow grete plesaunce,
Hir porte is suche, hir manere is trewe and playne;
She with glad chiere wil do hir busy peyne
To bryng yow there.[1]

The courtly love of medieval romances mostly belonged on the pages of illuminated manuscripts, highlighted in red or gold, or tripping off the lips of troubadours strumming their lutes. Lovers swooned in neatly clipped gardens, pining for their beloved to notice their existence or else engaged in Herculean labours to win their favour. Such books were owned by many of the aristocracy of England and Norman France but, in reality, these stories bore little resemblance to the financial and legal negotiations by which they were partnered for life.

There was little that could be considered romantic about the majority of marriages made among the fifteenth-century nobility. Partners were chosen by a child's family for dynastic and financial gain; they might be significantly older or younger than their spouses, and papal dispensations were often required in order to dissolve close ties of blood, intermarriage or spiritual connection. Once the agreement had been reached, with its various clauses about obligation and payment, the ceremony itself was more like the final stage of a transaction than the romantic occasions of today. The exchange of vows was consolidated by physical consummation, without which the match could be questioned or even dissolved. In royalty and high-ranking couples this was a formal occasion, with the pair led to bed by their family and friends and then questioned the following day, or the sheets and clothing examined, to ensure that the act had taken place. Physical difficulties and failures could become public knowledge, as in the case of Edward IV's mistress Elizabeth (Jane) Shore's first marriage, which was annulled due to her husband's impotence.

The main purpose of marriage was procreation. If Richard and Cecily managed to consummate their match in 1429, no surviving children would arrive for another nine years. This poses the historian a number of questions which, after the passage of five centuries, can only be answered with speculation. In the simplest scenario, Cecily did not conceive because they did not sleep together at all, or enough, for whatever reason. This is not impossible; it may have stemmed from some physical, emotional or psychological cause now lost to history; they may have tried and failed to connect or suffered from some illness. Perhaps it took two young, inexperienced people a while to get it right. Henry VI and his young queen, Margaret of Anjou, would take almost eight years to conceive their only child. Not all marriages were consummated at once. The Duke of Berry waited before consummating his marriage to the twelve-year-old Jeanne of Boulogne, stating to the king that he would 'guard her for three or four years until she becomes a perfect woman'.[2] There are many reasons why a physical connection can fail to produce children, still imperfectly understood by modern science. Fertility can be affected by the onset of menstruation, irregular ovulation, sperm count, the ratio of fat to body weight and any number of illnesses. Equally it can be triggered by changes in lifestyle, so Cecily's lack of conception over the next eight years is a riddle; it may have resulted from a number of factors.

Cecily's prolific sisters had little trouble conceiving quickly after their marriages. Katherine had been married at the age of twelve and bore her first child three years later. Eleanor was left a widow in 1414 at the age of seventeen but soon remarried to Henry Percy, son of Henry 'Hotspur'. The match may have coincided with his creation as Earl of Northumberland in 1416, for she was pregnant by the following autumn, delivering a short-lived son in July 1418. More recently, Anne's marriage in October 1424 had borne at least one child in 1425. Their mother Joan had conceived within around a year of her first marriage, bearing her first daughter at fourteen. In February 1397, at eighteen, she had conceived soon after her marriage to Ralph Neville, with the birthdate of her daughter Eleanor often given as the same year. Equally, Joan's mother, Katherine Swynford, began bearing children young, in her early to mid-teens. There do not appear to have been any hereditary fertility complications in Cecily's maternal line to explain the delay in her conception.

It is possible that Cecily did conceive and experienced miscarriages. If so, this would not have been recorded, especially if it was in the early stages, the first trimester or so. It may have been a purely personal matter, known only to the couple and Cecily's ladies. Assuming they were sharing a bed, the pair must have begun to wonder whether there was a problem. They may have tried one of the medieval remedies for infertility, such as pine nuts and chestnuts boiled in wine and sugar, or various combinations of herbs and 'sympathetic' ingredients such as quail testicles, ewe's or mare's milk, sheep urine or rabbit's blood. Women trying to conceive were given a drink made from powdered rabbit's womb, or encouraged to recite certain charms or perform symbolic rituals, such as writing out prayers on cards to be worn around the neck.[3] It is most likely that Cecily appealed for a child in her prayers, to the Virgin Mary and her favourite saints. Children were considered to be a sign of God's blessing of the union. The thirteenth-century text on marriage *Hali Meidenhad* stated that 'if she cannot breed, she is called barren. Her lord loveth and respects her less and she, as one that is very bad, weepeth at her fate, and calleth them glad and happy that breed a family.'[4] Some couples simply had to accept, perhaps over the course of decades, that they would not produce a child; others remarried but conception still did not follow. Branches of certain families died out as a result of low fertility or infertility. The blame was usually attached to the woman but, in several cases, wives went on to remarry and conceive with different partners, like Catherine Parr a century later, who only fell pregnant by her fourth husband.

In the early days of their marriage, the young couple appear to have remained in London after Henry VI's coronation as, in January 1430, Richard acted as Constable of England at a duel in the king's presence at Smithfield. The Greyfriars' Chronicle describes that 'there was a grete battelle in Smythfelde betwene Upton and John Downe; and whan they had fowth longe, the kynge toke up the matter and gave them grace'.[5] One possible reason that Cecily did not conceive may be the simple fact that they were not together. In April 1430, Richard accompanied the young king to France. It is by no means certain that the fourteen-year-old Cecily went with him. Her presence is not recorded then, as it would be later, but it would go some way to explaining her lack of conception.

On 20 February, an order was issued at Westminster for the king's uncle Humphrey, Duke of Gloucester, to summon the barons of the

Cinque Ports 'to be with ships and seamen in sufficient array'[6] at the Kent port of Sandwich before 1 May. Fifty-seven ships, each containing twenty men and a master, were to be ready to set sail at forty days' notice. The master would receive 6*d* a day and the men 3*d*, in service of the king's 'expedition against his enemies'.[7] Henry had more than 300 people in his retinue, including 8 dukes and earls, 182 servants and 5 surgeons; for the year 1430–31, this cost £22,000, mostly spent in France.[8] Richard had a personal retinue of nineteen, plus twelve lancers and thirty-six archers, and was awarded £400 to pay for his expenses.[9] No wife is mentioned. The king's fleet was assembled at Sandwich but he set sail from Dover. When the crossing was made, in April, Cecily may have accompanied Richard into Kent and waved him goodbye from the castle overlooking the port. They disembarked at Calais at ten in the morning on St George's Day, 23 April.

Why Cecily should accompany Richard in 1440 and not 1430 might be explained by the change in his role. By the time Cecily can be definitely placed in Rouen, in 1440, she had already borne two children and been married for eleven years; her husband was now Lieutenant of France, which would have required his residency. If Richard left her behind in 1430, it may have been because, as a minor, his role was not yet fixed and his family was not yet established. He went to France in attendance on Henry, not as the head of his own establishment, as he later would. Married couples were often separated, with the husband leaving his wife behind at home for long periods away, as was the case with John and Margaret Paston, who married in 1440. Perhaps the duke and duchess also wrote to each other, like the Pastons did, with such phrases as 'I recommend me unto you, desiring heartily to hear of your welfare' and praying 'you heartily that ye will vouchsafe to send me a letter as hastily as ye may'; Margaret urges John to wear the ring with the image of St Margaret that she sent him 'for a remembrance till ye come home'.[10] Perhaps Cecily also gave Richard some token for good luck.

It seems reasonable to assume that Cecily awaited Richard's return at court with her mother. As members of the royal family, with Joan being the granddaughter of Edward III, they may have found positions in the queen's household. The widowed Catherine of Valois was still in her twenties and had played an active part in the upbringing of her young son. During his absence in France, she was living at Windsor Castle, so Joan and Cecily may well have been among her household at the solid Norman castle on the Thames in Berkshire. Windsor had played a central role during Henry V's reign, hosting the Holy Roman Emperor in 1417 and being the location for the birth of Henry VI four years later. In 1428, it had been assigned as a summer residence for the king, where he was attended by young men, making it an 'academy for the young nobility'.[11] It also had romantic family associations, as the location where King James, King of Scotland, had fallen in love with Joan's namesake. Perhaps Cecily and her mother now witnessed another love affair unfolding.

Born around 1401, Catherine had been only twenty when Henry V died. Now, in the seclusion of Windsor, and perhaps also at other royal residences like Berkhamsted Castle, she drew close to her Welsh Keeper of the Wardrobe, Owen Tudor. Tradition has him falling in her lap during a dance. A Bill drawn up in 1428 had forbidden her from remarrying without the approval of the council, on the pain of her husband's lands being forfeited. The pair may have entered into a clandestine marriage, as her first two sons, Edmund and Jasper, were born during this time, in secrecy at Much Hadham and Hatfield. If Countess Joan and her daughter were trusted members of her inner circle, they might have been present, even assisting on these occasions. This is also suggested by Cecily's own choice to lie in at Hatfield when she bore a daughter in 1441.

Queen Catherine would have been among the first to receive news of the king's progress. In July, Henry VI arrived in Rouen, a city where the memories of the terrible siege of 1418–19, inflicted upon them by Henry V, were still fresh. The poem which survives in *Gregory's Chronicle*, 'The Siege of Rouen', describes how the vulnerable residents – the ill, old and young – had been forced out of the city walls to starve in ditches while those inside resorted to eating rats, cats, dogs and horses. Richard would have witnessed the trial of the French peasant girl Jeanne d'Arc, which began in Rouen on 9 January 1431, and her burning for heresy in the marketplace that May. He then attended the French coronation of Henry VI in the Parisian cathedral of Notre Dame in December, where he is listed among the attendant lords by the French chronicler Monstrelet as 'the rich duke of York'. He describes Henry walking under an azure canopy, sprinkled with fleurs-de-lys, presented with three crimson hearts containing violets and white doves. Before the church of the Innocents, a pageant had taken over the street, making it into a sort of forest where a living stag was hunted by dogs and horsemen, finally finding refuge at Henry's feet. At the ceremony itself, York was among the lords who assisted 'according to their various offices'. No mention was made of York's duchess, and the reference to ladies applauding the tournament held on the following day is too vague to confirm her presence. York was among the party who returned home with the English king the following January.

Henry VI was triumphantly received in London. Cecily may well have been there in order to meet Richard, on the occasion recorded in a poem by John Lydgate called 'The Comynge of the Kynge out of Fraunce to London'. It was a Thursday, towards the end of a windy February, according to Lydgate, making it 21 February by the reckoning of Victorian editor Nicholas Nicolas. She would have been among the citizens who 'hallowed' the day with 'great solemnity' and enjoyed the sun's beams, shining on London, making them all 'glad and light', welcoming their 'sovereign lord' with 'pure and clene intente' before the 'noble devyses' prepared in his honour. The pageants, featuring towers, champions, heraldic beasts and abstract virtues, with beautiful women and the sun god Phoebus, must have reminded some witnesses of the return of Henry V in 1415. The young married couple would have been reunited after an absence of twenty-two months. They must have changed; he was now twenty and she was sixteen. It was time to set up home together.

On 12 May 1432, Richard was granted 'livery of his estates'. This meant his uncle's full inheritance was put in his hands, as his 'heir of entail' who was found 'now of age'. During his minority, 'grievous waste' had been done to his lands and estates, and he was owed recompense for 'the good and unpaid service which by command of the King he had performed in France and in England at his great cost and charges'.[12] For Cecily, this marked a significant rite of passage in the eyes of medieval society – she and York were finally able to act as an independent, autonomous couple, taking on the reins of their estates, as well as dealing with the many challenges that such a large inheritance would bring. The lands were divided between two administrative centres, Ludlow and Fotheringhay, but they owned many other castles and manors around the country, and their existence during these early years of marriage must have been fairly peripatetic.

York's earldom of March had brought him significant lands and responsibilities in Wales. In May 1433, he was bound to pay Queen Catherine £53 6s 8d every year for the castle and lordship of Montgomery, in Powys, Mid Wales.[13] This might suggest that Richard and Cecily were resident there during part of this time, or that they used the castle on a regular basis. Now in ruins, Montgomery Castle was situated on the border, or Marcher lands, between England and Wales. According to the

1433 order, it had been given by Edmund, Earl of March, to Catherine for the duration of her life.[14] The castle had been refurbished around 1360. It had rectangular towers and an eastern range, accessible from the courtyard, and contained a chapel and three upper floors of private rooms. There was also a brewhouse and bakehouse with a large bread oven. The records between this time and the 1538 refurbishments are lacking and it has often been assumed that the castle went into decline or was used as a prison.

Standing high on a promontory, surrounded by ruins, Montgomery Castle must have been bleak. The surrounding market town had been razed during a siege of 1402 but the castle had held firm. Richard may well have been paying Queen Catherine an annual rent for the property because he and Cecily were using it as one of their residences, perhaps a temporary one. Richard's duties on inheriting the title of Earl of March would have involved regular visits to the borders, and Montgomery Castle was perfectly placed to facilitate this. Interestingly, in July 1433, Richard was asked to surrender a prisoner in his care, a Maurice ap Madoc ap Eyngnoun, or Eynoun, into the care of Richard de Beauchamp, Earl of Warwick, his kinsman through his marriage to Cecily's niece.[15] In September, Eynoun was transferred to imprisonment in Windsor Castle. This may have been the same person as Maurice ap Evan Lloyd ap Maurice ap Madoc ap Einion, who was vicar of St Michael's church in Kerry, Powys, Wales, in the 1440s. Kerry is less than 10 miles from Montgomery, suggesting that Richard, or his agents, were active in the area.

The Yorks were also in possession of Wigmore Castle, which had been granted to Richard in 1424. It had long been a Mortimer property and, although some sources have claimed it was in disrepair by this time, recent archaeological excavations by English Heritage have indicated that it underwent some 'extensive work' in the fifteenth century. The report also found good evidence of an upper-class diet being consumed, with cattle as the main food source, along with game and wildfowl, cod and herring. There were also suggestions that the castle had fish ponds for freshwater fish and that oats were used for hop making, rather than the traditional barley. There was also a garden within the castle walls. Stone and ceramic roof tiles were found, along with floor tiles, painted plaster and painted window glass, indicative of high-quality living. Also found were pieces of plate armour and other military objects.[16] No doubt Cecily spent some time in this beautiful location, high on a promontory south of Ludlow, overlooking the Welsh Marches.

In spite of their many properties, the young couple's main home was at Fotheringhay Castle, in Northamptonshire. Richard had inherited it in 1415 and it probably came into his full possession in September 1432, with the death of his aunt Anne, widow of the Earl of March. Although little of the castle remains, even less than at Montgomery, it was once a significant place, more than suitable for the residence of the Duke of York. It had been rebuilt and enlarged by Edmund of Langley, Richard's grandfather, and further improvements were made during the early fifteenth century, which may have been instigated by Richard and Cecily. In early July 1433, Richard was granted the right to raise £200 in Yorkshire, on condition that he pay £100 annually towards the completion of the collegiate church at Fotheringhay, according to the will of his grandfather, Edward of Langley.[17]

A mid-fourteenth-century description of the castle when occupied by Marie de St Pol described it as having a tower and being built of stone, 'walled in, embattled and encompassed with a good moat. Within are one large hall, two chambers, two chapels, a kitchen and bakehouse ... a porter's lodge with chambers over it and a drawbridge beneath.' Within the walls there was also a modern manor house, which contained offices and chambers 'and an outer gate with a room over it. The site of the whole contains ten acres.' An outer bailey was added in the 1430s and it was suggested, in a work of 1821, that this was deliberately created in the shape of a fetterlock, one of the heraldic devices of the House of York. The same book, Bonney's *Fotheringhay*, explains that in the early nineteenth century you could still see a staircase leading to 'fine lodgings', as well as a 'wonderful, spacious hall' and 'goodly and fair court'. It lists a buttery, brewhouse, bakehouse and yard, along with offices, a great house, barn, orchard or garden and another ruined house within the outer wall. Work began in 1434 on the new parish church of St Mary and All Saints, where Richard and Cecily now lie at rest. For seventeen months, in 1432 and 1433, Richard's duties indicate that he had the opportunity to live with Cecily as man and wife. Yet still there was no child.

Life for Cecily as a medieval duchess in the 1430s would have been quiet enough. Dividing her daily routine between acts of religious piety and managing her household, she was, in many ways, typical of many women of the aristocracy. Their lives were shaped by obligation; to their king, husbands, family and those dependent upon them for their livelihood. The ordinances survive from Cecily's household late in her life, after 1483, and, while her status then as a widow was significantly different from that which she held early in her marriage, some of her preoccupations would not have changed. In both cases, she was conscious of what was due to her status; the ordinances open with the recognition that it was 'requisite to understand the order of her own person, concerning God and the world'.[18] She would also have accompanied Richard to court, especially when he was required to attend council meetings. As his duchess, she would have had some ceremonial roles to play as well as receiving petitions on his behalf. Letters surviving from her widowhood in the 1460s and 1470s show she was actively involved in disputes concerning the land, wardships and property of her tenants; in the earlier years, she probably had some involvement in such events on a smaller scale.

There was certainly plenty to keep Cecily busy. It has been estimated that in the 1420s, Richard's estates brought in an annual income of over £4,000, spread across eighteen counties, in addition to the fact that he was the largest landowner in Wales.[19] These were grouped into nineteen receiverships, administered in Ludlow and Fotheringhay. Even with the employment of trustworthy deputies, this was a task that required much energy and skill. Whenever Richard was obliged to attend Parliament, or to oversee court sessions, Cecily was the next in command, required to provide the public face of their partnership, whatever situation might arise. The surviving evidence suggests that Cecily was actively involved in legal affairs; apart from her correspondence, she appears in a 1462 grant to determine a wardship, a 1476 land dispute in Essex and in a 1480 Court of Common Appeals for Devon, in pursuit of an errant receiver. She would have learned how to instigate and submit such cases to the legal processes during her early years as a duchess.

In May 1433, Richard was summoned to attend Henry VI's ninth parliament at Westminster. He travelled to London for the opening session on 8 July and was occupied there until it dissolved that December. Cecily probably went too. At this parliament, her mother Joan's legal dispute was raised again. Her petitioner suggested that 'if a judgement [was] rendered ... against the ... [new] earl', she would 'content the king' with £800 raised from the family coffers.[20] Richard and Cecily may have returned to Fotheringhay for a few months before the next summons came the following July. They had plenty of time to organise the move before travelling back to court for Henry's tenth parliament, which sat from 10 October until 23 December 1434.[21] Cecily was probably back at Fotheringhay in September 1435 when the news arrived of the death of the king's uncle, John of Lancaster, Duke of Bedford. He had been Governor of Normandy from 1422 to 1432 and his second wife, whom he married in 1433, was the young Jacquetta of Luxembourg. She would go on to become the mother of Elizabeth Wydeville, who would be Cecily's daughter-in-law and her queen. It opened up an important vacancy in the king's service overseas.

In 1436, Richard of York was still a comparatively young and inexperienced man. However, after much debate on the Royal Council, he was appointed Lieutenant General and Governor of France for a trial period of twelve months. The port of Winchelsea in East Sussex was chosen as the place of departure. Now it sits high on a landlocked promontory overlooking fields of sheep, but then the little town was a thriving port. A century before, it had grown prosperous on importing wines from Gascony, shipping in 737,000 gallons in a single year and providing passage for pilgrims to Santiago de Compostela, in ships of up to 200 tonnes. In 1434 alone, two years before Richard left the port, 2,433 people set off for the Spanish Way of St James.[22] On 20 May, Parliament granted 'our beloved Richard, Duke of York, in general our lieutenant', power 'to treat for perpetual peace or ill with France'.[23] York's party left the port days later, taking Cecily's brothers Richard, Earl of Salisbury, and William, Lord Fauconberg, with him, as well as Sir John Fastolf and others. This time, Cecily must have been with him, as she fell pregnant for the first time during his term of office.

Their destination was Rouen, the capital of Normandy and seat of English rule. Until recently it had been governed by the Duke of Bedford, who continued the plans of his brother Henry V to conquer and defend the north of France. Bedford had overseen a number of sieges and operations since 1422, winning significant victories and territories. However, after 1431 the French had made significant gains and reconciled with their former enemies in Burgundy, humiliating the English in the Treaty of Arras in September 1435. Bedford's death, a week before its conclusion, left a vacuum that remained unfilled for nine months. During that time, the French had recaptured Paris, and all the English there had been evacuated. Richard, Duke of York, knew he had a difficult task ahead.

On arrival, the Yorks moved into Rouen Castle. Only one tower now survives, but in the fifteenth century it was circular, with six towers and a demi-tower and two thick curtain walls; those of the surviving donjon are over 4 metres thick and 30 metres high.[24] Inside were a set of royal apartments and those previously inhabited by Bedford, which York and Cecily would have occupied. There was also a robing room, three chapels and a large inner courtyard. It had been built by Philip II between 1204 and 1210, and stood slightly to the north of the medieval city, being the main seat of administrative power for the whole region until the sixteenth century. Bedford had also built his own manor house in Rouen, the Castle of Joyeux Repos, a 3- or 4-acre site in the east of the city on which he lavished money in the early 1430s, adding fish ponds, planting trees and making tennis courts. Later the possession of a Celestine priory, the site is presently occupied by the Hôpital Charles Nicolle in the Rue de Germont.[25] It is more likely that this property went to his widow than that it remained in possession of the Crown and available to Richard and Cecily.

A castle book of hours, dating from the fifteenth century and from Rouen, is now in the possession of Bryn Mawr College, Pennsylvania. It features Latin prayers, the Gospels and eight miniature illustrations of the life of the Virgin along with other devotional scenes, beautifully illuminated with gold and floral decoration. There is no indication of ownership through the inclusion of heraldic devices but, given her wealth and piety, it is not too difficult to imagine this book, or one like it, being used by Cecily during her stay in the castle. Bedford is one possible candidate for the commissioning of the manuscript, as he was a well-known collector of early books, and ordered the creation of the Bedford book of hours in 1423 as a gift for his first wife. There was another candidate, too, active in Rouen between around 1420 and 1450. Known as the 'Fastolf Master', he worked on a number of manuscripts commissioned by the Hundred Years' War veteran, Sir John Fastolf, completing the *Livre de Quatre Vertues* around 1450. Both Fastolf and Bedford had Rouen connections with the Yorks, so Cecily may have had access to the libraries or works by the scribes and illuminators they employed. They may even have made recommendations for the Yorks to commission their own works.

It was during this period that another significant marriage took place. Bedford's widow was the beautiful Jacquetta of Luxembourg, Cecily's exact contemporary, descended from the Count of St Pol and, further back, from Henry III. She had been granted her dower settlement by Parliament on 6 February 1436, on condition that she did not marry again without a special licence. It is likely that she remained in Rouen after Bedford's death, probably at his castle of Joyeux Repos, as Henry VI ordered the loyal Lancastrian knight Sir Richard Wydeville to bring her back to England. It was a decision that would have huge future implications for the monarchy. Wydeville had previously been Bedford's chamberlain and would have been known to Jacquetta during these years in Rouen. The couple may already have been in love or else the circumstances threw them more closely together. They were married in secret sometime before 23 March 1437. Perhaps Jacquetta was already pregnant with their first child, Elizabeth, the 'White Queen' of popular fiction, whose birthdate is also given as 1437. They travelled back to England and confessed to the match. Henry VI imposed a fine of £1,000 for the violation of her dower terms, but officially forgave the couple that October.

An account of July 1439, written by English ambassadors negotiating a treaty in Normandy, gives a flavour of the sort of diplomatic engagements in which Richard and Cecily would have been engaged. As guests of Cardinal Beaufort and the Duchess of Burgundy in Calais, they dined at the home of the Archbishop of York and supped with the Duke of Stafford. The following morning, oaths of loyalty were sworn on the altar in the cardinal's oratory. On St Swithin's Day, 'pavilions or tents were erected on the spot selected for the meeting' and the cardinal gave 'a solemn entertainment to all the ambassadors and others of high rank'. A description of the cardinal's tent shows the impressive formality of these temporary structures and the lifestyle they offered:

> Built of timber, covered with new canvas, [it] was upwards of one hundred feet in length, and contained almost all necessary offices, as a pantry, butlery, wine cellar and two chambers; in the centre was a hall, covered and lined in scarlet tapestry, sufficiently large for 300 persons to sit at table and kitchens at the end.

In one tent belonging to the duchess was a 'seat covered in cloth and cushions of gold'. Long conferences were punctuated by dinners where Masses were preached to guests wearing cloth of gold, and diplomatic negotiations were fuelled by wine and sweetmeats.[26]

During the winter months at Rouen, news arrived from London that the king's mother, Catherine of Valois, had died at the age of thirty-five. Having borne Owen Tudor several children, her death on 3 January was probably the result of complications following childbirth. Given the secrecy surrounding her liaison, this may not have been common knowledge, although if Cecily and her mother had spent time in the queen's household, the duchess may at least have suspected the cause. It would have served as a reminder of just how dangerous the business of bearing children could be, although this would have been of little consequence to the young couple who were hoping to continue their dynastic line. Then, in the late spring, after eight years of marriage, Cecily may have finally conceived. Richard was relieved of his duty and replaced by the more experienced Richard Beauchamp, Earl of Warwick, that July, so the duke and duchess could anticipate returning to England.

The death of another English queen that year was to delay their departure. On 10 June, Henry IV's second wife, Joan of Navarre, passed away at her home at Havering-atte-Bower in London. She had proved a controversial figure, being convicted of attempting to poison Henry V in 1419 and spending four years in prison as a result. Now, though, she was given a state funeral and interred next to her husband in Canterbury Cathedral. Warwick's attendance delayed his departure for France slightly but then his plan to sail at the end of August was ruined by bad weather. In the end, he arrived in Rouen on 6 November. York and Cecily departed a few days later.[27] They would have been back at Fotheringhay in time to celebrate Christmas.

5

Becoming a Mother
1438–1442

And the froyt [fruit] that coms hom betwene,
Hit schal have grace to thryve and the;
Ther other schal have turment and tene,
Fore covetyse unlaufully[1]

Cecily Neville is particularly remembered today for her motherhood
and her piety. These were the defining features of women's lives in the
fifteenth century, the standards to which they aspired in order to establish
their worth in the eyes of society and the Church. After a slow start,
Cecily would more than prove her fertility. Over the next seventeen
years, she would bear at least twelve children, perhaps more. They
arrived at different locations, in England, France and Ireland, suggesting
that she remained at her husband's side throughout this time, and with a
regularity and speed that implies their relationship was close. The piety
may have come later.

As with so many issues concerning women's health, suggestions that
Cecily first gave birth in 1438 can be neither confirmed nor refuted. Such
events were rarely written down in any sort of reliable way, even in the
cases of important families. Those records that have survived have done
so almost against the odds. The national parish register system of births,
marriages and deaths, which revolutionised the way in which people's
lives were recorded, was still a century away in 1438. When births were
recorded, it was often in family Bibles or retrospectively, in dynastic
histories. For example, Edward's own commission, the *Edward IV Roll*,
or the *Chronicle of the History of the World from Creation to Woden*
only lists five of the king's siblings. The fullest list is found in a poem in

the Clare Roll, which records Cecily's surviving children and those who died at birth or in their infancy, making twelve in total, but there is no mention of this reputed first child. The poem does not include any who were lost before the full term of a pregnancy; miscarriages and short-lived children frequently went unrecorded, particularly if the loss had occurred before baptism had taken place. It was written in May 1460, when the Yorks were a large, established family. The author is unlikely to have known of any premature losses Cecily suffered as a young woman or to have seen any reason to include them. The only thing that can be stated without question is that if she bore a child in 1438, it did not survive.

The next time that Cecily can be identified at a specific time and place is 10 August 1439. On that day she was at Fotheringhay Castle, where she was preparing to give birth. This meant she had conceived early the previous November, which is not incompatible with another pregnancy in the same year. The prospect could be terrifying for a first-time mother, given the potential for injury and loss, in spite of the rudimentary pain relief offered by herbs and pseudo-religious rituals. Cecily would have withdrawn into a chamber at the castle with her womenfolk, perhaps with the assistance of her mother Joan and her married sisters. It was usually a group affair, allowing for the women to share their experience, with the assistance of a local midwife and female servants to ensure the room was kept well stocked with refreshments, firewood and clean linen.

Cecily could have afforded icons of her favourite saints, a rosary and a cross, and may even have borrowed some of the relics that religious houses regularly loaned out to high-status women during labour. Less than 10 miles away from Fotheringhay was the city of Peterborough, with its impressive Norman cathedral. The records of twelfth-century monk Hugh Candidus list in the reliquary such fantastical items as a piece of Aaron's rod, sections of Jesus's swaddling clothes, part of the original manger in which the baby Jesus lay and pieces of the five loaves that had fed the 5,000! More significantly, though, it claimed to house an item of clothing belonging to St Mary. Saints' clothing, in particular those such as shifts and girdles, were favoured by medieval mothers as offering some protection against the dangers of childbirth. Later, Cecily's granddaughter, Elizabeth of York, would rely on the girdle of St Mary from Westminster Abbey. There was no pain relief, but the regular chants and prayers, in addition to the belief in the goodwill and guidance of the saints, may have provided Cecily some relief in what frequently proved to be a terrifying and fatal ordeal for medieval women. Eventually, a baby girl was born. She was named Anne, perhaps in honour of Richard's mother.

Cecily recovered at Fotheringhay. Her infant daughter was baptised soon after her birth, which would have been arranged by her godparents, perhaps in a chapel inside the castle itself, or in the new parish church of St Mary and All Saints, which had been completed in 1430. It was customary for new mothers to lie in for up to a month following the delivery, to allow themselves a full chance of recovery. After that, in early September, Cecily would have been led, veiled, to the church, to undergo the ceremony of purification, later known as churching. A nursery would have been established for the baby at Fotheringhay, with wet nurses and rockers, overseen by a trusted lady governess. After the years of waiting, Cecily had proved she could produce a healthy child. Her next duty was to bear a son.

Richard, though, may not have been in England to greet the new arrival. His future had been in question since Warwick had taken over as Lieutenant in Rouen. On 7 April 1437, he had been formally thanked for his services, and directed to 'remain in France until other chieftains should be appointed to go there'.[2] Later in April, more of York's old powers were transferred to Warwick by royal command, so he was sitting idly in Rouen with little to do but watch and help keep the peace.[3] Some sources suggest he travelled back and forth between France and England over the next two years and, on this occasion, did not return until November 1439. By then, he was less than happy with the way he had been treated by Henry's parliament; apart from wasted time, his activities in France had left him seriously out of pocket and the Crown owed him around £18,000.[4] The situation soon changed again. Warwick had died in Rouen on 30 April 1439 and so, once more, the opportunity arose for York to return there in a permanent capacity. Less experienced than both Bedford and Warwick, York's appointment had something of a second-best feel to it but, finally, he was given a more secure role. On 2 July 1440 he was appointed to the position on a five-year commission, and that October he was granted protection for his servants, goods and properties in his forthcoming absence. However, he would not travel back across the Channel for another year. This may have been because, nine months after the birth of her daughter, Cecily had fallen pregnant again. Perhaps it was as a gift for her, in reward for this conception, that Richard spent a huge £23 15s buying crimson damask cloth from Italian merchant brothers Andrea and Federico Corner.[5]

Something kept Richard in England while Normandy was in a volatile state. It is quite likely that he was ensuring he was leaving his affairs in the hands of men he could trust, such as Bishop Brown of Norwich, Bishop Aiscough of Salisbury, Alnwick of Lincoln and Lord Sudeley, who, with many others, had made the transition from the household of the Duke of Bedford into that of York. On 19 November, the council encouraged Richard to leave for France, 'as his welbeloved cousin Richard Duc of Yorke shall mowe ye better do hym service in his royalme of France and duchie of Normandy ... to encorage to said Duk ... to be the redyer forthward so as for tareying of him none inconveniens follow'.[6] Another reason for remaining was the death of his mother-in-law. Joan Beaufort passed away at the age of sixty-one, on 13 November, at Howden in Yorkshire. In an interesting move that stressed her royal lineage, she chose to be buried with her mother at Lincoln Cathedral, rather than with either of her husbands. After all, it was the location where her father, John of Gaunt, had married her mother, Katherine Swynford, legitimising a union that had lasted for years. The double tomb, now positioned one after another, head to foot, stands under a stone canopy in the sanctuary at Lincoln, decorated with brass plates and shields. Originally, the pair had been side by side, as indicated in a seventeenth-century sketch, before being damaged during the Civil War. Cecily may have travelled the 50 miles from Fotheringhay to attend the funeral, but at this point she was six months pregnant. Within a few weeks, she would have gone into retirement, awaiting the birth. When this came, in February 1441, she was around 120 miles from Lincoln, in Hatfield, Hertfordshire.

Hatfield has long been a site with royal connections. The present Hatfield House, built by James I's minister Robert Cecil, stood on the site of an earlier palace, constructed at the end of the fifteenth century by Archbishop Morton. Originally a quadrangle of buildings around a courtyard surrounded by gardens, the banqueting hall still survives as testimony to the wealth of its traditional owners, the bishops of Ely. However, this was probably an extension of an even earlier building called the manor of Bishop's Hatfield, used as an episcopal palace in convenient proximity to London. Between 1437 and 1443, the manor was in the possession of Lewis de Luxembourg, Archbishop of Rouen and Bishop of Ely *in commendum*, that is, in custody while the position was vacant. He is not known to have visited the house but may have lent it to the duke and duchess as a result of their Rouen connections.

It is interesting to speculate as to why Cecily lay in at Hatfield. It has associations with the delivery of the late Queen Katherine's son Jasper, but none of Cecily's other children were born there. Was it an actual choice, or perhaps just the location where she found herself at the salient moment? Given that Cecily would follow Richard throughout his career and deliver children in France and Ireland, they may have been en route to or from London when it became necessary to stop. Perhaps Cecily was leaving the capital to travel home to Fotheringhay, where she had borne Anne and, presumably, where Anne's household and nurses were, when she went into labour. It was not always possible to predict exactly when a child was expected; there were no reliable pregnancy tests, and indicators such as belly size or foetal movement could be misleading. There is a chance that Cecily thought she had more time, or else her next baby decided to arrive early. Another possibility is that she became ill or began the process of miscarriage while travelling nearby and was taken to the manor.

The child she bore on 10 February 1441 did not survive long. At Westminster, four days later, he was believed to be alive, so he may have lived long enough to be christened. They had planned to name him Henry, in honour of the king; in the weeks before his birth, this news had been imparted to Henry VI himself, who was delighted.[7] The subsequent loss must have been a crushing personal blow for the duke and duchess. Perhaps Cecily needed a change of location – on 16 March, Richard petitioned the Crown for 'various manors in the counties of Dorset, Essex, Gloucester, Suffolk and Surrey, to the use of the said Duke and Cecilia his wife, and the heirs of their bodies'.[8] Out of these, Richard granted Cecily nine properties in East Anglia, Marshwood in Dorset, and Bisley and Pirbright in Surrey. It was convenient for Cecily to have various bases around the country, especially on occasions when she was travelling to visit York as he went about his business; those in Surrey were of particular use as stopping posts between London and the South Coast. It is not certain how often Cecily visited these places, or even that she did at all; the property was useful to her alone for the revenue it brought in. Of the three, Cecily may have most desired to visit Bisley in order to visit the nearby holy well of St John the Baptist, whose waters were said to have healing powers.

Cecily was busy again soon after her lying-in. While she underwent the purification ceremony that saw her progress solemnly and veiled to give thanks and receive forgiveness in church, arrangements were being made for her departure with Richard. Commissions for raising troops had been issued as early as 8 February, with the intent that York should muster on the south coast on 1 April. The timescale of Cecily's delivery seems to underpin the failure of this plan. In April, York's retinue was mustered at Portsdown in Hampshire, a long chalk hill overlooking Portsmouth and the Solent. The duke himself, with Cecily, did not leave London until 16 May. When they arrived on the coast, they would have stayed either in a specially erected tent or, more likely, in the old town itself, spread along the seafront. A constant victim of French raids, its recent defences included the Round Tower, begun by Henry V and finished in 1428. Almost a century after Cecily's stay, her great-grandson, Henry VIII, would watch as his famous flagship the *Mary Rose* disappeared beneath the waves there. Parliamentary papers for early May recorded a payment of £10 to a John Yerde, who had mustered 200 lances 'and the proportionate number of archers' for the duke, followed by further similar payments advanced to him. Elsewhere, £50 was also paid to a Sir Lewis John, who was travelling with York into Normandy 'to be of the King's Council there'.[9] On 23 May, the minutes of the council recorded that a letter was sent to York, 'informing him that sufficient shipping was in residence to carry him and his whole army over the sea at one time, and urging his speedy departure in consequence of the progress of the French'.[10] They must have sailed soon after this, arriving back in Rouen that June.[11] Prayers were issued for their success on 25 June, suggesting a possible date of departure.

It was in Rouen Castle, in 1441, that Cecily's later reputation for opulence was first recorded. The accounts of their officer of the household listed items such as jewelled dresses and a cushioned privy seat;[12] according to historian Michael Jones, York himself had to keep a watchful eye on the purse strings of this 'late medieval big spender'.[13] On one occasion, her shopping list included 60 yards of crimson silk lined with ermine, set with over 8 oz of gold, thirty pearls costing £6 each and another 300 smaller pearls. York's financier, John Wigmore, settled one clothing bill of hers that cost around £608 and paid £45 for a gold cup she ordered from a London goldsmith.[14] Other records that survive from the households of duchesses contemporary with Cecily indicate the standard of living to which she was entitled; these highlight, in particular, the upper-class privileges at mealtimes. The Duchess of Brittany's accounts show that she was regularly the recipient of unusual, luxurious birds such as swans, herons and larks, which replaced the usual domestic fowl on her table. She also feasted on fresh fish, including porpoise, sturgeon and whale meat, rather than the usual dried or salted fare.[15] Given that a piece of porpoise cost 3s 4d when the daily wage for a labourer as late as 1450 was 4d, such foods were part of the hierarchy of social difference, significant as symbols to the duchess. Soon after her arrival in 1441, Cecily was called upon to act as hostess to the representatives of the dukes of Brittany and Alençon.

One surviving book of French cookery, dating from the 1420s, gives a fairly accurate idea of the fare that would have graced Cecily's table in Rouen Castle. *Du Fait de Cuisine* was written for a similar ducal household, and lists the methods of preparing food as well as organising the cooks and the provisions of linen for the table. Its set menus for meat and fish days are generous and varied, including beef in lamprey sauce, fried fish with verjuice and gilded boar's heads, followed by a four-coloured blancmange, almond milk flans and an 'entremet' of a castle. It also has a section on food for invalids, with the type of fare that French cooks in the kitchens at Rouen may have prepared for Cecily during her pregnancy or in the period of recovery. 'Food for the sick' was bland fare – cooked pears and apples, green purée, blancmange, semolina, oatmeal and barley – although Cecily might have been tempted by some quince pastries or stuffed crayfish.[16]

When archaeologists at Leicester University were analysing the remains of Cecily's son, Richard III, in 2012/13, the high concentration of marine fish in his diet meant a readjustment of the usual parameters concerning the dating of his bones. The upper classes were used to the very best lifestyle and, given that Cecily was Edward III's granddaughter, she maintained this and more in her attire and at her table. It also had an important political dimension, widening the gap between the rulers and the ruled, providing a visual code for the Yorks' status in a city and region that had seen much conflict. Given the description in the anonymous poem 'The Siege of Rouen', which shows that its starving inhabitants were forced by their English adversaries to eat domestic animals as they 'lacke[d] mete and brede', the English, ensconced within Rouen Castle, must have been the focus of considerable resentment. Cecily's ostentation was in marked contrast to the city's recent experiences and the Yorks must have been conscious of potential threats to their regime. Rouen would actually fall to the French in 1449 and York was frequently engaged in repelling attacks and incursions, such as that at Pontoise in 1441.[17]

The display of wealth was consistent with the expectations of late medieval aristocracy. Eating, dressing and living well were expected of the Yorks; in fact, when figures in authority did not do so, it incited comment, such as with Henry VI's more pious lifestyle. If anyone during this period was going to have a padded toilet seat, in a draughty and ancient castle, it would be the Yorks. Visual signifiers were a common part of fifteenth-century lifestyles, found in clothing and sumptuary laws, personal devices, heraldry and symbols, decorated items such as manuscripts and jewellery, window glass and wall paintings. In May 1449, the Parliamentary Rolls list that a page named John Dowty was pardoned for stealing an item of Richard's, a silken sword girdle garnished with gold, which was symbolic beyond its monetary value. It is difficult to locate many contemporary examples that accuse Cecily of being unduly extravagant, yet the idea of her pride persists into popular culture and novels. She may have later styled herself 'queen by rights', which appears on her documents and letters from 1464,[18] but she did indeed have a claim to this title. Still, in modern works of non-fiction, Cecily is described as 'acting imperiously, as a queen-in-waiting [and having] an innate sense of pride in her own lineage', and 'receiving guests with all the state and dignity of a reigning monarch' in her own 'throne room'.[19] This does not necessarily denote vanity; it was considered an essential part of the demonstration of status and Cecily would have emphasised her and York's royal descent in this way, as well as giving a powerful message about York's status as Henry VI's heir. Henry himself was actively criticised when he failed to conform to expectations of royal appearance; Cecily and Richard were reinforcing their own claim by presenting what had all the hallmarks of an alternative court.

According to the religious texts to which Cecily would devote herself in later life, vanity was a mortal sin. The author Christine de Pisan, writers of saints' Lives, and others offering models of behaviour, such as in the childrearing manuals of the day, were united in rejecting wealth for wealth's sake. Yet the Yorks clearly revelled in their position and the trappings it brought, fulfilling expectations that they would set the standard in fashions of the day. A surviving portrait of Ralph Neville and Joan Beaufort's family, in the Neville book of hours, depicts the young daughters dressed in the popular forked headdresses, or 'hennins', of the day. It is often the case that only one half of this image is shown, captioned as representing Ralph and his twelve children, with Cecily at the back among the three girls. However, Ralph had twenty-two children across his two marriages, of which eleven were girls. Six more are depicted in a partner image, standing behind Joan. As the youngest, Cecily is likely to have been placed towards the back, if not the actual last figure itself. Typical of contemporary family depictions in manuscripts, glass and stone, the girls look very similar and are all dressed in the impressive two-coned or butterfly 'hennins', draped with veils. Writing in the 1420s to

1440s, poet John Lydgate wrote a satire on the wearing of such headgear, repeating the refrain that 'bewte will shewe, thouh hornys were away'. He continues,

> Clerkys recorde by gret auctorite
> Hornys wer yove to beestys for diffence
> A thyng contrary to femynyte
> To be maad sturdy of resistance
> But arche wyves egre in their violence
> Fers as tygre for to make affay
> They have despyt ageyn conscience
> Lyst nat of pryde, ther hornys cast away.

As the highest-ranking Englishwoman in Rouen, Cecily would have set the tone in terms of fashion and protocol. In the city there were a number of other wives of king's administrators, some of whom were her relations, and others who would prove to be powerful players in her future and those of her children. She would have known John Talbot, Earl of Shrewsbury, whom Richard would trust with several missions to England seeking royal funds to offset the thousands of pounds he was owed for his outlay in France. His first wife had been Cecily's cousin, Maud Neville, the daughter of her uncle Thomas. She bore four children who were close to Cecily in age. After that, he had married Margaret Beauchamp, daughter of the Earl of Warwick. The future would connect Margaret and Cecily's families through marriage; the countess's niece Anne would marry Cecily's son Richard and her two daughters, Eleanor and Elizabeth Talbot, would further shape the course of English history – Eleanor through a possible secret marriage with Cecily's son Edward and Elizabeth by being the grandmother of Anne de Mowbray, wife of Cecily's grandson. The close nature of a small number of aristocratic families meant that many of the seeds of the future royal court were together in Rouen in the mid-1440s.

Also present in the city at some point was the Duchess of Bedford, Jacquetta of Luxembourg. Her husband, Sir Richard Wydeville, is recorded in *Gregory's Chronicle* as accompanying Richard from Portsmouth in 1441 and Professor Griffiths states that the duchess accompanied him.[20] This may have created an uneasy dynamic, as Jacquetta's previous status had been that of wife of the heir to the throne, a position which Cecily now held. Although the dates are unclear, Jacquetta had already borne two or three surviving children at their Northamptonshire home of

Grafton Regis. She may have delivered Anthony already, or else borne him in 1442. As her childbearing did not resume until 1444, there is a chance she accompanied her husband to Normandy in the summer of 1441; he was also charged to accompany Margaret of Anjou back to England in 1445. It is interesting to speculate whether Jacquetta took her young children, Elizabeth and Anne, with her; Anthony may even have been born or conceived there. If so, the five-year-old Elizabeth would have been present in the city when Cecily gave birth to her future husband, Edward, the following year. As with Anne of York, it is equally likely that like the children remained in England.

The duke and duchess's quarters in the castle also contained a nursery. It is unclear whether the young Anne, then aged three, went with her parents to Rouen. There are arguments for and against; Weightman believes she was boarded out. Traditionally, daughters were left behind to be educated in convents while their aristocratic parents travelled. When Margaret Holland, Duchess of Clarence, travelled to Normandy to be with her husband in November 1419, her sons, who were then in their mid-teens, accompanied her but her two daughters, aged ten and thirteen, stayed with the Prioress of Dartford.[21] Yet the Yorks' absence in Rouen was planned to be of five years' duration, so perhaps they took their only surviving child with them. Also among the party was John de Vere, 12th Earl of Oxford, a loyal Lancastrian, and his wife of fifteen years, Elizabeth Howard. They would be in the city when Cecily gave birth to her next child, who would end up ordering de Vere's beheading twenty years later, when they found themselves on opposing sides.

Soon after they had arrived in Rouen, dramatic news reached them from England. That summer, a national scandal broke that directly affected Richard's position as heir to the throne. Since the death of Henry VI's uncle John, Duke of Bedford, his younger uncle, Humphrey, Duke of Gloucester, upheld his right to remain as regent to the teenage king. His second wife, Eleanor Cobham, was keen to conceive a child, as the marriage was reputedly childless. If she was successful, her offspring would be the nephew of Henry V, cousin to Henry VI and, as such, would take the place of Richard of York in the line of succession. Many women who wished to conceive employed a number of superstitious methods, from herbs and charms to pseudo-religious rituals and chants; Eleanor obtained powders from Margery Jourdayne, known as the 'witch of Eye'. In order to assist conception, Eleanor also consulted astrologers, which was also common; however, in Eleanor's case, they predicted that Henry

VI would suffer a life-threatening illness in 1441. This was classed as imagining the king's death, which was a heinous crime. These rumours reached the court and were investigated. The royal astrologers found no such illness in the king's chart and Eleanor, along with all her assistants and her confessor, was arrested on charges of treasonable necromancy. Eleanor denied all the charges except that of seeking assistance to fall pregnant; she was imprisoned for life and her marriage to Gloucester was terminated. Her 'accomplices' met with violent deaths. It was a stark reminder of just how vulnerable women could be when it came to their fertility and ambitions, even the most powerful ones. Cecily's experiences of conceiving and delivering a child would also give rise to scandal in her lifetime.

6

The Question of Edward
1442–1445

*'The rumours about his fathering reached England. Indeed, I was among
the few who swore that a great lady of your house would never stoop
so low. But I heard, we all heard, gossip of an archer named – what was
it?' She pretends to forget and taps her forehead.
'Blaybourne. An archer named Blaybourne who was supposed to be
in your armour. But I said, and even Queen Margaret d'Anjou said,
that a great lady like you would not so demean herself as to lie with a
common archer and let his bastard slip into a nobleman's cradle.'*[1]

The rumours of an archer named Blaybourne will not go away. The above
lines, spoken by the fictional version of Jacquetta, Duchess of Bedford, to
the equally fictional presentation of Cecily Neville, appear in Philippa
Gregory's novel *The White Queen*. When it was adapted by the BBC and
STARZ for a miniseries in the summer of 2013, the rumours of Cecily's
supposed infidelity reached an audience of over 10 million people in
the UK and USA combined. What started as a political slur against the
duchess in the fifteenth century was suddenly being debated worldwide,
a scope far beyond the dreams of her detractors. The story makes a good
fictional device. However, there are several factors that make it unlikely
at the least.

Cecily fell pregnant soon after her arrival in Rouen. The exact timing
of the conception has been the subject of much debate among historians
and would later prove a significant bone of political contention. Her
next child, Edward, would arrive on 28 April 1442. This would place
his conception sometime at the end of July 1441 or in the early days
of August, assuming that it was a nine-month pregnancy. Records

discovered in Rouen recently detail that Richard, Duke of York, was absent from Rouen on campaign at Pontoise for several weeks, returning to the city on 20 August. From this detail, several historians have inferred that Edward was not Richard's son. They believe this proves that Cecily must have had an adulterous liaison during his absence, which would render Edward illegitimate.

There are a number of problems with using this timing as evidence. If Cecily conceived on the night of Richard's return to Rouen, 20 August, this still allows for a pregnancy of thirty-six weeks. Today, nine months equates to roughly forty weeks but any delivery from thirty-seven weeks onwards is considered to be full term and falls within the bracket of a normal birth. In 2013, researchers at the National Institutes of Health in the USA were surprised to discover that the length of pregnancies can vary naturally by as much as five weeks, or thirty-seven days.[2] They also found that women tended to be consistent in their gestation, but no reliable evidence survives regarding Cecily's other pregnancies beyond the cartoon-esque descriptions of the birth of Richard III from the reign of the Tudors.

To be premature, a baby must be born before thirty-seven weeks and there is a fair chance that Edward might have arrived early. The nature of his christening is also cited as evidence that he was illegitimate, but again, there may be sound reasons for this. He was baptised in Rouen Castle, as opposed to the large ceremony his younger brother Edmund would receive in Rouen Cathedral. Yet, if Edward was slightly early, at thirty-six or even thirty-five weeks; if the labour was difficult, or he was small or gave any appearance of being sickly, he would have been baptised as soon as possible. It was common practice in such scenarios for baptism to take place in the bedchamber itself. In Rouen Castle, later maps show that as well as two larger chapels, the living quarters the Yorks occupied also contained a small chapel. Given that Cecily had recently lost a son soon after birth, it seems reasonable that she would wish to be cautious when it came to Edward's salvation. Every pregnancy can be different, even for those mothers who, as historian Michael Jones cites, experienced repeated pregnancies and therefore should have gained 'experience of the body and its sensations at these times'.[3] Yet all kinds of infections and complications could impact upon a fifteenth-century pregnancy and delivery. Nor does this bear any relation to the tall, healthy adult that Edward became.

Jones also states that the details of the birth of such an important heir would have been recorded if he was weak and sickly. Yet no details were recorded of the births of Cecily's other children; accounts of Richard III's birth a decade later would be made retrospectively, after his death. If Edward's life was briefly feared for, this concern may have lasted a few hours or a few days; this may not have been recorded, or it may have been recorded and not survived. It is also interesting that, in modern medicine, foetal lungs are considered to have finished developing at thirty-seven weeks. Accounts of Edward's premature death describe him lying on his left side, from which historians have inferred that he may have been suffering from pneumonia. If Edward was premature, and his lungs were not fully developed, they may have been particularly susceptible to inflammation. Thus, the date of his birth, his christening and premature death might be linked through this one simple explanation.

There is also the chance, though, that Cecily and York met away from the city of Rouen, while he was on campaign. Given that mothers can experience pregnancies that last as long as forty-two weeks, this allows for an additional six weeks of possible conception. Pontoise is a little over 50 miles from the city. It might have been a march of several days but, given that top racehorses can run at speeds of 30–40 miles an hour, it represents at most an afternoon's ride. There is every chance that the pair met at some midpoint, such as Gisors, with its motte-and-bailey castle, which was at that point in the hands of the English, with a garrison of ninety men stationed there in 1438 and forty-three in 1448. This suggests that it was a relatively quiet location, suitable for a romantic tryst. By each riding a little over 20 miles, the pair may have met at this location, or the equally accessible English-held Vernon or beautiful castle of La Roche-Guyon. Edward may have been conceived in one of these locations, or in one of the splendid travelling tents set up in the forest of the Val d'Oise. On at least one later occasion, Richard was keen to summon his wife to his side. On returning from Ireland in 1460, he was at Chester on 8 September and called for Cecily to ride and meet him as soon as possible. She left her children in London and went to join him: it is not impossible that a similar scenario occurred in Rouen in August 1441, meaning that she was already pregnant by the time she reached the city.

The suggestion that Cecily had an affair in Rouen also goes against what can be inferred about her character and marriage. As a proud aristocrat, conscious of her status as a descendant of Edward III and the position of Richard in the line of succession, Cecily understood there was a fair chance her eldest son would become heir to the throne. With York only hours away, it seems unlikely that she would have taken such a foolish risk regarding the paternity of this child in what appears to have been an otherwise companionable and fruitful match. She had been raised with a sense of her duty and, given the context of York's lineage, would have been very conscious that her children's pedigrees must be unimpeachable. Those who cite Edward's height and colouring as evidence of difference from his short, dark-haired father overlook the fact that Cecily bore other tall children and that she and York were both descended from Edward III, who was 6 feet tall and reputedly fair-haired. Perhaps it is most telling of all that York himself never questioned Edward's identity, accepting him fully as his son.

Poet John Audelay, who died in 1426, sums up much of the contemporary feeling about the problems inherent in aristocratic succession if wives were unfaithful. In his poem, 'The Chastity of Wives' (Carol 22), he expresses disgust for women who are promiscuous for the sake of lust, who 'disparage' the blood line of their lord with unlawful heirs:

> Bot now a lady wil take a page
> Fore no love bot fleschelé lust,
> And so here blod is disparage
> Thus lordus and lordchip al day ben lost.

Audelay expresses the view that a woman in Cecily's position would have held – that such behaviour brings the nobility and, by extension, England into disrepute and decline:

> Lordis and lorchip thus wastyn away
> In Englond in moné a place
> (That makis false ayrs — hit is no nay!)
> And lese worchip, honowre, and grace

Undeniably, there were cases of adultery and immorality during Cecily's lifetime. Men and women did ignore the teachings offered by the Church and break their marital vows, even those who were considered pious. Cecily's own son Edward would later prove to be a prime example of this. The Calendar of Letter Books for the City of London lists many cases of those who were convicted of immorality between 1400 and 1440: one was sentenced to stand in the pillories for three hours while others were fined and their sins proclaimed in public. However, women's behaviour tended to be censured more harshly, particularly those who were married and held positions of high status. Based on Cecily's position and what is known about her character, it is time for the rumours about her fidelity to be recognised as no more than political propaganda.

There was never any question about Edward's legitimacy until the late 1460s. Then, the Blaybourne rumour surfaced as a political slur against Edward's unpopular marriage, and later it was used to discredit his children. The idea did not derive from suspicions regarding the timing of York's presence in Rouen, as medieval medical texts show us that anything between seven and ten months was considered to be a normal pregnancy. If Cecily's contemporaries believed the rumours, it would have been dependent upon an affair in York's absence rather than the fact of his absence itself. The rumours were politically motivated and were never pressed to advantage, because they could not be proved. Cecily herself protested most loudly to the council about the slur on her reputation.

On 28 April 1442, Cecily gave birth to Edward at Rouen Castle. He was baptised in the one of the three chapels within the walls soon afterwards; besides the chapel in their apartments, there was a royal chapel and a free-standing one dedicated to St Giles inside the keep. Perhaps mindful of the fate of Henry, who had been born and died on the same day, his parents did not wish to take any chances with Edward's immortal soul. The larger christening that his brother Edmund would receive in 1443 may also have reflected York's intentions for his sons – Edward was to inherit York's titles and claim to the English throne, while Edmund was to become a landowner in the north of France. His nurse was a Norman woman, Anne of Caux, who would prove such a success with the family that she would return to England with them and preside over the nursery at Fotheringhay.[4] Cecily would have played a significant role in Anne's appointment, assessing her character based on her common fame, or reputation, her appearance and manner. Only healthy-looking women of sober habits were chosen to nurse the offspring of the aristocracy. In 1474, Edward would reward his nurse with a pension of £20 a year.[5]

Cecily's companion Elizabeth, Countess of Oxford, had also conceived that year, in December 1441, months after her own husband returned from assisting Richard at Pontoise, and gave birth to a son named John that following September. By the time he arrived, Cecily had conceived again. The following May she bore another son, named Edmund, who was christened in Rouen Cathedral. Barely two months passed before, in July 1443, Cecily fell pregnant for a fifth time. Just weeks before Edmund's first birthday, on 22 April 1444, she delivered another girl, whom she named Elizabeth. The baby was christened in Rouen Cathedral and one of her godparents was Jacquetta, Duchess of Bedford. There is also a chance that Jacquetta bore a child in Rouen too. The arrivals of her children are unclear but a 1465 reference to her son John being aged twenty years old may suggest that she was also pregnant and delivered at least one baby at this time, John, and perhaps also the daughter she named after herself. By 1446, the duchess was back at her family home of Grafton, where she delivered her son Lionel.

Already, Cecily's young son Edward was a valuable marital prospect. At the suggestion of the Duke of Suffolk, the possibility was discussed of a marriage between the baby boy and a daughter of the French king. These negotiations lasted for around two years and may have underpinned the Yorks' choice to give their second son, Edmund, a grander christening in Rouen Cathedral. It may well have appeared to them that their futures lay in France. Had there been any suspicion about his paternity, this would not have been the case. York was pleased by the idea and wrote to Charles VII of France, who by this time had a newborn daughter, Madeleine, who had arrived at Tours on 1 December 1443. On 18 April 1445, he addressed the king 'touching the matter of the marriage of one of my three honoured ladies, your daughters, and of Edouart of York, my eldest son', which made him 'comforted and joyful' because of his 'true desire' for friendship. He proposed to send his ambassadors to Charles 'in order to treat, discuss and conclude the business of the said marriage'. In June, he wrote back to Charles that he considered Madeleine to be of a 'very tender age' and proposed her sister Joan instead.[6] It is not difficult to imagine Cecily encouraging him to keep writing, to keep pushing for the lucrative match.

Of course, hindsight tells us there would be no such marriage. The course of English history would have run quite differently had this proposed union come about. The death of the dauphin's wife, Margaret of Scotland, that August, diverted Charles's attention to finding a new wife for his son and, as York wrote to Charles on 21 September, he had been summoned back to England by Henry VI. However, he still held firm to their intention and hoped that Charles would 'continue and hold to the intention declared', and would not be 'displeased'[7] by the delay, which sounds very much as if Richard and Cecily were anticipating returning to France. By that point, the Yorks were already at the Channel port of Honfleur. Back in London that winter, York was still pursuing the match. On 21 December, he wrote again, apologising for not having 'sent to you as speedily as I thought to have done; for my Lord the King ... has sent for me to come to him at all diligence, in order to assist at his parliament, in this city of London, where I have recently arrived'. Joan had been put aside again, in favour of Princess Madeleine, and York again proposed sending ambassadors to conclude the match. For Cecily, it must have represented a significant achievement, a real goal to strive hard for, representing her family's true status and importance. After this, though, the match was quietly dropped. This must have been a great disappointment.

By 1445, Cecily was the mother of four small children when a very important visitor passed through Rouen. A marriage had been negotiated for Henry VI, then aged twenty-three, with the fifteen-year-old niece of Charles VII of France. The match had been arranged according to the Treaty of Tours but was less advantageous for England, as the bride came without a dowry and was only related to the royal family by marriage. Margaret of Anjou was officially married to Henry in his absence, with the Duke of Suffolk standing in as his proxy, in the French city of Nancy in February 1445. Soon afterwards she set out for Paris, where she fell ill, but pushed on to arrive at Pontoise on 18 March. Here her French attendants handed her over to the English party, headed by the Duke of York. From there, they took barges along the Seine, arriving four days later. In Rouen, she was too unwell to take her place in the grand ceremonial entry that had been planned, so the Countess of Shrewsbury took her place instead.[8] The reception prepared for her entry into London, with its elaborate symbolism, gives an idea of what the citizens of Rouen would have witnessed, with pageantry of Peace and Plenty, Noah's Ark and 'old histories' accompanied by songs and poems. Margaret would have been conveyed to her lodgings, probably the royal suite inside Rouen Castle, where she was attended by Cecily herself.

The future English queen stayed in Rouen for two weeks over Easter. Here, a friendship may have been forged between the older woman and the girl, a connection which would remain like a thread between them through the difficult coming years, enabling them to still meet and share their experiences as women and mothers, in spite of the warfare between their men. York then accompanied her entourage to Honfleur, where she arrived on 9 April. Sending the young queen on her way, Cecily could not have predicted just how closely and fatally their futures would become entwined. Lydgate's verses in celebration of the match hoped that the marriage would bring peace to the two countries:

> Twixt the Reawmes two Englande and frraunce
> Pees shal approache, rest and unite
> Mars sette aside with alle hys cruelty
> Which to longe hath troubled the Reawmes tweyne.[9]

In 1445, York's tenure as Lieutenant of Normandy came to an end. He had been rewarded earlier in the year with the lordship of Mortimer, at Crickhowell, Powys, in appreciation of his service but his £83 annual pension had not been paid regularly and he was owed over £38,000 by the Crown.[10] Sir John Talbot was appointed in his place, which proved to be a lucky escape for Richard when Rouen fell four years later and Talbot was captured. After fulfilling his duties towards the new Queen of England, York and Cecily prepared for their departure that October. They fully expected to be returning soon, hoping that Henry would appoint York for a further term in Normandy but, as it happened, the pair would never set foot on French soil again.

7

Loss of Focus
1446–1452

The Falcon fleeth and hath no rest
Till he wit where to bigg his nest.[1]

Over the next ten years, Cecily's life was primarily a domestic one, as she delivered seven more children. However, it also had an undeniable political dimension, as her husband was drawn increasingly into national conflict that would turn her world upside down. With her sense of dynasty, Cecily must have taken a keen interest in her husband's advancement; as a close couple, there is every possibility that they discussed his advancement and shared a sense of disappointment that the promising start he had made in France seemed to dwindle in the new political climate. It was part of Cecily's role as a wife to support and advance her husband where possible by acting as a hostess, negotiator and administrator and by taking ceremonial roles. However, over the coming decade, the Yorks would see their aspirations stymied by the increasing opposition of key figures at court, who resented or feared the implications of Richard's claim to the throne.

The next phase of their lives started peacefully enough, in 1446. Cecily retired to Fotheringhay amid the green Northamptonshire fields spreading out on either side of the River Nene. She had conceived again before leaving Rouen and delivered her seventh child around the time of her thirty-first birthday, if not on the actual day itself, 3 May. It was a girl, whom they named Margaret, probably in honour of the new queen. York may have only just arrived in time, if he was there at all, being recorded as in London on 24 March to attend a session of Parliament that sat until 9 April. The baby would have been christened in the new chapel at Fotheringhay, perhaps by Richard Wancourt, who was the clergyman there from 1437, or else in the castle chapel. Wancourt may also have conducted the ceremony by which Cecily was churched about a month after delivery. Margaret's biographer Christine Weightman prefers William Worcester's theory that this new daughter was born at Waltham Abbey but concedes that the surviving annals of the abbey for 1445–47 make no reference to the stay of the duchess or the birth of a child. Such an event would undoubtedly have gone recorded given that the scribe even lists the changes in weather. It is likely that the couple stayed at Waltham Abbey, which had been beloved of John, Duke of Bedford, but that connection was not formalised until five months after their daughter's arrival. That October, York was granted an 'assignment for life' to 'come often to London for the King's business, to pay for his livery, horses and allot him the use of Waltham Abbey and town'.[2]

With another new baby in the nursery, the duchess soon resumed her marital duties. York was busy in London, anticipating being reappointed to the lieutenancy of Normandy and fending off the auditors who were examining his accounts. This came to an end around July, when he rejoined his family. They were probably together over the summer at one of their many estates, but in October they settled for a while at Bewdley in Worcestershire. They would have stayed at the Mortimer possession of Tickenhill House, which overlooked the town and was already established as a significant manor with a park, although it was extensively rebuilt in 1456. In 1446, corresponding with the period in which York visited, a new bridge was built over the River Severn, making access far easier for visitors and locals alike. It is not difficult to imagine York instigating this, as he was using the house as a base to deal with affairs concerning his estates in the south and west.

That October, Cecily fell pregnant again, probably at Tickenhill. Only four months had elapsed after she had delivered Margaret. By 30 November, York was back in London and attended council meetings through the first half of December at Westminster and Sheen. He spent the Christmas season at Fotheringhay, where he delayed until 26 January. Parliament met at Bury St Edmunds the following month, where Humphrey, Duke of Gloucester, was arrested on charges of treason and died a few days later. The duke had overseen many of York's estates before he had reached his majority and may have acted as something of a mentor to him; later, when he felt himself to be the subject of various whispering campaigns, York would identify his position with that of Gloucester. He may have been at Bury during these events, although his presence was officially recorded until 26 February, three days after the duke's death.

In the summer of 1447, Cecily bore another son named William, who died during, or soon after, birth. The Victorian writer Amelia Halsted gives his birthdate as 7 July and the location as Fotheringhay. Cecily had now lost three, perhaps four, babies out of eight (or nine), but this was not unusual. It has been estimated that, in English ducal families between 1330 and 1479, 36 per cent of male babies and 29 per cent of females died before their fifth birthday. The average family unit contained 4.6 surviving children.[3] It would be wrong to assume that medieval parents were more detached from their offspring or felt the loss of a child less keenly than we might today. It is true that infant and child mortality was far more common, and many families were larger, but surviving examples indicate the depth of feeling endured by royal parents on the loss of a beloved child. No doubt Cecily turned to her faith to console her, following the religious teaching that such things were the will of God, yet she would have had to bury her personal sorrow and continue with the life of a busy medieval duchess. She would have been aware that she had dependants in her household and on her estates and, while she could only pray for her lost child, she could actively seek to advance those that were still living. The Clare Roll poem that states 'Richard liveth yet' serves as a reminder of this dual state of endured loss and determination to fight on.

Although Cecily may have been mourning the loss of her latest baby, she and Richard were also mindful of the future. In 1447, their eldest child, Anne, was eight years old. It was a young age to become a wife, even earlier than Cecily's betrothal at the age of nine, but too good an opportunity to lose. That summer, Anne was married to the seventeen-year-old Henry Holland, who would inherit the title Earl of Exeter from his father that August. Young wives were usually sent to live in their husband's household, but in this case the groom may have come to Fotheringhay as, on 30 July, Richard was awarded 'the keeping of Henry, son and heir of John, Duke of Exeter, from the said John's death, Henry having taken to wife the daughter of the said Richard'.[4]

It was a good match for Anne on a dynastic level, with Holland descended directly from John of Gaunt; his grandmother Elizabeth had been the sister of Cecily's mother Joan, giving the bride and groom mutual great-grandparents. He had been born in the constable's lodgings in the Tower of London and christened in Westminster Abbey on the same day. It also meant that, after 1447, Henry was technically Henry

VI's nearest male relative as well as being his godson. The king had approved of the match, even encouraged it. York paid 4,500 marks as her dowry, a considerable sum, so he must have considered it to be a worthwhile investment. Holland was also closely related to York by marriage; his mother had been Richard's aunt by her first marriage to Edmund Mortimer.

York had returned to England with every expectation that his status would allow him to play a significant part in the government of the country. He might have anticipated being reposted in France and perhaps taking on some of the responsibilities of the king's late uncle, the Duke of Bedford. Many of Bedford's men had transferred their allegiance to York after his death in 1435[5] and it would make sense for him to step into those shoes, but he instead found himself squeezed out and sidelined. A new triumvirate at the heart of Henry VI's court had upset the balance of power against him, due to the claim he had on the throne and the potential damage he might cause to others who were attempting to control the impressionable king. The new queen, Margaret of Anjou, had been accustomed to the factional politics of France and made no secret of her partiality for two favourites, William de la Pole, Earl, and soon to be Duke, of Suffolk, and Edmund Beaufort, Earl of Somerset. York was dismayed to learn that, despite being significantly in debt as a result of his Normandy posting, he was being accused of favouritism and embezzling royal funds by Lord Privy Seal Adam Moleyns. Refuting the claims, he stated he 'feleth him grieved and his worship hurt'.[6] Withdrawing from court life, he was given various small grants and posts, such as the office of steward of the king's forest south of Trent, and in May 1447 he was given permission to build an embattled tower at Honesdon in Hertfordshire.[7] He spent much of 1446 and 1447 administering to his lands and estates.

The York household was changing at this time. They had brought back to England some of the loyal staff first employed in Normandy, who remained as familiar faces in Cecily's daily life, as well as other powerful associates who worked for, or with, the family. Returning from France with them were the family cofferer John Stanlow, treasurer John Cley and loyal servants William Browning, John Flegge, Walter Devereux, Simon Reynham and the Mulso brothers, Edmund, Thomas and William.[8] Cecily would have known Edmund as a man to be relied on since the earliest days of their marriage; he had accompanied them to Rouen in 1441 and after their return became Constable of Fotheringhay Castle. It must have been to his capable hands that York trusted his home and wife during such times as they were apart. Thomas Mulso was York's captain in Bernay, and William became his retainer.[9] Also in the ducal service were Sir John Fastolf, Thomas Lord Scales, Ralph Lord Cromwell, Sir Andrew Ogard, Sir William ap Thomas and Sir William Oldhall, who had been York's chamberlain since 1440. His councillors included Viscount Bourchier, John Lord Dudley and Reginald Lord de la Ware. Cecily would have known their receiver general, John Milewater, and the lawyers Robert Darcy, John Stork, Richard Quartermains and William Tresham, who must have visited their properties regularly to conduct business. More regular visitors would have been John Wigmore, York's financier from Rouen, who became his agent in London, and William Burley, who was entrusted with estate matters, including the initiation of ducal concerns.[10] There were also a small army of administrators who acted as York's receiver in his various estates. Records suggest he was paying around 190 salaries during the late 1440s.[11] Cecily herself would have overseen a significant number of servants in the different portions of her household, giving orders daily to the kitchens, cellars, chambers and hall, as well as being involved in all aspects of the hiring and firing of staff. She would have appointed trusted deputies to oversee its smooth running and ensure her wishes were carried out while she was busy with estate business. The image of the medieval lady sitting peacefully embroidering or playing the lute represents only a small proportion of what must have been a very busy and demanding life.

Cecily was used to travelling while pregnant, but with her pattern of regular childbearing she may have remained at Fotheringhay while Richard was travelling in Wales or else taken advantage of one of the intervals between her children to travel the 100-odd miles to Ludlow. She may also have been at Ludlow during part of this time to oversee the household that was established for her elder sons Edward and Edmund. It was customary for aristocratic boys, and particularly heirs to the throne, to be raised at court or in their own establishment, and by the time Edward and Edmund were five and six it was time for their education to be overseen in a permanent base. The solid and luxurious Ludlow Castle in Shropshire, close to the Welsh Marches, was the ideal location, having been enlarged by Roger Mortimer, 1st Earl of March. However, Cecily would soon leave England behind again.

On 30 July 1447, Richard was appointed Lieutenant of Ireland for ten years on a fee of 4,000 marks, followed by an annual salary of 2,000.[12] It seemed to be a decisive appointment, engineered to prevent York from taking a more active role in the government of Normandy.

A number of his contemporaries certainly thought it was designed to remove him from the heart of government, perhaps even to clear the way for Somerset's unimpeded advancement. One satirical poem had him 'exciled from our soveraigne lordes presens',[13] while *Benet's Chronicle* described him as 'banished' and *Gregory's Chronicle* had him 'exsyled into Irlonde for hys rebellyon as thoo a boute the kynge informyde hym'.[14] It seems that he may have spoken out in Parliament at some point against Somerset for his role in England's losses in France. This, coupled with Moleyn's accusations about his finances, even though he had been denied the money he needed to fulfil his obligations, was enough to give the king the impression that York could prove a dangerous thorn in his side.

The appointment was confirmed in the Parliamentary Rolls in December and cemented the following year with Somerset's appointment as his replacement in France. This came as a disappointment but was now no surprise. The months passed, but York delayed his departure. Fearing the influence of his enemies in his absence, he asked Cecily's brother, Salisbury, to read a letter in Parliament about his intentions to serve the king loyally. Perhaps it was for this reason that he did not leave England until 1449, a full two years after the appointment. He was in London for a Garter ceremony in November 1447 and his presence at Fotheringhay on 13 January 1448 suggests the family spent the Christmas period there. Cecily fell pregnant again that February, and by October he was back in London. Cecily's next child arrived soon afterwards; Halstead later has her at a place called Neyte, where she delivered a short-lived son, John, on 7 November. This was the manor and garden of La Neyte, belonging to the Abbot of Westminster, located near Ebury Bridge on the bank of the Thames. Here there was a great garden, an almoner's garden, a kitchen garden, a garden of the Warden of the Lady Chapel along with several others, stretching over 2½ acres.[15] The abbot at the time was Edmund Kyrton, who extended hospitality to the duchess while York was about Parliamentary business in London.

It was fairly common practice before the Reformation for women of all walks of life to be accommodated in monastic hospitals and lodgings while infirm or in labour; Cecily would no doubt have been given the best possible accommodation in line with her rank. She may also have benefited from the nearby infirmarer's garden, with its wealth of culinary and medicinal herbs, which feature so frequently in medieval remedies for childbirth and recovery. Her infant son is likely to have been buried within the grounds of the establishment, if not at Westminster itself. York may have hurried away on receiving news that she was in labour but, as husbands were customarily excluded from the birth chamber at this time, it is likely that he was in government until decisive news arrived. This does not lessen the bond between him and Cecily or his children, it simply serves as a reminder that their lives were lived according to different rules than those of today.

York was still dragging his heels about the Irish lieutenancy. The Elizabethan antiquarian John Stowe claimed that the spur to his departure was an uprising early in 1449, with York described as the fittest person to subdue the rebels, although this overlooks the fact that this was his duty given his promotion two years earlier. The *Herald of Peace* from 1831 suggested that he was deliberately underequipped by Queen Margaret and Somerset in the hope that he might be slain in the attempt. York's salary was confirmed by the king at Westminster in February 1449, but on 6 March he was still conducting official business at 'Fodrynggay', granting the friars at Bury St Edmunds the right to enclose land. A week later, he appointed Thomas Yonge and John Wyggemore as his attorneys in England during his absence.[16] Cecily would have been overseeing the household being packed up in readiness for their departure, organising the servants to collect linen and necessary items, although larger pieces like furniture would have been dismantled closer to departure. In April, James Manthorp, Henry Wyhom and Thomas Combe were commissioned to arrest ships, barges and other vessels, with their masters and mariners, for the Yorks' passage, 'so that they be at Beaumaris with all speed'.[17] The departure finally took place in June; they travelled north to Beaumaris on the isle of Anglesey, probably staying in the castle where Eleanor Cobham was a prisoner, before sailing straight across the Irish Sea to Dublin. By the time they landed at Howth on 6 July, Cecily was six months pregnant.

The Parliamentary Rolls list grants to a number of men who accompanied the Yorks to Ireland for 'the safe keeping of those parts'. From Richard's own household came William Oldhall and Edmund Mulso, as well as John Wykes, Roger Ree of Essex, Stephen Cristmasse of Kent and James Manthorp; perhaps some of their wives accompanied them, as part of Cecily's retinue.[18] They were heading to a city rich in ancestral associations; York's great-great-grandfather Lionel, Duke of Clarence, had also held the position and granted property to the dean and chapter of St Patrick's, on condition that they said Masses for the souls of himself and his duchess, their ancestors and posterity.[19] According to the *Annals of the Four Masters*, he was 'received with great honour, and the Earls of Ireland went into his house, as did also the Irish ... and gave him as many beeves [beefs?] for the use of his kitchen as it pleased him to demand'.[20]

There had been a castle in Dublin since the twelfth century. Lionel had made some changes to it, ordering the demolition of a house within the castle walls and the construction of a new roof, a new chamber adjoining the little chapel and a new house beside the bakery.[21] His grandson, Roger de Mortimer, had also been Lieutenant of Ireland, which then passed to Edmund de Mortimer, Richard's uncle. From him, York inherited the earldom of Ulster and lordships of Connaught, Meath, Leix and Ossory. The castle that Cecily would have seen for the first time that summer was set within the city itself, a solid rectangle with six towers enclosing a courtyard. Two sides of it flanked the River Poddle, which was diverted into its moat. They would have approached it from Cork Hill and entered through the Bedford Tower. This no longer exists but the huge, solid Record Tower gives a sense of its proportions. They soon moved to the castle of Trim, in County Meath, part of York's Mortimer inheritance and the largest Norman castle in Ireland, where they spent the Christmas of 1449.[22]

Any rebellion was swiftly suppressed in 1449. York was so successful that, in the autumn, one of his followers said that 'with the myght of Jesus ere twelvemonth come to an end the wildest Yrishman in Yrland would be sworn English'.[23] Richard's role included retaining men, letting land and maintaining law and order; the Irish Patent Rolls contain records of him licensing the election of a new Bishop of St Patrick's in August, granting subsidies and granting bishoprics and offices at Dublin and 40 miles north, at Drogheda.[24] To assist him, York appointed Richard Nugent, Baron of Delvin, as his deputy.[25] Almost straight away York began work, issuing summonses on 8 August to the leading lords and clergymen to attend a session of Parliament at Dublin on 17 October; the following March, he recalled them to Drogheda for 24 April.[26] Much of his work would have been conducted in the great hall, built of stone and wood, used for Parliamentary sessions and as a law court; on other occasions, Cecily would have jurisdiction over it, when it became the venue for feasting. Within a month of arrival, York had raised such support that he was able to lead a large force to overcome the O'Byrne territories and bring many powerful Irish figures into submission. On 21 October, soon after this, Cecily matched his political success with a personal victory, when she gave birth to another boy at Dublin Castle. Little George would be her third son to survive infancy.

Around the time Cecily rose from her lying-in to be churched, bad news arrived from France. Under the regime of York's replacement, the Duke of Somerset, French and English relations had been deteriorating for a while, with Charles VII complaining that he was now treated 'in a style derogatory to the honour of the king and different from what he had been used to in times past by the Duke of York'.[27] On 10 November, Rouen had been recaptured by the French, bringing the brief years of peace to an end. In a twist of fate, the conquering armies had been led by René of Anjou, the father of the new English queen. By the following summer, Somerset had lost almost all of England's territories across the Channel in ineffectual and costly campaigns, and York could not help but be bitter about such a dramatic change, following the success of his own lieutenancy. Things were also turning sour for York's other adversary, the Duke of Suffolk, appointed as Lord High Admiral since 1447. On the death of Henry VI's other uncle, Humphrey, Duke of Gloucester, Suffolk had been appointed Lord Chamberlain and was, in effect, the most powerful figure at court, after the king and queen. On 25 May 1447, York had been at Westminster to witness the accusation of disloyalty levelled against Suffolk, for relinquishing Anjou and other territories. Later it emerged that he had been conducting secret negotiations with France, possibly planning an invasion and betraying Parliamentary secrets; for this, he was impeached by the Commons in March 1450. He would be banished to Calais but, following a mock trial on board the ship carrying him, was beheaded and his body thrown overboard. It was later washed up near Dover beach. His adherent, Bishop Adam Moleyns, who had accused York of embezzlement, had been lynched by unpaid sailors in Portsmouth that January. It was to be the start of a turbulent year. Little by little, more news leaked through to Dublin.

For Cecily and Richard, the news was worrying but it also brought a vindication of the failings of their opponents. Already there had been a couple of minor uprisings early that year, in Kent, but by the summer, the rebels had swelled in number and rallied to the leadership of a Sussex man named Jack Cade. In early June, around 5,000 had gathered at Blackheath, demanding the end of fighting with France, high taxation and the removal of certain unpopular aristocrats, clergymen and even the king. The rebellion was crushed and Cade killed, but not before a number of leading figures had been killed, including the Bishop of Salisbury and Baron Saye. York was concerned to hear that Cade had been claiming descent from the Mortimer family, calling himself John Mortimer and that, in some quarters, this had developed into the belief that York himself had incited the men to rebel, before departing for Ireland. He and Cecily must have recognised this as a potentially dangerous turning point. Swift action was required to clear his name. He protested his innocence in a letter to Henry VI, which is included in *Holinshed's Chronicles*:

> I have been informed that divers language hath been said of me to your most excellent estate which should sound to my dishonour and reproach and charge of my person ...
>
> If there be any man that will or dare say the contrary or charge me otherwise, I beseech your rightwiseness to call him before your high presence and I will declare me for my discharge as a true knight ought to do.[28]

The response from Henry was reassuring, concluding that 'in all such matters, we declare, repute and admit you as our true and faithful subject, and as our faithful cousin'.[29] Yet, in the light of recent reprisals, York decided to return to England, to defend himself and perhaps to seize the moment. It also seems probable that he had decided to leave before the dispute broke, as he had been writing to Henry since the spring with some urgency regarding his finances in Ireland. In order to prevent the loss of certain territories he required more money, and when this was not forthcoming he wrote to Salisbury, saying that he would rather return to England than be known as the duke who had lost the province.[30]

Early in September, he and Cecily set sail from Dublin, possibly landing at Beaumaris, or maybe further down the Welsh coast, arriving in Denbigh on 7 September. His arrival caused a panic in Westminster, with troops sent to meet his 'sodyn coming withouten certain warnyng'. With an army of between 3,000 and 5,000 armed men, it seems likely that he would have left Cecily and baby George at Ludlow or Fotheringhay as he marched on the capital. It is quite likely that she was already pregnant again at this point, with the son, Thomas, whom she would lose in either 1450 or 1451. Arriving in the capital, he rode proudly through the streets in a display of power, before lodging with the Bishop of Salisbury. The previous bishop, William Ainscough, had been unpopular for marrying Henry VI to Margaret of Anjou, and was murdered in the Cade Rebellion. The new incumbent was Richard Beauchamp, already known to York in his capacity of Bishop of Hereford. The property would have been Salisbury House, also known as Dorset House, based on Fleet Street, between Whitefriars and St Bride's, with a frontage down to the river. Until they could acquire a suitable property of their own, York and

Cecily were often lodged in the homes of their allies in London, forming an important part of their support network in the capital.

York presented his suit to the king, offering himself as a figure of reform. Henry was aware that many of the recent rebels had proposed the duke as an alternative ruler, so responded with caution. Soon after this, York left court, possibly disappointed that he had been offered no concession, but also satisfied that he was not under any immediate suspicion and was now back at the heart of government. That October, he was expected at Walsingham, according to a letter received by John Paston: 'My Lord shall be atte Walsingham on Sonday next comynge and from thens he shall go to Norwich.' The letter asked that York be given 'as good attendance and pleasaunce' as possible and that the City of Norwich 'mete wyth him in the best wyse also'. In mid-October, he was in Bury St Edmunds, according to a letter from the Earl of Oxford to John Paston, describing how he met with the Duke of Norfolk and stayed with him until nine at night. On 17 October, he was at Fotheringhay and remained there for four days before he travelled to Ludlow, possibly with Cecily, for a stay of eight days.

In mid-November, York left his family behind and headed back to Parliament, to join in discussions regarding the defence of the realm. He knew it would prove controversial. Before he arrived, his close friend Sir William Oldhall was appointed Speaker of the House of Commons, which was an encouraging sign. When York arrived in London on 23 November, he rode with his sword carried upright before him, both provocative and defensive and a reminder of the recent challenges to his rightful status. The city crowds seemed to agree. Riots erupted among dissatisfied soldiers when the king refused to act against Somerset for his failures in Normandy; both *Bale's Chronicle* and *Benet's Chronicles* list their cries for vengeance and accusations that Somerset was a traitor. On 1 December, this led to an attempt to assassinate the former lieutenant, who escaped from Blackfriars by boat while his lodgings in the friary were sacked. Although the mob's demands tallied well with York's desires, giving rise to speculation regarding his involvement, Benet claims that Somerset was saved by the Duke of Devon, acting on York's orders. In spite of their differences, he did not want to see London descend into chaos and, as a fellow duke in a closed dynastic world, it was in his interest to nip army insurrection in the bud. He helped to quell the uprisings when they spread to Hoo and Tuddenham and, according to Bale, Benet and Gregory, dispatched the ringleader to the Earl of Salisbury for execution. A procession headed by the king through the streets on 5 December seemed to restore order before Parliament broke up for Christmas. York left London on 19 December and spent the season at Stratford-le-Bow.

It is unclear whether Cecily and her children joined York in Middlesex. Stratford, or Bow, was a place that had some aspirations to culture and learning, even something of a finishing school, as Chaucer commented in *The Canterbury Tales*:

> French she spake full fayre and fetisley
> After the scole of Stratford atte Bowe
> For French of Paris was to hire unknowe

They may have stayed at the nearby Priory of St Leonards or at the old palace at Oldford, still referred to as King John's Palace and also as Giffing Place or Petersfield by the historian Leland. This appears to have been within the manor of Stepney, and sections of the building survived into the nineteenth century. Some ancient remains of a building blew down in a storm of January 1800, but a section of the original palace survived until September 1863, when it burned down. It had comprised twelve rooms, 'standing on a kind of terrace, with elaborate chimney pieces and a large oaken staircase'.[31] It had been in the possession of Humphrey, Duke of Gloucester, so may have passed into York's hands on his decease. On New Year's Day, he returned to London and was listed there again on 10 January and at the start of Parliament's new session ten days later. This was an indicator of how critical the situation had become.

Once more, rumours and rioting spread through the city. Again, York's claim to the throne seemed to be at the heart of the malcontents' demands. In Kent, a Stephen Christmas is recorded in *Gregory's Chronicle* as making claims that the king intended to harm the country and should be replaced by Richard. He was executed 'for hyr talking a gayne the kyng, havynge maore favyr unto the Duke of Yorke thenne unto the kynge'. While it is likely that many Englishmen saw York as potentially better able to run the country than Henry, who appeared weak and easily led by his unpopular wife and the Duke of Somerset, this situation caused particular alarm as Christmas had been among York's retinue in Ireland. Henry left the capital and York was excluded from government. It had appeared that he might be granted the earldom of Pembroke, which was vacant following the death of Suffolk. Instead, he found this was given to the queen and in 1452 was bestowed on the Lancastrian Jasper Tudor.

Above left: 1. Henry V. Henry inherited the throne from his father in 1413, as the second Lancastrian king. Descended from John of Gaunt, the third son of Edward III, the Lancastrians deposed Richard II and replaced his heirs. In the year of Cecily's birth, 1415, Henry V led an English army to victory at Agincourt. The English sustained few losses but one of the notable dead was Edmund of York, uncle to Cecily's future husband.

Above right: 2. Henry V and Catherine of Valois. Henry married the young French Princess Catherine in June 1420, as part of a peace treaty with England. Catherine delivered a son in December 1421 but, nine months later, was left a widow at the age of twenty, when Henry V died on campaign in France.

Below and following page, top: 3 & 4. Raby Castle, County Durham. Cecily was born at Raby in May 1415. The castle was fairly new then, having been built in the mid-fourteenth century on the site of an existing manor house.

Above left: 5. St Mary's church, Staindrop. In 1408, Cecily's father, Ralph, Earl of Westmorland, founded the collegiate church in the village of Staindrop, near Raby. When he died in 1425, he was laid to rest there, flanked by the effigies of both his wives, although neither of them are buried there.

Above right: 6. Effigy of Joan Beaufort in Staindrop church. Cecily's mother Joan is depicted in alabaster beside her husband but she actually lies with her own mother in Lincoln Cathedral.

Right: 7. Julian of Norwich, from the front of Norwich Cathedral. Cecily's mother was interested in the lives of religious women. Julian of Norwich's contemporary Margery Kempe also had visions but had chosen a secular path, being married and bearing children. Joan summoned Margery to visit her and later wrote exonerating her of any wrongdoing.

Below: 8. Falcon and Fetterlock, the symbol of the House of York. The fetterlock was used by Edmund of Langley, 1st Duke of York and fourth surviving son of Edward III, the king who had used a falcon as his personal device. They were united by Cecily's and Richard's son Edward IV.

Bottom: 9. Falcon and Fetterlock misericord. This carved wooden image, on the underside of the choir stalls in St Laurence's church, Ludlow, is a lasting reminder of the associations of the Duke of York and his family with the town.

Top: 10. Ruins of Fotheringhay. Cecily's main residence after her marriage was at Fotheringhay Castle, in Northamptonshire. Little survives now of what must have been an imposing and well-defended castle, on the River Nene.

Above left: 11. St Mary and All Saints, Fotheringhay. Begun in 1434, the new church at Fotheringhay is all that remains of a larger, original collegiate church. It would prove to be a significant location for Cecily, as her husband and her second son, Edmund, would be reinterred there in 1476 and it would be the location of her own burial in 1495, in accordance with the terms of her will.

Above centre: 12. Window, Fotheringhay. A modern stained-glass window in the church of St Mary and All Saints contains several of the heraldic devices of the House of York.

Above right: 13. Richard, Duke of York. Cecily and Richard were betrothed in 1424, when she was nine. Their wedding took place in 1429, probably soon after her fourteenth birthday. The marriage appears to have been a successful one, lasting for over thirty years and producing thirteen children.

Above: 14. Rouen Cathedral. Cecily accompanied Richard to Rouen in 1441, when he was appointed Lieutenant of France. It was here, in Rouen Castle, that she gave birth to three children. Edward was baptised within the castle itself, suggesting that his survival may have been in doubt, but a year later, Edmund was christened in Rouen Cathedral.

Below and right: 15 & 16. Medieval Rouen. Many of the streets around the marketplace in modern Rouen give a sense of the city Cecily must have known during her five-year residence.

Left: 17. Rouen's *Gros Horloge*. Rouen's great clock sits in an archway in the city's Roman walls. Although the present clock face dates from the 1520s, a clock has been situated in this location since 1409. It is certainly a point of connection between the modern city and that which Cecily would have known.

Below: 18. Dublin Castle. At Dublin Castle, in October 1449, Cecily gave birth to George, the future Duke of Clarence.

Previous page, bottom, and this page, above and below: 19, 20, 21. Ludlow Castle. Part of the Mortimer inheritance, this twelfth-century castle became the main residence of Richard, Duke of York, and it was also the household for their sons Edward and Edmund in their youth.

22. Henry VI. The son of Henry V and Catherine of Valois, Henry inherited the throne in 1422 at the age of nine months, when his father died unexpectedly young from dysentery. The newly wed Cecily and Richard are likely to have attended his English coronation in 1429, while Richard certainly accompanied him to France for a second ceremony in 1431.

24. Edward IV. Cecily's third child and eldest surviving son, Edward was born in Rouen Castle on 28 April 1442. Edward became king after his victory at the Battle of Towton in 1461.

25. Elizabeth Wydeville. The daughter of Jacquetta, Duchess of Bedford, and Richard Wydeville, Elizabeth was a widow with two sons when she went through a secret marriage ceremony with Edward in 1464. She and Edward were married for nineteen years and had ten children together.

23. Millennium Bridge. Just to the right of the bridge, near the site of St Paul's Cathedral, stood Cecily's town house, Baynard's Castle. Excavations conducted by the Department of Urban Archaeology in 1974 and 1981 uncovered the plan of the castle, which had four wings around a trapezoidal courtyard; tiled floors, part of a fireplace and a staircase were uncovered from the time when Cecily lived there.

26. Caister Castle. Set on the beautiful Norfolk coastline, Caister was the fairy-tale dwelling of Sir John Fastolf, an associate of York's from his service in Normandy. Cecily stayed in the castle in 1456 and was so enamoured of it that she attempted to persuade Fastolf to sell it to her, but with no success.

This page: 27 & 28. Tonbridge Castle. One of the residences of Cecily's sister Anne, Duchess of Buckingham, the Kent stronghold was the location where Cecily was dispatched after her surrender at Ludlow in 1459. It was the arrival of her son Edward and his victory at Northampton that finally secured her freedom.

29. Tomb of Joan Neville, St. Nicholas's church, Arundel, Sussex. Joan was Cecily's niece, the daughter of her brother Richard Neville, Earl of Salisbury. She married William FitzAlan, Earl of Arundel, and bore him six children before her death in 1462.

Above left and above right: 30 & 31. Site of the Paston House, Norwich. A significant amount of information about the movements of the Duke of York and his wife can be gleaned from the letters written by the Paston family in the fifteenth century. Their Norwich house burned down in 1507 and another was built on the same site in Elm Hill by the city's mayor.

Right: 32. Sandwich, Kent. In 1469, Cecily travelled to the port of Sandwich in Kent with George and Warwick as they were about to depart for Calais, where George married Warwick's daughter Isabel Neville. Did the duchess accompany them in order to celebrate the marriage, or to try and persuade them not to go through with it?

Left and below: 33 & 34. Berkhamsted Castle, Hertfordshire. In 1469, Cecily left Fotheringhay Castle and spent the remainder of her life based at Berkhamsted. It represented a significant downscale for the duchess, but this may have been a reflection of her status as a widow.

Bottom: 35. Windsor Castle. Edward IV established a Yorkist mausoleum at St George's Chapel, Windsor. It was here that his body was carried and interred on his death in April 1483.

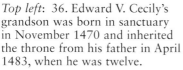

Top left: 36. Edward V. Cecily's grandson was born in sanctuary in November 1470 and inherited the throne from his father in April 1483, when he was twelve.

Top right: 37. Princes in the Tower. Edward V and his younger brother, Richard, Duke of York, were last seen playing in the gardens of the Tower of London in the summer of 1483. Historical opinion is divided over whether they met with a violent end or survived and fled to freedom.

Right: 38. Richard III. Cecily's twelfth child, Richard was born in October 1452 at Fotheringhay Castle. Richard proved a loyal supporter of his brother Edward, accompanying him into exile in 1470, but on Edward's death in 1483 it was Richard who became king, not Edward's son. What role did Cecily play in this process?

39. Anne Neville. Cecily's daughter-in-law, Anne married Richard, Duke of Gloucester, in 1472. Cecily witnessed the entire span of Anne's short life, including the arrival and death of her son, Edward of Middleham. Anne became Richard's queen in 1483 and died of an unknown illness, possibly tuberculosis, in March 1485.

Above left: 40. Elizabeth of York. The eldest daughter of Edward IV and Elizabeth Wydeville, Elizabeth emerged from sanctuary with her mother early in 1484 and was present at her uncle Richard's court.

Above right: 41. Tomb of Thomas Bourchier, Archbishop of Canterbury, Canterbury Cathedral, Kent. Thomas Bourchier was related to Cecily through his brother's marriage to Isabel, sister of Richard, Duke of York. He was sent to remove the younger of the Princes in the Tower from sanctuary and later officiated at the coronations of Richard III and Henry VII. Ten years older than Cecily, he lived a similarly long life, dying in 1486 at his Palace of Knole, in Kent.

42. Richard and Anne, Cecily's son and daughter-in-law, as portrayed by Edward Austin Abbey in 1896. Cecily outlived both Richard and Anne, long enough to see the Tudor regime established and a considerable degree of negative reaction against her son's brief rule. She is described in her household ordinances as the mother of Edward IV but Richard is not mentioned, perhaps reflecting the mood of the times.

Above left: 43. Madonna and Child. Piety and devotion to the saints was a particularly significant part of medieval life, but even by those standards Cecily was pious and devoted, ending her life as a vowess, something similar to living in holy orders.

Above right: 44. Margaret Beaufort. Margaret's third husband, Sir Thomas Stanley, played a significant role in supporting the 1485 invasion of her son, Henry Tudor, which ended the life and reign of Richard III.

Left: 45. Henry VII and Henry VIII. In 1486, Cecily's granddaughter, Elizabeth of York, married Henry VII, the victor of Bosworth Field.

Above: 47. Raby Castle. A romantic view of Cecily's birthplace, from a 1930s postcard.

Richard Plantagenet. Duke of York. Nephew to Edward Duke of York. and Father to King Edward 4th. was slain at Wakefield. in the 37 Year of Henry 6th 1459. and lies buried here with Cecily his Wife.

Cecily. Dutchefs of York. Daughter to Ralph Neville first Earl of Westmorland.

46. Fotheringhay memorial. The tomb erected in St Mary and All Saints' church, Fotheringhay, Northampton, to Richard and Cecily. The originals were in a poor state when their great-granddaughter Elizabeth I visited and she commissioned this new memorial in the 1570s.

That summer, England lost the territory of Bordeaux, which reinforced York's criticisms of Somerset. In July, a plan was reputedly hatched by Oldhall, York's chamberlain, now Speaker of the Commons, to seize the king that September. Oldhall was then leasing the manor of Standon from York and a number of his men there were arrested. His name had already been raised in connection with Cade's Rebellion, and York's reputation was further damaged by this plot. That September there were also uprisings in York's name at Ilminster and Yeovil, and then in Norfolk it was alleged that an Edward Clere had received letters from York attempting to incite further rebellion. Satirical verses penned by Sir William Tailboys, an enemy of York's associate Lord Cromwell, were also circulated, naming the duke as a rival claimant to the throne. It is difficult to know exactly what role York himself played in these manifestations of discontent. Clearly, they worked in his favour to an extent, demonstrating support for him and voicing lack of confidence in the current regime. It is possible that he played a role in generating them, by inciting his retainers and supporters to raise trouble, but the sort of low-level nuisance they created only served to isolate him from government and decision-making. York was no fool; he knew that he would only succeed in his aims to oust Somerset by either taking direct action or by some concerted, large-scale effort. If so, these sporadic outbursts in his name must have been frustrating and damaging to his cause. By September he was in Southwark, probably staying at the house of Sir John Fastolf, with an army of 2,000 men.

That November, York's supporter Thomas Yonge, MP for Bristol, proposed to the council that the duke should be named as Henry VI's heir, for which he was sent to the Tower. York's presence at the Parliamentary session bore little fruit and by the following year he was ready to use force. The family were at Ludlow again to observe Christmas and it was there, early in January 1452, that Cecily conceived again. It was probably her twelfth child, perhaps her thirteenth, but her last four pregnancies had only produced one surviving son. She would not yet have been aware of her condition, but it would have been apparent that conflict was brewing, as her husband lost patience with the continual goading of the Duke of Somerset and his allies. From Ludlow, Richard wrote a petition, dated 9 January, attempting once more to clear his name. He was aware that the king had 'a distrust by sinister information of mine enemies, adversaries and evil-willers', and had arranged to swear his loyalty to Henry upon the sacraments before the Bishop of Hereford and the Earl of Shrewsbury.[32] The influence of these enemies was damaging

York's reputation with the king and hindering his advancement so, as the unofficial royal heir, he determined to move against them. One political satire of the time demonstrates that the view that Henry was being manipulated by Somerset and his agents, as well as a fear of general lawlessness, was widely held:

> Trowth and pore men ben appressed
> And mischief is nothing redressed
> The kyng knowith not all ...[33]

The family were still at Ludlow on 3 February, when Richard wrote 'under his signet' to the burgesses of Shrewsbury, asking for their support in his cause against his enemies. His letter is reproduced in *Warkworth's Chronicles*, explaining that all his loyalty and efforts had been 'of none effect, through the envy, malice and untruth of the said Duke of Somerset ... [who] laboureth continually about the King's highness for my undoing, and to corrupt my blood, and to disherit me and my heirs'. The final straw might have been the news that Oldhall had been forcibly ejected from sanctuary by the duke, who believed York's chamberlain had been involved in an attack on one of his men. Oldhall was restored to St Martin's-le-Grand, where he remained until 1455, but trouble was fomenting elsewhere too. A few days later, the Mulso brothers began to muster support at Fotheringhay, with the intention of joining with York on the way to London. Through his English estates, groups of men gathered in assemblies and hastened to the side of their lord. With a personal force of at least 8,000 troops, York marched south, arriving at Blackheath by the start of March. The Cottonian Roll ii 23 contains a detailed description of his encampment there, with York in the middle, flanked by Lord Devonshire on the south and Lord Cobham beside the Thames, with seven ships full of 'ther stuff'.[34] York declined to attack the king's forces and welcomed the party sent to negotiate in the king's name. He repeated his desire for the removal of Somerset, and a tentative agreement appeared to have been made to allow him to speak to Henry in person. After the king pledged his safety, York dismissed his men and entered the royal tent. It was a trick. Somerset was not required to answer to any of the articles York had submitted against him. Instead, the duke was forced to make a humiliating oath of loyalty to Somerset and promise to act 'in humble and obeysant wise'. He was then sent to London, in the custody of two bishops. The news reached Cecily at Ludlow. York still had around 10,000 men in the Welsh Marches. According to the London chronicler Fabyan, York's son Edward, now almost ten years old, called them to arms and rode at their head to the capital.

Did young Edward's campaign actually happen? With the independence, determination and military precocity shown by Edward at the age of eighteen, it would seem to be in character. What role did Cecily play in it? Did she encourage her son or try to dissuade him from a potentially dangerous mission? She was two months pregnant at this point, perhaps suffering from the symptoms of the first trimester, but presumably she was aware of her son's plans. Given that Fabyan was apprenticed around 1470, making a birthdate of the 1450s most likely, he cannot have been a witness himself, although he may have drawn on the memories of older friends and family. After all, he was born in London, and served as its sheriff, alderman and an auditor of its accounts, and was proposed as Lord Mayor in 1503. With the Patent Rolls for 1452 filled with the names of men who were granted pardons for supporting York that summer, it is not stretching credulity too far to suggest that Fabyan may have had access to first-hand knowledge.

News of her husband's humiliation reached Cecily. On 10 March, York was forced to swear a public oath at St Paul's Cathedral that he would not take up arms again. His bitter response, submitted to the House of Lords and preserved in the Cottonian Collection, made clear his reasons for resenting Somerset's influence, particularly the losses he had incurred in France. After this, around 24 March, York retreated to Ludlow. If his young son Edward had been marching south at the head of an army, York may well have intercepted them and brought them back home. Cecily would have been relieved to see them return. Further trouble rumbled on through the summer, with small uprisings in York's name in Kent and Suffolk, and in May Oldhall was brought before the King's Bench and indicted. York was in Ludlow that June, and Tickenhill, Bewdley, that July. In mid-August, Henry VI visited Ludlow as part of a progress to the west[35] and would, no doubt, have been received and probably lodged in the castle. However, it seems that the duke was doing his best to avoid Henry, travelling to Fotheringhay and arriving there on 11 August.

At this stage, Cecily had less than six weeks to go before her next child was due. Presumably she gave the orders for the Ludlow household to be packed up and allowed others to carry them out; one source has the duke leaving Fotheringhay but returning by Michaelmas, 29 September.[36] By 2 October, Cecily was definitely in Yorkshire, where she gave birth to a son. Later writers would describe this birth with much invented detail but there is no indication that it was anything other than a straightforward delivery. If Cecily was able to travel over 100 miles in the preceding weeks, the delivery is unlikely to have been the nightmare that chroniclers like John Rous and Thomas More would make it out to be. The Yorks named their new son Richard.

That December, Sir John Fastolf was a visitor at Fotheringhay. By this point the old soldier was over seventy, with a long and varied career in France as well as being a significant patron of the arts. Given his history serving under York in Normandy, he may well have been received as a welcome guest, but there was also financial business to transact. On 15 December 1451, the pair drew up an indenture, by which York handed over some of his personal jewels into Fastolf's keeping as guarantee for a short-term loan of money. The items give an idea of the treasure in the family's possession, much of it bearing their personal iconography: a 'nowche of gold with a greet pointed diamond sette up on a roose enamelled white; a nowche of gold in facion of a ragged staf with 2 ymages of man and woman garnysshed with a ruby, a diamond and a greete peerle; and a floure of gold, garnysshed with 2 rubies, a diamond and 3 hanging pearls'. These covered a debt amounting to £437, which York was bound to repay by the Nativity of St John the Baptist, 24 June, upon which he would receive his jewels back.[37] The timing of this may indicate York had bills he anticipated paying as a result of the Christmas season, possibly following the usual tradition of demonstrating his loyalty to the king and queen with expensive gifts.

Since their return from France in 1445, Cecily's and Richard's lives had lost their direction somewhat. York was technically heir to the throne but, with the queen's advisers effectively squeezing him out, he was unable to take the role at the heart of government that his birth should have ensured. Frequently occupied with the rigours of pregnancy and delivery, Cecily must have continually hoped to hear that he had been acknowledged and promoted, in order to provide her children with a secure place in the world they were soon to enter, a world in which their birth gave them a certain entitlement. With only Anne already matched, their marriages would be crucial in the coming years, forming alliances that would signal the family's rise or decline. Edward and Edmund were established at Ludlow, and there were now two more girls who required dowries and husbands, and two little boys, still in the nursery. Finally, in 1453, an unexpected turn of events would put York at the heart of power.

8

The Lord Protector's Wife
1453-1455

All women that in thys world art wrought
By me they may ensample take
ffor I that was brought up of noght
A prince me chese to be his make.[1]

Queen Margaret of Anjou was pregnant. Seven years had passed since Cecily had encountered the fifteen-year-old girl suffering from illness on her way through Rouen to her English marriage. Since then, national politics had put them on opposing sides but they still had many things in common. Having spent years wondering whether she would conceive, Cecily must have understood Margaret's concerns over her own fertility in the intervening years. Whether this was down to infrequent relations with her husband or some medical condition, Margaret may well have asked Cecily for advice. The two certainly corresponded about pregnancy and birth, and the duchess would play a leading part in the queen's churching ceremony the following year. It would have been a bittersweet friendship, not incompatible with promoting her family's futures at court, but Cecily knew that the arrival of a royal heir would mean the relegation of her husband's status as next in line to the throne.

Early in the new year, 1453, Margaret conceived and, once her condition was confirmed, around Easter time, she travelled to the shrine of Our Lady at Walsingham to give thanks. It was part of a wider campaign to build support among the local gentry; Margaret Paston recorded that the queen spent three days in Norwich shortly before St George's Day and tried to encourage the Pastons' cousin Elizabeth to get married. On the queen's return journey, she stayed with Cecily at Hitchin,

in Hertfordshire, then an important town that served as the receivership
for the whole county. It is not impossible that the two women travelled
together to the Norfolk shrine, one to give thanks for a safe delivery and
the other to ask for guidance through the coming birth. They would have
stayed at the manor or mansion house attached to the priory at Hitchin,
known as the Biggin. The small convent house there had been established
in 1317 and dedicated to the Virgin; it still stands on the south side of the
town and is currently used as a hotel, with one external flint wall dating
from the early fifteenth century and internal stone walls and features.
Built by Adam le Rous, it had once been in the possession of Edward III's
mistress, Alice Ferrers, but by the 1440s it was owned by Richard, Duke
of York.[2]

Hitchin historian Reginald Hine describes the approach to the house,
through the gatehouse, along a cobbled pathway and through a formal
garden. Then, on the right, lay the L-shaped building, or four buildings
under one roof, known as the 'owlde halle', which contained the chapter
house along its ground floor, and upstairs in its western-facing section
were the prior's lodging and two little chambers. There was also a holy
well, dedicated to St Winefride, the waters of which the queen and
duchess may have drunk.[3] It was common for pilgrims of all ranks to
make the journey to Walsingham, staying along the way in establishments
dedicated to Mary; Cecily and Margaret would have stayed in the prior's
lodgings and, perhaps, offered their thanks to the patron saints of
motherhood at the nearby parish church of St Mary, which still shows
the evidence of its fifteenth-century refurbishment. It seems, from details
in a later letter, that Cecily used this opportunity to speak with Margaret
on behalf of her husband, regarding his fall from favour, in the hope that
he would be restored to his previous position of trust. Her plea may have
been written, too, as she later refers to things that were 'specified in the
said supplication'.

That summer, Cecily wrote to Margaret continuing these themes
by thanking the Virgin Mary for helping the queen to 'fulfil your
right honourable body of the most precious, most joyful and most
comfortable earthly treasure that might come unto this land'. She then
pressed Margaret further to consider Richard's plight. The letter gives
an indication of the effect the recent years had had upon the couple's
prospects and the closeness with which they shared their grievances.
Cecily had recently been ill, her 'sloth and discontinuance' being caused
by 'the disease and infirmity that since my said being in your highness'
presence hath grown'. Written at least six months after she had given

birth to Richard, and perhaps more, it is not clear if this illness relates to, or was a consequence of, pregnancy and delivery. It may have been a result of bearing another child, or a post-partum complication; it may not have been connected at all. Cecily's use of the word 'labour' may mislead, as this was not necessarily the way she would refer to a delivery and more commonly denotes effort. In the letter, it may relate to the pain she took in supplicating the queen.

York's lack of favour with the king had clearly affected his family deeply. Most remarkable about the letter is Cecily's tone of humility, in such contrast to many popular depictions of her vanity and pride. The two are not incompatible, but this letter serves as a reminder of just how the late medieval social machinery worked, with its elaborate set phrases of devotion and loyalty, which appear nonetheless genuine as the duchess pleads for her husband's fair treatment. It is difficult to doubt the 'immeasurable sorrow and heaviness' she expresses, which did 'diminish and abridge' her days as well as her 'worldly joy and comfort', that she felt in York's estrangement from the Crown. Whether she was acting independently in writing this, trying to build on an existing female bond, or whether York was at her elbow, it demonstrates that Cecily could certainly be persuasive and humble. So few of her letters survive that it is worth reproducing in full, if only to get a sense of her voice:

Cecily, Duchess of York, to Queen Margaret of Anjou, 1453
Beseecheth with all humbleness and reverence possible your lowly obeisant servant and bedewoman, Cecily, Duchess of York that whereof the plenty of your good gand benign grace it pleased thereunto in your coming from that blessed, gracious and devout pilgrimage of our Lady of Walsingham to suffer to coming out of my simple person, replete with such immeasurable sorrow and heaviness as I doubt not will of the continuance thereof diminish and abridge my days, as it does my worldly joy and comfort, unto your most worthy and most high presence, whereunto that [you pleased] full benignly to receive my supplication to the same, made for your humble, true man and servant, my lord my husband, whose infinite sorrow, unrest of heart and of worldly comfort, caused of that that he heareth him to be estranged from the grace and benevolent favour of that most Christian, most gracious and most benevolent prince, the king of our sovereign lord, whose majesty royal my said lord and husband now as ever, God knoweth, during his life hath been as true, and as humble, and as obeisant liegeman and to the performing of his noble pleasure and

commandment as ready, as well-disposed, and as diligent at his power, and over that as glad, as specified in the said supplication, I beseech your highness and good grace, at the mercy of our Creator now ready to send His grace to all Christian persons, and of that blessed Lady to whom you alte prayed, in whom aboundeth plenteously mercy and grace, by whose mediation it pleased our Lord to fulfil your right honourable body of the most precious, most joyful, and most comfortable earthly treasure that might come into this land and to the people thereof, the which I beseech His abundant grace to prosper in you, and at such as it pleaseth Him to bring into this world, with all honour, gracious speed and felicity, with also of furthermore supplication of blessed and noble fruit of your said body, for the great trust and most comfortable surety and weal of this realm and of the king's true liege people of the same, to call the good speed of the matters contained in this said supplication into the gracious and tender recommendation of your highness.

Whereunto I should for the same hath without sloth or discontinuance and with undelayed diligence have sued, nor had the disease and infirmity that since my said being in your highness presence hath grown and growth, upon me caused not only the encumberous labour, to me full painful and uneasy, God knoweth, that then I took upon me, but also the continuance and addition of such heaviness that I have taken, and take, for the consideration of the sorrow of my said Lord and husband; and if it please your good grace not to take to any displeasure of strangeness that I have not diligently continued the suit of my said supplication unto your said highness, caused of the same infirmity not hid upon my wretched body. Wherefore I report me to God; and in reverence of whom, and of his said grace and mercy to you showed, it pleases [eftsones] unto your high nobility to be a tender and gracious mean unto the highness of our sovereign lord for the favour and benevolence of his hand to be showed unto my lord and husband, so that through the gracious mean of you, sovereign lady, he may and effectually obtain to have the same. Wherein I beseech your said highness that my said labour and pain may not be taken frivolously nor unfruitfully, but the more agreeable for my said lord unto your good grace. Whereunto, notwithstanding my infirmity, I should not have spared to have recontinued my suit, if I could or might have done, that it should have pleased your nobility if that I should so have done the which, as it shall please thereunto I shall not let, not sparing pain that my body now suffice of any probability to bear, or suffer, with God's grace, whom I shall pray to prosper your high estate in honour, joy and felicity.[4]

Margaret's response to the letter is unknown. As the summer advanced and she prepared herself for her coming confinement, the court dispatched to Clarendon Palace. There, circumstances beyond the control of both women were to propel Cecily's husband to the very pinnacle of government.

In August 1453, Henry VI was taken ill. The causes and nature of his affliction are still debated by historians today, but, whether he was suffering from hereditary 'madness' or a nervous breakdown, he fell into a catatonic and unresponsive state and could no longer even give the impression of ruling. For a while this was kept secret, as doctors attempted to remedy the situation, but Henry's condition did not change. When Margaret went into labour that October, delivering a son on 13 October at Westminster, Henry was unable to recognise her or his heir. A witness, John Stodeley, described how the Duke of Buckingham took the baby in his arms 'and presented him to the Kyng in godly wyse, beseeching the Kyng to blisse him; and the Kyng gave no maner answere'. The queen did the same 'but alle their labour was in veyne for they departed thens without any answere or countenance savyng only that ones he loked on the Prince and caste doune his eyene ayen, without any more'.[5] Somerset was the boy's godfather.

The inevitable rumours about the boy's paternity redoubled as Henry stared at his son without acknowledgement. Cecily and York were in London at the time, having arrived with a 'modest retinue' on 12 November, according to *Benet's Chronicle*. Richard had been summoned to attend a session of Parliament and Cecily was listed among those attending the queen at her churching ceremony in November. With childbirth as a female preserve and only high-ranking women allowed to touch the queen's body, it is highly likely that the experienced Cecily was present at the prince's birth, along with the duchesses of Suffolk and Somerset, who accompanied her at the purification. Her experience would have made her a valuable addition, and her rank made her an ideal choice, in accordance with contemporary practice. Although history had written their menfolk into the roles of enemies, it is important to remember the close family ties that bound this tiny segment of the aristocracy and frequently facilitated their physical proximity. Their rivalries and conflicts are one small part of a much wider blood connection, which flared up as the result of disagreements precipitated by this proximity. In 1453, the wives of York and Lancaster were still on terms of sufficient familiarity that Cecily may well have been one of Margaret's 'gossips' in the birth chamber.

As winter approached, it became clear that the king was not improving. Although Henry now had a son, who had superseded York in the succession, the reins of government now fell to him. One of his first acts in this transitional autumn was to order Somerset's arrest; the duke was committed to the Tower on 23 November, probably while his trial was being planned. It must have seemed to York and Cecily that all the obstacles of the past years were melting away. In December 1453, Richard stood before the council and declared himself a true 'liegeman' and subject of King Henry, who would work for the 'welfare of the king and his subjects'. However, 'divers persones' had withdrawn their counsel from him, causing 'greet hurte' and he now required them to 'freely without any impediment resort unto him'. All the lords 'condescended and agreed as to that thing that was thought unto theim juste and resounable'.[6] He and Cecily left London for Christmas, probably returning to Ludlow, as was their custom, but York took the opportunity to gather his support for the return to Parliament. This included his son Edward, Norfolk, Warwick and, surprisingly, the king's half-brothers Jasper and Edmund Tudor, who at this stage supported York over Somerset.

Then there was a surprising development. Until this point Margaret of Anjou had played little active part in politics, but, early in 1454, she submitted a Bill of five articles requesting the full rights of a regent. They were recorded in a newsletter written by John Stodeley on 19 January. She desired to have 'the hole reule of this land' and the right to appoint 'the Chauncellor, the Tresorere, Privy Seelle and alle other officers of this land'. She wished to have all the bishoprics and benefices under her control as well as having sufficient 'livelihoods' for herself, the king and her son. Stodeley also wrote that Somerset 'hathe espies goyng in every Lordes hous of this land' and that every man was of 'th'opynion' that he 'maketh hym redy to be as strong as he kan make hym'.[7] If the queen's articles were passed, it would prove a disaster for York's cause.

York returned to London promptly, being welcomed into the city by an official delegation led by the mayor and aldermen, and, according to the Paston Letters, established in 'his household meynee, clenly beseen and likely men', including Warwick, the Tudor brothers Richmond and Pembroke and his eldest son, Edward, Earl of March.[8] Travelling with them and waiting to see how the future would unfold, Cecily must have been impatient as she re-established herself in the capital. With Henry incapacitated and his heir still an infant, someone was required to run the country. Given his status and descent, her husband looked like the best candidate for the job. He would be king in all but name, making her something very like a queen.

Soon, York brought good news. Margaret's proposals were not popular. In March, the council assented to give York power to hold a parliament at Westminster in the king's name.[9] Then, on 3 April, he was officially named as Lord Protector 'in consideration of the King's infirmity whereby his attendance to the protection of the realm and church of England would be tedious and prejudicial to his swift recovery'. No one knew how long Henry's illness would last, or if he would ever recover, so Richard's authority was established until 'Edward, the king's first-born son, arrive at years of discretion, if he shall then wish to take upon himself the charge of protector and defender'.[10] With his enemy Somerset in the Tower and Cecily's brother the Earl of Salisbury as his chancellor, York's future had dramatically altered for the better. Richard was as good as king and this put Cecily in the position of almost being a queen. However, there was someone else close to home who thought they had a better claim.

Cecily's sons were back in their establishment at Ludlow. A letter sent from Edward and Edmund to their father probably dates to around this time and shows that they were aware of the developments in his career, that the twists and turns of recent events were shared among the family. They gave thanks for their father's 'honourable conduct and good speed in all your matters and business, and of [York's] gracious prevail against the intent and malice of your evil-willers'. The letter was written during Easter week. In 1454, Easter Sunday fell on 21 April, so it was probably written soon after York's appointment as Lord Protector, allowing for enough time for the news to travel north. A later composition seems unlikely, as this would place it in the weeks preceding battle, when the duke's 'evil-willers' were once more in the ascendant. The letter also speaks of green gowns and fine bonnets, as well as the 'odious rule and demeaning'[11] of the Croft brothers, their tutors at Ludlow, which tends towards an earlier interpretation of the boys' ages at the time of composition. At Easter 1454, Edward was about to turn twelve and Edmund was ten. Sir Richard Croft was the second husband of their lady governess, Eleanor Cornwall, who had previously married into the Mortimer family. It has been suggested that Croft was too young to have been the boys' tutor but a possible birthdate of 1427 would put him in his late twenties and may reflect the confusion caused by the fact that he had a younger brother who was also named Richard.

A second letter, dated from 3 June, also survives, acknowledging the receipt of a letter written by their father on 29 May at the city of York, which had been brought to them by the family servant William Cleton. Their father had commended them to 'attend to our learning in our young age, that should cause us to grow to honour and worship in our old age'. They requested that York send them Harry Lovedeyne, groom of the kitchen, 'whose service is to us right agreeable'.[12] By then, the Croft situation appeared to have been resolved. The boys' gratitude for the father's success over his enemies was soon to be replaced by concern, as another rival rose from within the family ranks. Richard remained in York until after 20 June, the Feast of Corpus Christi, according to a letter received by John Paston from an R. Dollay. The duke was received there with 'great worship'. As the birthdates of her children suggest, she travelled regularly with her husband, Cecily may well have been staying with him in the medieval city.

The Yorks had so many properties that it is more helpful to think of their household as a body of people rather than a physical place. This was concentrated on the immediate needs of the family but had a number of branches, spread through their estates in England and Wales. Some of their staff were attached to specific locations by a particular role, such as parker or steward. They often fulfilled other, more general, unspecified positions as councillors or general aides. In the last decade, York's household had undergone some changes and now comprised a mixture of loyal friends and associates from Normandy and Ireland, as well as new faces who had transferred their support from the households of Bedford and Gloucester, and those who were dissatisfied with Somerset and Henry VI. The retinues of great magnates offered protection and opportunities to those aspiring to better themselves; any slight connection with social betters brought prestige and the opportunity to serve. Even the wearing of a lord's livery was something most medieval people aspired to. To enter the service of the heir to the throne was, in itself, an achievement and people were wise enough to try to support those who had the promise of being more powerful in the future. Without question there were many who were personally loyal to the family, but it would be unrealistic to expect that to be motivated by anything other than a desire for self-advancement.

As York's duchess, Cecily would have known the family servants well. The book of the *Ménagier de Paris*, a series of guidelines for medieval wifedom, states that it is crucial for a woman in her position to be able to deal with servants on a regular basis. She must be wise enough not to be cheated by them and ensure that they carry out their duties properly, particularly in the absence of her lord. Cecily would have known John Cotes, parker of Fotheringhay by the early 1450s, who was paid £2 a year for his work. There was also John Leyland, seneschal of Fotheringhay, and Thomas Willoughby, already auditor and newly appointed treasurer in 1453. Their old associate Edmund Mulso, a loyal Yorkist, was now steward of the castle; William Burley remained as their lawyer; their cofferer, John Kendal, would go on to become secretary to Cecily's new baby, Richard. Roger Crosse was listed as York's chaplain on 3 September 1452, perhaps replacing James Hamelin, who was listed as performing this role in the 1440s; William Wilflete acted as the duke's confessor. Given that in their early married life they applied for a joint confessor, he probably served Cecily as well. Their auditing clerk was Thomas Aleyn, who would later work more closely with Cecily and was clearly trusted by her.[13]

The members of the household who assisted with the daily running of the hall and hearth would have been accustomed to receive their orders from the lady of the house. Roger Ree was usher of the chamber, Richard Stalworth was the valet, and John Thykkethorpe groom of the chamber. John Malas, valet of the Yorks' wardrobe from 1453, had been valet to the Duke of Gloucester and previously had an annuity paid. Along with his wife, Joan, he had been with them in Ireland, making it likely that Joan, if still alive, was also in Cecily's household in the early 1450s. The Yorks' domestic servants in the early 1450s included John Boyes, Richard Chapelyn, Thomas Grey, William Kirby, William Cleton, John Harpsfield, John Lardener and William Mayell.[14]

Preparing the family's food was Henry Cook, a yeoman of the kitchen, from the Welsh valley of Usk. John Hemmingbrough was also a cook in York's service by 1451, and would go on to be chief cook to his son, Edward IV. Harry Lovedene was the groom of the kitchen, Walter Moyle was valet of the cellar and John Walden was clerk of the kitchen, having progressed from being responsible for buying poultry a decade before. John Oram was clerk of the spicery in the 1430s, but had become clerk of the itinerant household by the early 1450s. They were overseen by Richard Wigmore, steward of the household, possibly the son of John Wigmore, who served York in the 1430s as an attorney. The extent of the ducal household reached far beyond this; their names represent only a fragment of those who lived and worked in the Yorks' service, at one or many of their properties. They also relied on the service and supplies of London men like fishmonger Richard Drax, broker John Snow, draper

Henry Wever and goldsmith Robert Butler.[15] Servants came and went; some drifted in and out of their employ, while others remained with the family for three decades and went on to serve Cecily's sons.

Although her existence was a peripatetic one, Cecily would have been a regular visitor to Ludlow, overseeing the household and the education of her two eldest sons. As well as a traditional academic grounding and the obligatory lessons in polite behaviour attested to by surviving manuals, they were being prepared for a chivalric life as knights of the future. No doubt their reading would have encompassed the French romances that told of such struggles and the heroic accounts of historic and legendary figures, but there was also a practical element to this preparation, involving riding at the quintain, the handling of weapons, agility in armour, throwing and climbing.[16] While their exact regime does not survive, the best indicator for its nature is the set of Ordinances that Cecily's son Edward drew up for his own 'first begotten' son, in 1473.

Under these ordinances, the three-year-old Edward was allowed to rise at a convenient hour according to his age and be interrupted by no one except for his uncle Anthony Wydeville, his chamberlain and chaplains. The chaplain would say matins in his presence before Edward headed to chapel for Mass, where he was to be uninterrupted. Immediately after this, he was to have breakfast, honourably served at a convenient hour. While he ate, he was to listen to 'such noble storyes as behoveth a Prince to understand' and go from there to his learning, followed by disports and exercises 'as behoveth his estate to have experience in'. He attended evensong before supper, followed again by such 'honest disportes' that may be 'conveniently devised for his recreation'. Dinner was to be served at ten, or eleven on fast days, and supper at four. He was to be put to bed at eight, and his servants were to make him 'joyoux and merry towards his bedde'.[17] Standards of behaviour were important too. No one in the household was permitted to be a 'swearer, brawler, backbiter, adventurer or use words of ribaldry' in the prince's presence. If one person struck another within the house he would be punished, but if he drew a weapon he was to be set in the stocks, losing his position on the second offence. No one should be absent without sufficient licence and the gates were closed and opened at set hours and 'guarded well and all servants furnished and harnessed according to their degrees'.[18] Cecily's youngest boys, George and Richard, would have been following a similar regime in the nursery at Fotheringhay, under the careful eye of Anne of Caux.

When it came to the education of her daughters, Elizabeth and Margaret, Cecily may have had a more direct input. In 1454, Elizabeth was ten and Margaret eight. Their education would have been overseen by a lady governess, but Cecily herself may also have instructed them in reading and writing. The ordinances drawn up for her household in later life display an extensive library, including the popular *Golden Legend*, Nicholas Love's *Mirror of the Blessed Lyf of Jesu Christ*, Walter Hilton's *Active and Contemplative Lives* and other saints' lives. Her will, drawn up in 1495, lists breviaries, Mass books, psalters and gospels. She may have read her daughters stories and histories herself, as well as modelling feminine behaviour and accomplishments. Most of all, they were trained to be wives, administering to their husbands, children and their estates. In this, female relatives were traditionally the first guides, as the husband in the *Ménagier de Paris* wrote to his wife in the late fourteenth century – 'the women of your lineage are good enough to correct you harshly themselves' – although for a long time she had none of her 'kinswomen near you to whom you might turn for counsel in your private needs', and she, in turn, would 'be able to teach better wisdom to [her] daughters'.[19] Devotional and instructional literature also cites female examples, such as the loyal wives Sarah, Rebecca and Rachel and the patience of Chaucer's Griselda, as well as the examples set by the lives of female saints in the popular hagiographies of the day. One of Cecily's daughters would be in need of such patience and endurance in the coming years.

By this point, the couple's eldest daughter, Anne, had consummated her marriage to Henry Holland, Earl of Exeter. Around this time, at the age of seventeen, she fell pregnant with their only child. The young earl, though, had proven himself to be imprudent and impulsive, allying with York's enemies, the Percy family, in a bitter land dispute with the king's chamberlain, Ralph, Lord Cromwell of Tattershall. Now he was resentful that York had been appointed Lord Protector instead of himself. In May 1454, Holland led an uprising from the Percy Manor of Spofforth towards the city of York, under the standard of Lancaster. However, he did not get very far. York quickly marched north; he was in London on 13 May and in the city of York eight days later, where he passed sentence on the Percys, imposing huge fines so they were imprisoned as debtors.[20] It also emerged that Holland had been planning his father-in-law's death; York may have even survived an assassination attempt, and although Exeter eluded capture and fled, he was apprehended in London and sentenced to be imprisoned in Pontefract Castle. York was in London in June and back again in July when he received the commission to deliver his wayward son-in-law to his confinement on 24 July. Once at Pontefract, he could leave Exeter under the watchful eye of Cecily's brother, Salisbury. This cannot have been an easy time for Cecily, watching Anne's husband develop such intentions towards her family while Anne was carrying his child. Around this time, at the age of thirty-nine, Cecily herself also fell pregnant again.

One of York's first tasks as Lord Protector was to plan for England's future in Normandy. He guaranteed the debts owed to the garrison at Calais, succeeded in revoking some of the more punishing trade conditions with the Merchants of the Staple and calmed a major rebellion. In July he was in London to be appointed Captain of Calais, and ordered the assembly of a fleet to defend it and England's right to trade in the Channel.[21] On 3 August, he was again at York, then progressed to his castle at Sandal, from where he wrote to John Paston regarding his patronage of Walsingham. On 19 September, he was overseeing the local courts of oyer and terminer in Derby. Most significant of all, a date for the trial of the Duke of Somerset was established, for 28 October.

Calais having been dealt with, Richard turned his attention to Henry's court. It had become an unwieldy and wasteful establishment and needed to be thoroughly investigated and the essential roles redefined. If the duke and duchess were not actually living at court at this time, they must have been close by, in order for York to oversee this huge operation. No provision is made for them within the court itself, which may well indicate that they were elsewhere. At this point, Baynard's Castle was still in the hands of Henry VI and Richard is not recorded as living there until 1457, but it is quite likely that, as Lord Protector, he had the use of the property. The castle had four wings enclosing several courtyards but recent excavations have shown that the wall flanking the river had five smaller, projecting towers. Its great hall was 40 feet long by 24 feet wide and could accommodate several hundred people. In addition to the riverside entrance, granting easy access to Westminster, there was a cobbled land entrance to the north. Inside, archaeologists recently found tiled flooring and the remains of a fireplace. Cecily would have established herself here, at the head of a household that included her husband's retinue of 400 men and the nursery for her young children. While she was laying out the domestic roles at Baynard's, York was doing a similar task on a much larger scale.

Finally published in 1455, York's household ordinances of Henry VI provide an interesting snapshot of the English court on the eve of war. Allowances were made for the permanent residence of the king's confessor and his staff; the two Tudor earls, Jasper of Pembroke and Edmund of Richmond, each with seven men; then there was a viscount, then the

Lord Chamberlain and two barons. After that came the officers of the king's household: carvers, physicians, chamberers, secretaries, chaplains, squires, ushers and so forth. All the names are male, from the scullery and kitchens to the launderers and poultry keepers. Queen Margaret was allocated 120 people and Prince Edward was granted 38, although Margaret had retreated to Greenwich during York's ascendancy. The document has twenty-eight signatories, starting with the new Archbishop of Canterbury, Richard's kinsman Thomas Bourchier, who is followed by nine more bishops. After that came York's turn to sign but, instead of writing his name beneath that of the Bishop of Ely, he began a new column and wrote his name highest of all. The other signatories were his nephew the Earl of Warwick, the earls of Devon and Buckingham, the Tudor brothers, York's brother-in-law Salisbury, along with Stanley, Say and others.[22] A significant number of them would lose their lives in the coming conflict.

The call to arms came fairly quickly. One moment York was at the pinnacle of government, reshaping the royal regime, with his enemies under control, and the next he was on the outside again. He was in London attending Parliament on 7 November, by which time the proposed date for the commencement of Somerset's trial had passed without any appearance of the necessary legal proceedings. It may have been postponed due to the riots that took place in the city that autumn against Italian merchants. The event that precipitated the change in Richard's fortunes happened on Christmas Day 1454. He would have been with his family, perhaps at prayer, or feasting, when the news came. King Henry had come to his senses. He was able to acknowledge his son and was made aware of the events of the previous year. The brief taste of power was over.

Early in the New Year, York resigned his position as Lord Protector with 'great honour and the love of all'.[23] He had little choice but to do so. Yet it was not quite with the love of all; once restored to power, Henry freed Somerset from the Tower in February 1455. 'The duke said that during the king's disease he was committed to the Tower of London and kept there a year, ten weeks and more',[24] and asked for exemplification of the act that had committed him there. On 4 March, Somerset was with the king and queen at Greenwich, where he secured a declaration of his innocence regarding all the criminal charges levelled against him, with others to be put to arbitration. Exeter was also released from Pontefract Castle but, worse still, York was relieved of his captaincy of Calais, which had been intended to last for seven years, only to find it awarded to Somerset. The reprisals he had feared soon materialised. Other small privileges and benefits were removed from him and his allies, and when a special session of the Great Council was called at Leicester for 21 May, York and his allies believed it would seek to question their loyalty. At least York was not alone this time, having the powerful Neville family members of Cecily's brother Salisbury and his son, Warwick, at his side. They withdrew from court without seeking permission and attempted once more to intercede between the king and the Lancastrian faction before they reached Leicester.[25] Henry's confessor, John Blackman, wrote of York, 'Sullenly the disgraced nobleman retired to his estates in the North and there, brooded over the affront put upon him by the Queen and her party.'[26]

But York was a man of action, never one to brood for long. With Somerset fully restored to power, it was clear that he would seek to move against York and attempt to remove him permanently from government, and thus a group of councillors was summoned to attend secret meetings between 15 and 18 April. This was followed by a declaration that the Great Council would meet at Leicester. York suspected, probably quite rightly, that on this occasion steps would be taken against him. He needed to pre-empt the meeting. On 18 May, he sent out summonses to his estates for men to rally to his side. In a letter dated two days later, he wrote from Royston in Hertfordshire to the king regarding the 'subtle means' of their enemies and that he must 'be of power to kepe oureself oute of the daungier whereunto our enemies have not ceesed to studie, labour and compass to bring us'.[27] On 21 May, the king was at Watford, and York was just over 20 miles away at Ware. Between them lay the small Hertfordshire market town of St Albans. It must have seemed to Cecily and Richard that they were back to square one again. This time, it meant war.

9

Fortunes of War
1455–1459

Myssereule doth ryse ans maketh neyghbours werre[1]

Outside the little Hertfordshire town of St Albans, the opposing sides drew up their armies. Yet, even at this stage, not many of those involved really expected an actual fight. The king, flanked by the dukes of Somerset, Exeter and Buckingham and the earls of Northumberland and Devon, headed boldly into the marketplace and unfurled his banner. Just as at Blackheath three years earlier, a series of difficult negotiations began, with messengers running back and forth. The townsfolk looked on, alarmed, wondering what would happen next. They could not have predicted the course of that afternoon, which left them and much of the English nobility in a state of shock.

York's grievances followed familiar lines. He protested his loyalty to Henry while asking for the removal of his evil counsellor, asking for Somerset to be handed over. His intention may well have been to put the duke on official trial so that he could level formal charges of incompetence and corruption against him. He may have had in mind a similar process that Suffolk had undergone in 1450. In 1453 he had gone as far as to have Somerset committed to the Tower, but on that occasion it is possible that Somerset's life was saved because Henry recovered before York was able to move against him. The king and queen had been deeply upset by Suffolk's death and, mindful of this, Henry refused to comply. Instead, he appointed Buckingham as Constable of England, with control over the royal forces, such as they were in their state of half-readiness. This could have been a reconciliatory move, as Buckingham was married to Cecily's sister Anne and had little desire to see actual fighting take place or York and his party alienated further.

York had not forgotten that, back in 1452, circumstances at Dartford had forced him to swear an oath to not raise arms again in opposition to the king's supporters. To this end, he had received a papal dispensation to permit him to do so,[2] which indicates the extent of his dissatisfaction, the long-standing nature of the dispute and the extent of his piety. It also indicates his intentions. The past few years had proved so frustrating, with constant threats to his person and undermining of his position, that conflict seemed the only recourse. There seems no reason to doubt that his chief objective was the removal of Somerset. At around ten in the morning of 22 May 1455, when negotiations broke down, fighting began. The battle was bloody but brief. Somerset was backed into the prophetic Castle Inn, symbolic for the duke as it had reputedly been predicted that he would die in a castle. This may be romantic legend but, at any rate, he was killed fighting his way out of a building on the square. His death brought the battle to an end; it was the outcome York had probably hoped for. In one step, it removed the man who he believed to have been working against him and it would allow him to take a key role in government again. He submitted to the king and asked for his forgiveness.

News of the events would have been dispatched quickly. Cecily was probably miles away, at Fotheringhay or Ludlow, having retreated from London with York when the Leicester parliament was called. The days must have passed anxiously, as she supervised her household and the nursery containing her small children while heavily pregnant; no doubt she had confidence in her husband's abilities and his right to act, yet there was always a risk involved. A messenger would have reached her within the next day or so, at a distance of just over 60 miles to Fotheringhay. If she was at Ludlow, around 130 miles from the battle scene, she may not have heard the news until York had returned to London. The news had reached Lamberhithe in London by Whitsun, three days later, on Sunday 25 May. From there, John Crane wrote to John Paston with the news that Somerset was dead and York was victorious; 'as for any other Lordes, many of theym be hurt'.[3]

Cecily probably received a letter containing news of her husband's victory before this time or, at the very latest, on the same day. On Whit Sunday, Crane may well have witnessed York staging a crown-wearing ceremony at St Paul's Cathedral. From St Albans, the victorious party had headed for the capital, taking Henry with them – a matter in which the king probably had little choice. On 25 May, York placed the crown on Henry's head with his own hands. Finally, after years of being overlooked and generations of his family being bypassed, the duke's position was being acknowledged. As his duchess, Cecily would have been considered a queen-in-waiting. While the victory was a relief, as was the removal of the Yorks' implacable enemy Somerset, the way in which it had been achieved must have caused Cecily to fear for the future. Dependent still on the patronage and goodwill of the king and queen, they had taken a huge risk in jeopardising this connection. It is highly likely that, on receiving the news, Cecily dispatched her own letter to Margaret, attempting to use words to heal the wounds of the battlefield.

York soon acted to secure himself and his followers; with King Henry now virtually under house arrest, he took Somerset's old position as Constable of England, and Richard Neville, Earl of Warwick, became Captain of Calais. York's brother-in-law, Henry Bourchier, husband of his sister Isabel, was appointed as treasurer. The king was simply not able to provide the strong rule that the country needed; he is often described during this period as being unresponsive or bewildered; and many pockets of lawlessness had broken out.[4] To many, it seemed that York was the only magnate capable of restoring England to stability. In his chronicle, John Hardyng addressed the duke:

> O worthy Prince! O duke of York I meane
> Discendid downe of highest bloodde royall …
> By whiche knowledge your discrete sapience
> All vyce evermore destroye maye and reprove
> By virtuous and blessedfull diligence
> And vertue love, that maye not ought greve
> How ye shall rule your subjects, while ye lyve
> In lawe, and peace, and all tranquyllite
> Whiche been the floures of all regalyte.[5]

Feelings were clearly running high following the Battle of St Albans. A letter, written to William Worcester from William Barker in June 1455, recorded a planned attempt on the duke's life: 'It was said forsooth, that Harper and two other of the King's Chamber, were confederated to [have] sticked [stabbed] the Duke of York in the King's chamber, but it was not so, for they have cleared them thereof.'[6] That summer's parliament absolved York and his party from all guilt in the death of Somerset and the others who had died at St Albans. With his old adversary out of the way, York could now expect to take a central role in national politics again. He could anticipate playing the role that his descent and position as a leading magnate of the day should have facilitated since the mid-1440s.

Then, King Henry fell ill again. If he had not suffered a relapse in his mental health, at the very least he was incapable of performing key offices, and was in need of assistance. Rymer places this occurrence as early as mid-June, but the development did not become general knowledge until much later. It may have been that Henry experienced some lucid moments rather than the state of complete catatonia that he had experienced in 1453–54, which made diagnosis more difficult. In June, according to the Barker letter, York was staying at the Franciscan friary at Ware. Now a priory, it was founded in 1338, and part of it still stands in the Hertfordshire town of Ware, as a convenient stopping point on the road to London. Details such as the grotesques carved on corbels, doorways and roof trusses give an idea of the scale of the larger building that York knew. He may well have been lodging here as a traveller in June 1455, or else, in the weeks after St Albans, the pious duke was making his amends with God for the bloodshed. He might even have been at the friary when the news of the king's illness reached him. Doctors had attended him in June and July but the outbreaks of violence in London, Derbyshire and Devon showed that a strong leader was again required. That November, York was appointed Lord Protector for the second time.

For Cecily, at the age of forty, their ambitions were finally within reach. However, as was often the lot of women, victory on one level overshadowed a personal tragedy. In the summer of 1455, perhaps in July, she gave birth to her last child, a girl named Ursula. Little is known about the pregnancy or delivery, or even the location of Ursula's birth, which is assumed to have taken place at Fotheringhay, yet it is clear from the Clare Roll poem that she had died by spring 1460. No christening is recorded. It may have been another stillbirth or a loss to an early childhood illness. Writing to Margaret of Anjou back in 1453, Cecily had described the heaviness of pregnancy, and now, after possibly thirteen births over a period of sixteen years, she had seven surviving children. The recent decades had been marked for her by a string of births, which had not prevented her from travelling abroad but which must have led to significant periods of incapacity. Pregnancy customs required a woman to follow strict guidelines regarding diet, activity and superstition, as well as a month of lying in before the birth, and a similar period of recovery afterwards. As such, it was an experience that tended to unite women in spite of political differences, such as with Cecily and Margaret, connecting them through the experience on a religious, practical and emotional level.

Increasingly, though, the coming years would make this less possible for the wives of the king and his leading magnate.

This year also marked another personal transition for Cecily. With her experience, she may have been present in person to see the arrival of her first grandchild, Lady Anne Holland, daughter of Anne and the rebellious Earl of Exeter, then still incarcerated in Wallingford Castle. After Exeter fought on the side of the king at St Albans, their marriage now had little chance of success; the young pair would go through a formal separation in years to come. Anne would have had need of her mother's support on a number of levels and may well have called her to her bedside, as childbirth was most commonly supported by families of women of several generations. Yet, for all her ambitions and love for her children, Cecily would have still understood Margaret of Anjou's position; if she could not sympathise with her as a queen, perhaps she did as a mother.

Early in 1456, Queen Margaret left court with Prince Edward and established herself at Tutbury, which was more favourable to the Lancastrian cause than London. Here she set up a safe base for herself and her son, probably at the fourteenth-century Tutbury Castle, with five towers and walls 7 feet thick, or possibly at the nearby manor house, which was then owned by the Duke of Buckingham and his wife Anne, Cecily's sister. Although it was not a good omen for national unity, it removed her temporarily from York's way. His return to London on 9 February was recorded by John Bocking in a letter to Fastolf: 'This day my Lordes York and Warwick comen to the Parlement in a good array, to the number of 300 men [in armour] whereof many men mervailed.'[7] However, Henry VI was showing signs of being able to conduct some limited aspects of royal business and, as Bocking recounted, 'it was said on Saterday [7 February] my Lord shuld have ben discharged this same day'.[8] Henry's fluctuating mental health afforded him moments of clarity but denied him a consistent ability to steer the reins of government, even if he had been inclined, or able, to do so. The terms of York's November appointment specified that he could not be dismissed 'at the king's pleasure', as he had before, but only by the king himself, which gave him a little more security.

In Parliament, they spoke of 'a greet gleymyng sterre that but late hathe been seen diverse tymes, merveilous in apperyng'.[9] Such things were often considered as omens, either for good or bad. It did not bode well for York, whose position was called into question as the delicate balance of power between king and protector continued. He resigned his position on 25 February: 'in the king's presence the Duke of York resigned his office and withdrew from Parliament before the session ended'.[10] That May, York went to Sandal Castle and was still there in June, when Bocking wrote to John Paston that he 'waytith on the Quene and she up on him'.[11] It was an uneasy truce. The uncertainty of Henry's mental state coupled with the influence of the queen and her new favourite, Henry Beaufort, the new Duke of Somerset and son of York's old adversary, made for a volatile political situation. A further source of tension remained in the unpaid debts that Parliament still owed the duke, which were now of several years' standing. At the Yorkshire stronghold, Cecily and Richard must have reflected on their current position and the future of their children. As the summer days passed, within the thick walls of the castle, set high on the motte overlooking the River Calder, they were aware that their rightful power was close to hand but could easily be snatched away from their grasp. As a strong couple of royal descent, with a growing brood of children, they presented a very real alternative to the partnership of Henry VI and Margaret, possessing many of the qualities that would have made them more successful rulers of the country.

Later that June, an occasion arose that necessitated York taking the part of king. While he was at Sandal, James II, King of Scots, sent a letter to Henry VI, threatening to invade. It was York who made the formal response to try to bring them back in line, later chiding James for his border raids.[12] In August the court moved to Coventry and, once again, York feared that the queen and young Duke of Somerset would influence the king in his absence. They were to remain there for the next four years, making an alternative power base in the North, further dividing the country and its leaders. Additionally, a number of new appointments were made to the council, of men who were sympathetic to the Lancastrian cause. When York travelled there that autumn, the meeting was less than satisfactory. A letter from John Gresham to John Paston that October described how 'my Lord of York hath be with the Kyng, and is departed ageyn in right good conceyt with the Kyng but not in gret conceyt with the Queen and sum men sey ... my Lord of York had be distressed at his departyng'.[13]

In early September, *Benet's Chronicle* records that York was in London, staying at Salisbury House, the property of Richard Beauchamp, Bishop of Salisbury, in Fleet Street. While there, his enemies made a threatening display that left him in no doubt that, although Somerset was dead, the war was far from over. Impaled on the railings outside were the heads of five dogs, each with a verse of anti-York satire clamped between their jaws. Known as 'The Five Dogs of London', it is held in the collection of Trinity College Dublin and worth quoting fully:

Whan lordschyppe fayleth, gode felowschipe awayleth
My mayster ys cruell and can no curtesye
ffor whos offense here am y pyghte [put]
hyt ys no reson that y schulde dye
ffor his trespace and he go quyte.

Offte beryth the sone the faderis gilte
None so gylteless as y compleyne
ffor ones that y barked a-geynys the mone
With mighty force here was y sleyne
My tyme was come; my defenys ys done.

The tonge breketh bone, yet in him is none
ffor fawte of curasse [caress?] my throat was cutte
y cryed for helpe, y was not herde
y wolde my mayster hadde provide my butte
thys hadde y for hym to my rewarde

Off folowynge adventurous, the judgement is jeperdous
Wat planet compelled me, or what signe
To serve that man that all men hate?
Y wolde hys hede were here for myne
ffor he hath caused all the debate

Happy is the man whom perils provided
The blasynge starne with his late constellacioun
ys pleynly determined weyis batayle
To soche a remedye y holde yt geson
And yn rancur with-owte remedy ys none avayle

Maysterys, taketh for no grewe thewgh that we be dede
ffor they will walke by your fleke [flank/side] in despyte of your hede.[14]

The content and tone of this give the impression of disgruntled employees or former employees. In the last few years York seemed to attract those who wished to rebel under his name, only to find that he was still implacable in his adherence to the throne. Only that spring two of his men, Sir William Herbert and Sir Walter Devereux, had begun fresh trouble by seizing the mayor of Hereford and attacking local property, which developed into an attack on Kenilworth in June. Although he had planned to be, Henry was not actually in residence at the time, which scuppered the intention to capture and kill him. When they then attacked the Earl of Richmond in Carmarthen Castle, they overlooked the fact that the property was, technically, in York's hands. The grisly warning of the five dogs reminded York of the many enemies who still opposed his claim, and of the need to play by the rules and suppress lawbreaking, no matter who lay behind it. From London he went to Sandal, then back to the capital on 11 October, and five days later he obeyed the summons to attend Parliament at Coventry. The situation was becoming increasingly tense, with the queen's party dismissing those of York's supporters in key roles. In November, Warwick was ambushed by Exeter and the young Duke of Somerset. Holding the Yorkist lords responsible for his father's death at St Alban's, the twenty-year-old Henry Beaufort turned his attention to Richard in Coventry. According to *Bale's Chronicle*, he attacked York, who was only saved after the intervention of the city's mayor.[15]

Cecily was far removed from these political tensions. In autumn 1456, she stayed at Caister Castle in Norfolk, with Sir John Fastolf, in an environment as far removed from the dangers of Coventry as possible. Reputedly the inspiration for the character of Falstaff, Sir John had been a veteran of the Hundred Years' War by the time he served under Richard, Duke of York, in Normandy. He had retired in 1440 and his moated castle at Caister was considered a 'ryche juelle',[16] and one of the most desirable in the country. Although little of it survives now, following a siege in 1469, the castle Cecily stayed in was a beautiful and comfortable retreat, with a garden, swannery, fish ponds, chapel and mill approached across a causeway. Accounts from 1431–32 reveal that there was a permanent staff of twenty-four, with departments for the kitchen and cellar, buttery and pantry, and bakehouse. Extensive rebuilding was undertaken at that time, costing over £1,372 and continuing through the next decade, including five turrets along the moat side, a flat roof for viewing the countryside and a gallery of glazed windows opening onto an inner courtyard which featured a mechanical clock that struck the hours. There was also a stew, or bathhouse, and there may have been an early prototype of the stacked accommodation that soon became fashionable in royal residences.[17]

‚ The private rooms of Fastolf and his wife (who died long before Cecily's visit) were particularly impressive. They had three rooms each, with a bedchamber, withdrawing room and outer chamber, as well as latrines; a 1448 inventory listed that Lady Fastolf owned two little ewers of blue glass powdered with gold. The castle was unusual in having two halls, with the larger one measuring 28 feet wide. In the 1440s it was decorated with gilt copper wall plates and a cupboard with silver-gilt plate, arrows tipped with swan feathers and a multitude of cushions.[18] Many of the walls were white, and accounts show that the furniture was painted red, green and yellow. Impressive arras hangings woven with gold kept out the draughts and lay across Fastolf's bed. Cecily was probably housed in the South Tower, an independent range of buildings across the moat used for important visitors.[19] No wonder the duchess fell in love with the place. She was so enamoured of it in 1456 that she tried to persuade Sir John to sell it to her, as York had lands in the area but no manor house. He wrote on 15 November that 'my Lady of York has been here and sore moved me for the purchase'.[20] On his death three years later, Fastolf intended to establish a chantry college at his home, but legal wrangling over his will ensured this never happened. Cecily was among the last guests to appreciate the place. The beautiful Caister Castle was damaged by a siege in 1469.

An inventory of Fastolf's goods made at the time of his death paints a vivid picture of the kind of lifestyle to which the duke and duchess would have been accustomed. His collection included ewers of gold and flagons of silver, with silver chargers, plates, saucers and dishes. There was a great salt cellar shaped like a bastille, or small tower, in gilt, adorned with roses, silver pots enamelled with flowers and branches and flagons decorated with chains. He had a pair of gilt basins with a carved antelope in the middle and a spice plate, gilt with red roses and a small version of Fastolf's helmet set in the centre.[21]

Among Fastolf's extensive wardrobe there were gowns of cloth of gold, French russet lined with silk, blue and black satin and a red velvet jacket bound with red leather. He had scarlet hose, damask hoods of deep-green velvet, a hat of beaver fur lined with damask gilt and set with a girdle, buckle and pendant. He had detachable pockets embroidered with white roses and red crosses, jackets of deer leather and white linen petticoats stuffed with flocks; also among his effects were four cloaks of dark murrey (maroon), a 'coat of armour of white silk of St George' and a silver dagger.[22] To adorn his bed, he had a choice of pillows in white with blue fleurs-de-lys, red velvet, purple and gold silk and a little green silken one stuffed with lavender. His covers were in colourful silks, embroidered with gold leaves, lined with buckram and a feather bed of pearl silk.[23] His walls were draped with gold-woven tapestries, depicting bears holding spears, giants, savages holding children in their arms, women harping, archers, the Assumption of Our Lady, gentlemen holding hounds and hawks, all fringed with red, green or white silk. The list continues over many pages detailing the contents of every room, from the plain green work beds and bolsters in the 'chamber for strangeours', to the pipes of red wine in the cellar to the 'kervyng knyvys' in the buttery.[24]

Cecily also stayed at Fastolf's London home, Fastolf Palace or Place, in Southwark, near the Blur Boar Inn, which he also owned. He had built this in the 1440s, and excavations in the 1980s and 1990s suggest it was a moated manor house on the site of an old manor owned by the Dunley family and the house called the Rosary, built by Edward II.[25] Fastolf Place contained a counting house and had a 'round tabull'. It was surrounded by a large, buttressed brick wall with two gatehouses and two causeways, as well as a brewery with its own river access.[26] Cecily was definitely there in 1460, after Fastolf's death the previous November, probably as a result of her connections with his cousins, the Pastons. It seems likely that Cecily and her family had been guests there in the intervening years.

Cecily was also concerned with family matters while the political situation worsened. Sometime before February 1458, the Yorks' second daughter, Elizabeth, was married to John de la Pole, eldest son of the Duke of Suffolk. This was just before her fourteenth birthday, which fell at the end of April. The bridegroom had already been through one arranged match, at the age of seven, to the Lancastrian heiress Margaret Beaufort, but this was annulled in February 1453. The dukedom had been forfeited at the time of his father's disgrace but it was still a good marriage for Elizabeth, with the de la Poles based at Ewelme Manor in Oxfordshire and Wingfield Castle on the Suffolk/Norfolk border. The young bride had reached the age of consent so probably went to live with her husband soon after the ceremony.

By January 1458, there had been over two years of official peace, yet tension brimmed under the surface. Several attempts were made to ambush York and Warwick as they endeavoured to attend a council at Westminster, although Londoners themselves had proved to be welcoming to the pair. The opposing factions at court contrived to make a show of unity in a bizarre event that came to be known as the Loveday, held on 24 March. Forming a procession to St Paul's Cathedral, they walked through the streets of London hand in hand, with York leading Queen Margaret and Warwick, with Exeter and Salisbury with Somerset. 'At Poules in London, with gret renoun, on our ladi day in lente this peas was wrought; the king, the Queen with lords many oone, to worship that virgine as they ought … in token that love was in heart and thought,' as one surviving poem claimed. Another pro-Lancastrian verse written the same year depicted the tempestuous political situation through the metaphor of a ship tossed on the waves, while a reconciliation poem recorded in the Cotton MS Vespasian B xvi describes York, Somerset and Warwick as being full of 'love and charity'. Much of the orchestration of this theatrical feat was achieved by the new Archbishop of Canterbury, Thomas Bourchier, York's kinsman, whom he had appointed as chancellor during the first protectorate.

It is tempting to read Cecily's influence in this event; perhaps through her friendship with Margaret she was writing letters to try to reconcile her husband with the queen, as she had in 1453. While she had no real political influence, her role as a duchess, and the connection she had forged with the young girl in Rouen, would have placed her well to have some sway over the personal aspect of their relationship. York lodged at his new London property, Baynard's Castle, with a retinue of 140 men, so it is fairly likely that Cecily went too and visited the queen, who was staying at the Bishop of London's palace. There, Cecily may have renewed her supplications to Margaret of Anjou and given thanks when they appeared to have borne fruit. She would have attended the Mass of celebration at St Paul's and the jousting at the Tower in the queen's presence.

Although those involved were all smiles in March, the peace was brief, and tension had broken out again by the autumn. The real question had remained unaddressed: that of who was to rule the country, Margaret or York. Further attacks were made on the Yorkists, including an attempt on Warwick's life, after which he fled to Calais. The queen issued a warrant for his arrest, and, early in the new year, began to prepare for further confrontation by ordering the collection of weapons in the Tower of London, with sheaves of arrows and bows.[27] An anonymous poem, 'Take Good Heed', warned York and his party to be careful, using their heraldic symbols as a code:

But pray we al to god that died on a spere
To save the rose [York], the lion [Norfolk], the eagle [Salisbury] and the bear [Warwick].[28]

This warning was very apt. Through 1459, hostility was mounting and, when a meeting of the Great Council was called at Coventry at the end of June, York was convinced that the queen was planning to pass an Act of Attainder against him and his allies. This would remove their rights to hold titles and property, which they would not be able to pass on to their heirs either. The Yorkists decided their best chance was to make a personal appeal to Henry but he was at Kenilworth Castle and they were scattered over the country, with York at Ludlow, Salisbury at Middleham in Yorkshire and Warwick still in Calais. Witnessing her family poised on the brink of conflict again, Cecily would now have far more to worry about than her husband. At the ages of sixteen and seventeen, her two eldest sons were of an age to participate actively in politics, even to fight in battle. Yet she knew the significance of an attainder for her sons. She may have tried to intercede on their behalf by sending letters to Queen Margaret, but it is more likely that, by this point, she recognised that those weak ties had been broken. With her younger children – Margaret, aged fifteen, George, aged ten, and Richard, seven – she watched the men ride off to try to save the situation.

Marching down from Middleham Castle with a force of around 5,000 men, Salisbury intended to meet up with York's forces. By 23 September, he had covered most of the distance to Ludlow when he was ambushed by the queen's forces, led by Lord Audley, at Blore Heath in Staffordshire. Separated from the much larger enemy army by a brook, Salisbury pretended to withdraw. This provoked a Lancastrian charge and Salisbury was able to launch an attack while they were crossing. Several hours of close fighting followed, in which Audley was killed and the Lancastrians turned on themselves in confusion. Salisbury finally won the day, although two of his sons were captured and imprisoned in Chester Castle. Next, he headed straight for Ludlow, anticipating further conflict.

A fortnight later, the decisive clash occurred. York, Warwick and Salisbury were denounced as traitors, although the Parliamentary Rolls record that Henry offered pardons to the first two, if they were to submit to him within six days. York wrote to Henry twice, restating his loyalty and offering complete submission if he could be guaranteed safe passage to the king's person; however, according to *Whethamsted's Chronicle*, he refused the pardon as meaningless and degrading given that the king's relatives acted as they pleased. The trio then signed an indenture and swore an oath in Worcester Cathedral that they were the true liegemen of the king and taking up arms only against his councillors. Although it is possible to read other motives into these actions, they do have the appearance of earnestness and represent the real divide they experienced in attempting to serve their king while recognising that the queen was now their enemy. Significantly, on 9 October, Warwick's position as Captain of Calais was given to the young Henry, Duke of Somerset. It was the king's armies who advanced on York's position on 12 October. This was dangerously close to home, at Ludford Bridge, over the River Nene on the edge of Ludlow. The castle containing his wife and younger children was only a few minutes' walk away. Perhaps it was this that caused York to panic and possibly led to him making a mistake.

A rumour circulated among York's troops that the king was dead. *Stowe's Chronicle* states that York brought forth witnesses to swear to this effect and Masses were said for his soul.[29] This may well have originated with the duke himself, aware that his men were reluctant to fight against an army which was flying the royal standard. Did York actually believe it, or was it a ploy to dispel his men's fears of being charged with treason? The misunderstanding, or deception, was swiftly unravelled. That very evening, Henry was visible among his troops, with the royal standard still flying above him, which had a devastating effect on morale. Under cover of night, a number of Warwick's forces defected, including those under Andrew, Lord Trollope, who had travelled with him from Calais. It seemed pointless to embark upon a fight under such conditions, when defeat, death and the attainder of titles and properties, preventing the inheritance of heirs, seemed inevitable. Self-preservation must have underpinned their decision to abandon the field. Leaving their banners where they lay,[30] York, his elder sons, Warwick and Salisbury withdrew into the darkness. York fled to Ireland with the sixteen-year-old Edmund. His elder brother Edward headed for Calais with his Warwick uncle and cousin.

The next day, King Henry's army realised their opposition had fled and rampaged through the streets of Ludlow. Despite romantic legends to the contrary, which depict a heroic Cecily standing at the Market Cross to meet her enemies, only two contemporary sources place her in Ludlow. *Hearne's Fragment*, a chronicle written by a servant of Edward IV, recorded that the troops 'burnt and pillaged the [town]; and the Duchess of York, residing there, had her wardrobe rifled and her furniture spoiled'.[31] Whethamsted states that 'the toune of Ludlow longyng thane to the duk of York, was robbed to the bare walles and the noble duches of York unmanly and cruelly was entreted and spoyled'.[32] Sheltering with her three young children, it must have been a terrifying experience, if it happened. Codes of chivalric conduct were designed to protect women from physical harm. However, the recent wars had seen an escalation in violence and many of those old chivalric boundaries had been breached. The looters would have been common soldiers and while, theoretically, still bound to respect their social superiors, the unpredictable mentality of a mob, coupled with the absence of the duke, would have made the duchess an easy target. Even so, the suggestion that she was spoiled, or despoiled in a physical sense, being subject to a violence or rape, seems unlikely. Nor is there any evidence to support the romantic theory that she stood in the Market Cross to meet her enemies. Once the moment had passed, the duchess would certainly have been vocal as she sought reprisal and her subsequent treatment by the king suggests he would have been more than prepared to punish the culprits. Even when warring among themselves, the aristocracy represented a narrow clique of interconnected families. Cecily, York and Henry VI shared common ancestors; she was of royal blood and such a slur against her would have constituted a crime against them all.

When it was safe, Cecily went to the parliament at Coventry and deferred to the king. This is agreed by most sources, including Fabyan and the *English Chronicle*, and there is a very real possibility that she was not at Ludlow at all, given its proximity to the fighting, but that reports of rampaging troops despoiling her property were exaggerated. Her submission may have been in response to Henry's offer on 30 November to pardon all those who submitted within eight days. It was the wisest thing to do under the circumstances and reinforced York's previous stance of loyalty. A witness there, John Bocking, wrote to John Paston on 7 December that 'the Duchesse of York come yester-even late, as the bringer hereof shall more plainly declare yow'. It can only be imagined how the bearer of the letter described Cecily's plight. Fortunately, she was shown mercy. On 20 December, she received an annual grant of 1,000 marks 'for the relief of her and her infants who had not offended against the king',[33] although all York's other lands and estates reverted to ownership of the crown. The Fotheringhay account rolls for 1459 would remain blank. At Coventry, Cecily may also have interceded for many of the duke's followers, thus lessening the penalties they suffered.[34] However, it was deemed likely that she would attempt to contact York, so she was sent to the custody of her sister Anne, Duchess of Buckingham, at Tonbridge Castle in Kent. Had she attempted to flee the country and join York in Ireland, her fate would have been considerably worse. Her sister-in-law, Alice, Countess of Salisbury, fled with her husband to Calais and was subsequently included in the Act of Attainder that was passed against the rebels that autumn.

What were Cecily's feelings towards York while she stood her ground and protected her children at Ludlow? She probably had imperfect news of his flight at that moment; while the castle was being sacked, he was probably still heading for the coast. The retreat has the appearance of a last-minute decision but, if there was time for him to get a message of warning to her, she was unable, or unwilling, to flee. Perhaps neither she nor York predicted the rampage of the Lancastrian troops, even given the proximity of the castle. Perhaps it was a strategy the pair discussed before the duke departed for battle. There may have been moments when she felt alone, abandoned even, but her actions in October 1459 show courage and determination.

10

Fickle Fortune
1459–1460

Her tears will pierce into a marble heart;
The tiger will be mild, whiles she does mourn[1]

Tonbridge Castle, in West Kent, is a Norman motte-and-bailey construction, of which little now remains. In the mid-fifteenth century, it was in the hands of Humphrey Stafford, Duke of Buckingham, who was a loyal Lancastrian. Even though he had fought against York at St Albans, he had been reluctant to do so, with marital ties placing him in a difficult position; his wife, Anne, was Cecily's closest sibling in age, but their eldest son, Humphrey, was married to Somerset's daughter Margaret. The castle was considered strong and secure, with its great towers connected by massive curtain walls, its solid keep and double gatehouse. Even when it had fallen into disrepair in the 1520s, Henry VIII was able to describe it as 'the strongest forteres and moste like unto a castell of any other that the Duke had in England or Wales'.[2] In 1451, it had been the location for the court that had been held in judgement upon Richard Lennard, who confessed to being one of those who had killed the Duke of Suffolk.[3] It was there that Cecily and her three children found refuge at the end of 1459, until such time as their luck changed again. In the new year, word arrived that York and Edmund had reached Dublin, and that Edward was safe in Calais. It was then a matter of waiting for them to make their next move.

There has been some suggestion that Cecily and her children were kept at Maxstoke Castle in Warwickshire, also in the possession of the Stafford family. This may have been the case briefly, but a detail in the Paston Letters makes it seem more likely that she was at Tonbridge. Initially, she was kept closely guarded – 'fulle strayte and many a grete rebuke'[4] – but very early in 1460, a letter from William Botoner to John Berney records that 'my Lady Duchesse ys stille ayen receved' in Kent, which suggests she had been given permission to make visits in the vicinity of the castle. As she remained in her sister's custody until June, this would have been impossible were she based in Warwickshire. Having been the hostess in Rouen, where she dressed in jewels to welcome the young Margaret of Anjou, Cecily now found herself suffering the slings and arrows of fortune, dispossessed of her home, estates and titles. Most of her sister Anne's children had been born in the 1430s and 1440s, so there was no nursery or schoolroom for Cecily's children to join. A new tutor may have been hired to continue to teach George, then ten, and Richard, aged seven, while Cecily herself may have taken responsibility for her thirteen-year-old daughter Margaret. There was precious little else for her to do, deprived as she was of all her previous duties.

Luckily, York had found refuge in Ireland, where his first brief stint as lieutenant was still fresh in the memory of the people. Technically, he still held the role, as his term had been extended in December 1457. Following his attainder, James Butler, the Lancastrian Earl of Wiltshire and son-in-law to the dead Duke of Somerset, was appointed in his place, but never took up the position. York's lands were parcelled out soon after Ludford Bridge, with Northumberland, his chief enemy in the Percy family, receiving a grant for life of Scarborough Castle and a number of other properties for 'attendance about the King's person against Richard, Duke of York, and other rebels'.[5] John Middleton was rewarded in January 1460 for good service against the rebels, with the lordship of Multon and the 'keeping of the conies', or rabbits, there.[6] William Browning was granted all his possessions in Dorset and Somerset 'forefeit by his high treason'[7] and John, Earl of Shrewsbury, was granted the lordship of Ludlow.[8] His allies were also punished. The lordship of Cranborn, belonging to John Ausytn, 'servant of Richard, Duke of York ... with the Duke in the field against the King', was awarded to a loyal Lancastrian.[9] The Lancastrians also attempted to get their hands on York himself, with several demands being made for the Irish to relinquish the exiles. They refused to comply. Richard also had his sixteen-year-old son Edmund and a little band of loyal supporters with him, of whom twenty-one can be identified with certainty, many from the Neville estates. He remained fairly settled in Ireland until the summer, apparently without making any plans to return to England; according to Whethamsted he had been 'hailed there as a messiah'. In Calais, though, his eldest son Edward and cousin Warwick were planning an invasion.

At Tonbridge, news would have reached Cecily in the new year of the activities of her nephew and her son. Perhaps she smiled to herself as she learned that they had raided the Kent port of Sandwich in January, where the young Earl of Somerset was constructing a fleet to invade Calais. He had been made the new constable but, loyal to Warwick, the town had refused to admit him. This was the infamous occasion when Sir John Dynham surprised Lord Rivers, Jacquetta and their son Anthony asleep in their beds in Sandwich and carried them to Calais with the fleet, where they were berated by Warwick and Edward for their disloyalty and presumption. Events had placed Cecily's son and his allies on the opposing side of their old friends from Rouen. Rivers and his wife had known Edward as an infant in Normandy; it must have grated on them to be accused of being social climbers. John Paston relates how the youth derided Rivers as a knave's son, which appears such a great irony in hindsight, given that Edward would soon become his son-in-law. Perhaps it was the old connection that spared them the fate of the Captain of Sandwich, who was beheaded; Jacquetta was sent home but the two men remained prisoners for another six months.

Again in March, Cecily would have heard that, just as Somerset had repaired the damage from the raid, Edward and Warwick had struck again and destroyed the fleet as it sat waiting to sail. That March, a general pardon was issued by Parliament 'to any captains, patrons, merchants, pilots, galleymen, sailors and mariners of any carracks [sailing boats] and galleys arrested to serve on the sea against Richard, Earl of Warwick and his accomplices'.[10] Parliament also offered payment of all loans and moneys owing to it that month, using the estates of the rebels in order to preserve their own funds and to better defeat them and 'the king's adversary in France'.[11] That April, a commission was given to Robert Basele, Mayor of Winchelsea, to resist York, Warwick and Salisbury, whom, it was rumoured, planned to enter the town. Basele was ordered to 'arrest and commit to prison or expel all suspected persons'. The same was extended to the Mayor of Southampton and those in other prominent ports. Men were put on watch around the coastline of Dorset, Devon and Cornwall.[12] The Buckinghams were still very much in royal favour that summer, with Anne receiving the 'wardship of all the possessions' of Sir Robert Grey, until his son Humphrey came of age, as well as the right to arrange the boy's marriage. Humphrey was then twelve and may have come to live at Tonbridge Castle; he would not be married until

1470.[13] Along with other leading Lancastrians, including Cecily's half-brother Ralph Neville and her son-in-law Exeter, Buckingham was given a commission to call together all men 'able to labour ... as soon as they hear that Richard, Duke of York, Edward, Earl of March', and the others, were ready to 'enter the realm or cause to be made any congregations, combinations or unlawful gatherings'.[14]

On 26 June, Edward, Salisbury and Warwick landed at Sandwich. Relying on Kent's reputation for rebellion, as well as the relationship Warwick had established with the sailors since his days as captain, they marched to Canterbury, where welcoming verses were pinned to the city gates:

> Send hom most gracious Jhesu, most benygne
> Send home thy trewe blode unto his proper veyne
> Richard, Duk of York, Job thy servant insygne ...
> he may nat be slayne ...
> Edwards, Erle of Marche, whos fame the erthe shall spread
> Richard, Erle of Salisbury, named prudence
> wythe that noble knyghte and floure of manhode
> Richard Earl of Warwick, sheelde of our defence.[15]

It seems almost inconceivable that, as the rebels passed through Kent on their way to the capital, Edward would not try to contact his mother at Tonbridge, if he knew that she was there. It would also follow that, if he saw her in person, or visited her at the Buckingham's home, he may attempt to bring about her release. However, *Gregory's Chronicle* states that Cecily remained put 'tylle the field was done at Northampton', so it would seem that Edward may have sent words of encouragement to her but marched on in order to meet his opponents. By the time he and Warwick had reached London, on 2 July, they had raised an army of 10,000 men. A list of points, preserved in Harleian Manuscript 543, outlined the reasons why Kent was so keen to support the rebels' attempt to remove Henry from his evil council. Their first statement asserted that 'the king, by the insatiable covetousness, malicious purpose and false-brought-of-nought persons, daily and nightly about his Highness, is daily informed that good is evil and evil is good'. Their eighth point related specifically to the spread of slanders regarding the Duke of York, making the king 'hate and destroy his friends'.[16]

The Yorkist army clashed with the Lancastrians in the grounds of Delapré Abbey, at Northampton, on 26 June. It was an encounter that would turn the tables for Cecily and her sister. Her nephew Warwick and eighteen-year-old son Edward, now almost 6 feet 4 inches tall, were drawn up in opposition to her sister Anne's husband, Humphrey Stafford, Duke of Buckingham. The weather was terrible, with the ground sodden from days of rain, rendering the gunpowder in the Lancastrian cannons worthless. Midway through, the defection of Lord Grey of Ruthin turned the tables and the battle was won in little under an hour. About 400 men lay dead. The poem 'The Battle of Northampton', preserved in Trinity College Dublin, uses heraldic devices and the extended metaphor of hunting to describe the action and its outcome. Warwick (the bear) and Edward (the bearward) kill the buck (Buckingham) and others (the dogs).

> The bereward asked no question why,
> But on the dogges he set full rounde ...
> The game was done in a litel stounde
> The buk was slayne and borne away.[17]

The same poem urged York to return from Ireland and protested his loyalty and innocence of all charges against him,

> ... whom treson ne falshod meuer dyd shame
> But euer obedient to his sovereign.[18]

Both women must have spent an anxious few days at Tonbridge, watching the road for signs of messengers. When they finally arrived, weary from the long ride south, they brought the news that both women dreaded and longed for at the same time. For Cecily it was a resounding victory, but for her sister Anne it was the terrible confirmation that her husband had been killed in battle. King Henry had been captured in his tent, at prayer on bended knee. The victors were marching him to London to establish a government in his name, while Queen Margaret and her son had fled to the protection of Jasper Tudor at Harlech Castle, after being robbed along the way. The Great Seal, the symbol of power, had been entrusted to the hands of Cecily's nephew, George Neville.

Once again Cecily's personal and political life came into sharp contrast. While sympathising with her sister, her thoughts were turning to the future. Shortly after the battle was won, she would have heard news of the murder of an old friend, Thomas, Lord Scales. Scales had fought in Normandy under the Duke of Bedford and Fastolf; in 1442, at Rouen, he had been made Edward's godfather. However, he had supported the Lancastrians against Cecily's brother, the Earl of Salisbury. As Constable of the Tower, he had turned its guns on the city with disastrous results. In addition to the cannon, he was indiscriminate in the use of 'wildfire', a weapon developed to repel enemy ships, which burned when doused with water, and killed innocent bystanders in the streets. According to Wyrcester, he was dispatched while trying to escape from the Tower, possibly by seamen carrying him across the Thames to sanctuary, and his naked body was dumped in the cemetery of St Mary Overy in Southwark. The tide of support in London turned very decisively in favour of Edward and Warwick as a result of this, although they did give Scales a dignified funeral.

Soon, Cecily left Tonbridge with her children and headed for London. Edward may even have ridden down himself to inform them of his victory and liberate them. The nineteenth-century biographer Caroline Halsted suggests that Anne allowed Cecily to escape and that she travelled to London in secrecy, avoiding her own property of Baynard's Castle and staying instead at John Paston's law chambers at Temple Inn, before moving to Fastolf's Southwark mansion.[19] On 15 September, a delegation, including the harbinger of the Earl of March, had approached Paston's servant Christopher Hausson 'desyryng that my Lady of York might lye here untylle the coming of my Lord of York and hir tw sonnys, my Lorde George and my lorde Richard and my Lady Margarete hir dawztry, which I granted them … to lie here till Michaelmas [29 September]'.[20] By this time, Cecily had received news that York had landed at Chester. Whethamsted claimed he had been summoned by an encouraging letter from the king. Shortly afterwards, he sent for her to come and meet him at Hereford, so they could make a triumphant entry into the capital together; possibly as early as 23 September.[21] She departed London in a chair of blue velvet, pulled by four pairs of horses.[22] According to Hausson's letter, which is dated 12 October, the three children were left behind at Fastolf's but were visited daily by Edward, Earl of March, who remained in the city.

The cathedral city of Hereford lies around 130 miles to the west of London. There are a number of possible places where the long-anticipated reunion between York and Cecily could have occurred. Firstly, there was the impressive Hereford Castle, long since vanished. Built before the Norman Conquest, it was described by Leland as nearly as large as Windsor Castle and 'the fairest and strongest in all England'. During the thirteenth century, an inventory listed the place as including great and small halls, royal apartments for the king and queen, a counting house and exchequer, stables, kitchen, bakery and two gaols.[23] However, Leland also states that it was decaying from around the time of Edward III. York had owned a number of properties in the area at which he may have awaited Cecily's arrival, not least the solid Wigmore Castle, which Edward would use as a base the following spring. Before the attainder, he had also held the manor of Marden, or Mawardine, a Mortimer inheritance, 7 miles to the north of the city. If Cecily arrived before Richard, she may have prayed for his safe arrival in the church of St Mary the Virgin and taken the waters from the holy well there, traditionally supposed to have sprung from the place where St Ethelbert was first buried. York paused briefly at Ludlow, perhaps to survey the damage and learn the whereabouts of his family and possessions. Halsted places his reunion with his wife there, based on the evidence of Wyrcester. York was received there by an assembly of local gentry, who encouraged him to assume the throne; if the idea had not already occurred to him, this seemed to confirm his next move. He went on to Shrewsbury and remained there for four days with Warwick before travelling to Hereford.

The details of this reunion suggest the Yorks were close; surely before their departure, or during the long ride back to London, Richard would have confided his intentions to Cecily. As an attainted traitor, he had been forced into a corner. The king's forces had been soundly defeated and Henry was little more than an ineffectual puppet in the Yorkists' hands. It was time for Richard to claim the throne of England. Did Cecily approve of her husband's scheme? Did she listen intently and advise him to act at once, or did she counsel caution, aware that such a decisive act would prove disastrous should it fail? Perhaps she had such confidence in York's abilities and such conviction in the right of his claim that the possibility of failure did not appear realistic. After all, it had been his choice to leave Ludlow; it had been a desertion rather than a defeat. No doubt the couple discussed the sack of their home and the aftermath.

Sadly, it is impossible to know now what Cecily's attitude was towards York's plans. Her prompt obedience to his summons suggests support, and her long-standing belief in their joint royal lineage was perfectly consistent with his intentions. She may have welcomed the idea of him replacing Henry VI as King. Equally, she may have questioned it, or doubted it, as her eldest son would do. There was a general feeling of discontent brewing against Henry VI, whose illness and ineffectualness was being seen as leading the country into ruin, which was summarised well by the tenth statement of the men of Kent:

That our Sovereign Lord may understand that he hath had false council; for his law is lost, his merchandise is lost, his commerce hath been destroyed, the sea is lost, France is lost, himself is made so poor that he may not pay for his meat nor drink; he oweth more and is greater in debt than ever was King in England.[24]

Cecily and York were at Gloucester on 2 October, the day of their son Richard's eighth birthday, before moving to Abingdon in Oxfordshire. The Paston Letters also place them at Leicester, Coventry 'and other divers towns', where York presided over the local courts 'to punch them by fawtes to the Kyngs lawys'.[25] The attainder that had been passed at Coventry the previous autumn was successfully revoked. On 10 October, Cecily and York rode into London and headed to Baynard's Castle, where the family were reunited.[26] Other sources have him travelling straight to Westminster from Barnet, marching into the royal palace and taking possession.[27] If this was the case, Cecily may well have been with him and witnessed what followed.

What followed was a terrible political miscalculation. York rode with a troop of 500 men to Westminster with his trumpets sounding and his sword carried before him. It was the third day that Parliament had been sitting; they were expecting him, as Warwick had announced his approach. He entered the king's chamber and put Henry under his own guard. Approaching the throne, he laid his hand upon it and boldly declared his right to claim it. He waited for applause but was met by an awkward silence. The Earl of Worcester's secretary wrote to him in Venice, describing the scene, assigning York 800 horsemen, 'with his swerde born uppe right by for him thorowe the halle and parliament chamber. And there under the cloth of estate stondyng he gave them knowliche that he purposed nat to ley doaune his swerde but the challenge his right and so toke his loggyng in the qwenys chamber.'[28]

Ireland's 'messiah' had misjudged the political mood in London. His brother-in-law, Archbishop Thomas Bourchier, refused to sanction the deposition of Henry. It fell to Warwick to take him aside and attempt to negotiate a compromise, with the blunt news that 'the lords and the people were ill-content against him because he thus wished to strip the king of his crown'.[29] According to William Wyrcester, 'few of the Lords countenanced him' and 'every state and grade, whatever age or sex, order or condition, began to whisper against him'.[30] Unsure of what to do next, he wisely accepted a suggestion to withdraw and speak with the king. Henry's response was, for once, decisive. Stating his descent from Henry

V, he reminded them 'my father was king, his father was king; I have worn the crown forty years from my cradle, you have all sworn fealty to me as your sovereign and your fathers have done the same to my fathers. How can my right then be disputed?'[31] Yet somehow, in spite of the embarrassment of his coup not being supported, the situation began to turn around. In the ensuing parliamentary debate, begun on 16 October, York's claim was objected to on the grounds that he was descended from 'females' and that he did not bear the arms of Lionel, Duke of Clarence, Edward III's third son, but those of Edmund of Langley, his fifth son. However, things were gradually going York's way and on the night of 31 October, *Gregory's Chronicle* relates that King Henry was removed from court, against his will, to the house of the Bishop of London. York visited him there and one historian speculates that he may have attempted to persuade him to abdicate.[32]

On 9 November, the Act of Accord offered York the concession of being Henry's heir, displacing the seven-year-old Edward, Prince of Wales. He was named as Lord Protector during the king's lifetime, Prince of Wales, Duke of Cornwall and Earl of Chester and awarded an annual income of £10,000; it was also considered treason to imagine or 'encompass' York's death. It was a situation Margaret of Anjou would never accept. The Milanese ambassador even suggested that the queen had given Henry VI poison and planned to 'unite with the Duke of Somerset', Henry Beaufort, adding the tart little comment that 'at least he knew how to die, if he did not know what to do else'. Cecily now found her old friend pitted against her husband. It was a fight for the rights of their children. She declined to return to London and place her son in the care of her enemies, taking him north instead. Even York's own supporters believed he had gone too far according to William Wyrcester.

Early that December, 'the right high and myghty Prynce Richard Plantagenet Duke of York' swore that

> I, Richard, Duc of York, promise and swear by the faith and truth that I owe to almighty God, that I shall never doo, consent, procure or stir … anything that may be to the abriggement of the natural lyfe of Kyng Henry the Sixth or to the hurt of his reign or dignity royal.[33]

His two eldest sons, Edward and Edmund, now next in line to the throne after their father, swore a similar oath. For Cecily, this act was the final vindication she and her husband had longed for and seemed to guarantee that the inheritance would pass intact to her children. It was a dramatic improvement on the situation she had found herself in exactly twelve months before – alone, disinherited and stripped of all her titles and lands. All that stood between her and the throne was the life of the fragile Henry, now aged thirty-nine, patently unstable and within her husband's control. There must have been celebrations at Baynard's Castle that month.

Parliament passed the necessary legislation that

> it is appointed that the said Richard Duke of York ... be entitled, called and reputed from henceforth very and rightful heir to the Corones, Royal Estate, Dignity and Lordship aforesaid and after the decease of the said King Henry ... the said Duke and his heirs, shall immediately succeed to the said Corones, Royal Estate, Dignity and Lordship.[34]

Yet, just at the pinnacle of her success, Cecily must have known that there were some who would never accept her husband and sons as kings. In November 1460, the Lancastrian Earl of Northumberland, Lords Clifford, Dacre and Neville met in the city of York and 'destroyed' the tenants of York and Salisbury.[35] The queen summoned all those loyal to the crown to join her in Hull, whereupon 15,000 Northerners rallied to her side, making a huge, ominous force that could only portend a coming battle. In December she travelled to Scotland to ask for assistance, knowing that she would receive a welcome from the new king, James III, who had already denounced York for supposedly sending him letters inciting rebellion against Henry.[36]

The early days of December were spent planning the Yorkist attack, with York, Edward, Edmund, Warwick, Salisbury and their allies meeting at Baynard's Castle. Cecily may have been involved as an active participant in the discussions, or at least may have overheard the men's business as her husband, sons and brother sat up late into the night debating what the queen's next move might be and how they could best meet the challenge she posed. In the end, it was decided that Warwick would remain in London to guard the king and Edward would head into Wales to drum up more support and prevent the queen's armies joining with those of Jasper Tudor. The plan was to meet at Wakefield, once a sufficient army had been raised, and face the queen's forces together. Then the time came to say goodbye. Cecily watched as her husband and son Edmund climbed into the saddle and rode out of the gates of Baynard's Castle. She would never see them again.

On 9 December, York left London with Edmund, Salisbury and a few hundred men. They headed north, gathering troops as they went, although a minor skirmish with Somerset's men at Worksop depleted their forces. According to Whethamsted, 'they gathered a great force of people as they went, by authority of a royal commission, as a protection for their own persons, to put down and repress the multitude of their adversaries', but assistance from Edward's Welsh army was still required. On 21 December, York reached Sandal Castle, set high on a ridge overlooking the River Calder, 2 miles from the town of Wakefield. Recent studies and excavations have established that it was surrounded by cultivated fields and a paled deer park, with good views for miles around.[37] The Lancastrian army was not too far off, based in and around Pontefract, 10 miles to the east.

At Baynard's Castle, Cecily spent Christmas with her younger children, Margaret, George and Richard. Her sister-in-law, Alice, Countess of Salisbury, may have kept her company, having recently returned from exile with the rest of her son Warwick's family – his wife and two small daughters, Isabel and Anne, who were Cecily's great-nieces. Perhaps Cecily was also joined by her eldest daughter, Anne, seeking respite from her difficult marriage to the Duke of Exeter along with Cecily's five-year-old granddaughter? They may have waited together at Coldharbour House, but it is more likely to have been Baynard's Castle, which was considered impregnable. The family party may even have included the newly married Elizabeth and her husband John, Duke of Suffolk, who were gathered in the capital to celebrate York's recent success. For Cecily, there would have been some entertainment – feasting, singing, disguisings, tumblers, players and the reading of romances – but there would have been much prayer and religious devotion. The day of 28 December was traditionally held as Holy Innocents' Day and spent in fasting and penance.

They passed Christmas safely inside Sandal Castle too, in planning and prayer, anticipating the coming battle. Keith Dockray suggests that a brief peace may have been negotiated for the season, which usually extended for the twelve days through to Twelfth Night, on 6 January. This would go some way to explaining why the Yorkist lords took the decision to emerge from the solid walls of Sandal on 30 December and render themselves vulnerable, a theory found in several chronicles of the time and the report of a Milanese visitor to London soon afterwards. After almost ten days inside engaging in the seasonal festivities, they must have been running low on supplies. A letter written on 9 January by Antonio de la Torre to Francesco Sforza, Duke of Milan, includes the foraging story:

> Although they were three times stronger [più forti tretanti], yet from lack of discipline, because they allowed a large part of the force to go pillaging and searching for victuals, their adversaries, who are desperate, attacked the duke and his followers. Ultimately they routed them, slaying the duke and his younger son, the Earl of Rutland, Warwick's father and many others.[38]

The fact that the battle was fought, unusually, in the afternoon, suggests it was a surprise attack, unplanned and opportunistic. The *Short English Chronicle* describes it as an ambush, while the *English Chronicle* and Jean de Waurin believed that York was lured out by Somerset's men wearing the livery of Warwick's bear and ragged staff. The usual suspects include Anthony Trollope (who deserted at Ludford Bridge), but this theory originated only in Waurin, who does make other errors, and it is not corroborated elsewhere. The *Davies Chronicle* places the blame on Cecily's uncle, George Neville. The timing also suggests that the attack may well have been a planned assassination of York. The Milanese ambassador wrote that 'the Duke of York seems rather to have been slain out of hatred for having claimed the kingdom than anything else'. Coming so soon after the Act of Accord, which confirmed his position as Henry's heir to the exclusion of Prince Edward, this disregard of the usual codes of battle, coupled with the many ambush attempts the Yorkists had survived in recent years, presents a convincing case for the deliberate targeting of York.

It might seem a rash act to venture out from the safety of Sandal Castle. Sir Davy Hall, an ancestor of Tudor writer Edward Hall, was present with York in 1460 and advised York to remain put until Edward arrived with reinforcements from Wales, but the Duke 'would not be counselled' and went into a 'great fury,' saying 'their great number shall not appal my spirits but encourage them'.[39] It appears, from several sources, that York went out to support a foraging party which had come under attack. Whethamsted wrote that the Lancastrians attacked on the day before the Christmas truce was due to expire. York was cut down in the midst of the fighting. Although *Whethamsted's Register* states explicitly that York was taken alive, his is the only source to state this; most others place his death on the field of battle. Salisbury was captured and beheaded at Pontefract the following day, while his seventeen-year-old son Thomas

Neville also died, along with Salisbury's eighteen-year-old son-in-law William, Lord Harrington, who left behind a newborn daughter named Cecily. That left Edmund, Duke of Rutland, Cecily's own seventeen-year-old son, described by *Gregory's Chronicle* as 'one of the best-disposed Lords of the land'.

Initially, York may have believed he had saved his son's life. Edward Hall suggested that Richard had put Edmund in the care of his tutor, Sir Robert Aspall, who hurried him away from the scene but not before Lord Clifford had spotted them and given chase. Hall does get Edmund's age incorrect, stating that he was only twelve at the time, but local legend supports the location of his death, so it may well have happened in this way. The *Annales* relates that Edmund was killed by Lord Clifford on the bridge at Wakefield, perhaps in revenge for the death of his own father at St Albans. This was a long, nine-arched bridge, already a century old, a mile away from the battle site. If this report is true, Edmund may have been attempting to reach the sanctuary of the Chantry Chapel of St Mary the Virgin, located on the south side, when his enemies seized him. According to Hall, Robert Aspall was spared in order to 'bere the earles mother and brother worde what he had done'.[40]

The severed heads of York, Edmund, Salisbury, Neville, Harrington and others were displayed on Micklegate Bar in the city of York, York's reputedly dressed in a paper crown. The bodies were buried in Pontefract. Whether it was brought by Aspall or some other messenger, the terrible news reached London on 2 January,[41] so, if Cecily was at Baynard's Castle, she would have soon been apprised of her husband's fate. It was the start of a new year, 1461, but the life she had known was over.

II

In the Name of the Father
1461–1464

Now is the Winter of our discontent
Made glorious summer by this sun of York[1]

It must have been difficult for Cecily to stomach the Lancastrian justification for the death of her husband. Her one-time friend, Margaret of Anjou, announced to the city of London that York had 'of extreme malice long hid under colours, plotted by many ways and means the destruction of [the King's] good grace'.[2] Even amid her grief, Cecily's first thought was for the safety of her remaining sons. Edward was still in the Welsh Marches and was now old enough to defend himself but George and Richard could prove potential targets for Lancastrian attack. With the assistance of Warwick, who was Admiral of England and, until lately, Captain of Calais, she sent them away into the care of Philip, Duke of Burgundy, at Utrecht. Presumably she entrusted them to some loyal servants but it was a considerable act of trust, sending her two boys, aged eleven and eight, across the perilous North Sea in winter. It speaks volumes about the level of danger she believed her family to be in and her ability to act quickly and decisively. She must have spent much of January and February in prayer for their safety, as well as that of Edward, and for the soul of her husband.

Cecily was then alone except for her daughter Margaret. Their location early in 1461 is unclear, although she was back in the capital by the start of April. She may have remained in London, in the familiar safety of Baynard's Castle, retreated to the family home at Fotheringhay or gone to stay with relatives. Grief must have mingled with the desire for revenge; Cecily and her nephew Warwick might have met, or exchanged letters, to share the burden of their loss. The execution of Cecily's brother, Salisbury, at Pontefract only added to the horror of the reports that reached them from the battlefield. Grieving for his father's loss, Warwick marched north to confront the queen's army. He was optimistic about his chances, writing to Pope Pius II from London on 11 January that 'with the help of God and the King, who is excellently disposed, all will end well'.[3] However, before it could be said that all did, indeed, end well, the earl was to be thoroughly beaten and the Yorkist cause was saved instead by the military prowess of Cecily's eighteen-year-old son Edward.

Edward had grown into a tall and impressive youth, strong and commanding, standing at almost 6 feet 4 inches. Croyland described him as being 'of vigorous age, and well fitted to endure the conflict of battle, while, at the same time, he was fully equal to the management of the affairs of the state'.[4] He may well have still been at Gloucester, where he spent Christmas, when the news arrived from Wakefield. He acted quickly, allowing himself little time to grieve, and, like Warwick, sprang instead to action, keen to avenge his father's death. Edward marched his army south, having amassed a significant number of Welsh lords, although others had joined the Lancastrian forces under the leadership of the Tudors. One of these armies, led by the king's half-brother Jasper, was close to Wigmore Castle, where Edward was then staying. Instead of heading to join Warwick, he decided to engage with Tudor instead and prevent him from swelling the ranks of the main Lancastrian forces. On 2 or 3 February, he won a decisive victory at Mortimer's Cross, after having witnessed the phenomenon of a parhelion or sundog – three suns in the morning sky. This was taken to be a portentous omen by Edward's men, until he convinced them that it was a manifestation of divine approval, representing the Holy Trinity. They went on to scatter the Lancastrian army, who were pursued all the way to Hereford. Jasper Tudor escaped but his father, Owen, widower of Catherine of Valois, was beheaded either in the marketplace or on the steps of the cathedral.

Meanwhile, Warwick was left to meet the approaching queen's army as best he could. Two weeks after Edward's victory, he encountered Margaret's forces at St Albans, and a lengthy battle was fought, from dawn to dusk. As darkness fell, Warwick realised he was outnumbered and withdrew his men. He lost custody of Henry VI, who was reunited with Margaret; she now had a clear march ahead to London, to retake the capital and reinstate the royal family. However, incredibly, she turned her army north again to Dunstable. This may have been because London was terrified of her approach, having heard stories of the Lancastrian troops looting and rioting through towns like Grantham and Stanford[5] without restraint, and was preparing to close its gates against her. The terrified city formed a very unusual delegation to approach its queen. Cecily's sister and former gaoler, Anne, Duchess of Buckingham, along with the newly widowed Lady Scales and Jacquetta, Duchess of Bedford, travelled with a group of clergymen to plead with the queen for mercy. Under other circumstances, Cecily might have been among them. She was in London, at Baynard's Castle, throughout this dangerous time, grateful for the building's solid walls and 40-foot great hall, capable of accommodating 400 men easily. Perhaps Cecily was asked to lend her support, but the role the queen had played in the path to York's death, coupled with her hopes for Edward, would have made it unthinkable. The women met with some success, returning to the city on 20 February. However, London was still wary. When a party sent to supply the queen's army returned home, the gates were barred to them. According to the *Croyland Chronicle*, they were thrown open in rapturous welcome and 'unbounded joy' a week later, as Edward and Warwick approached. The poem 'The Rose of Rouen' gave Edward credit for saving England from the queen and the lords of the North. For the first time since their bereavement, Cecily was reunited with her eldest son.

Edward now took on his father's title and rights, declaring himself 'by the grace of God of England, France and Ireland, vrai [true] and just heir'.[6] The *Great Chronicle of London* relates how he mustered his troops in St John's Fields, where he outlined the various failings of Henry VI and asked the people whether the Lancastrian was fit to rule them, 'whereunto the people cried hugely and said "nay nay"'. The Milanese ambassador estimated that 5,000 people were in attendance when Edward and Warwick celebrated that day by 'going in procession through the place amid great festivities'. Edward was fortunate to have the city on his side; even York's misjudged attempt at the throne in December 1460 had not wiped away his good rule during his two protectorates and this, coupled with the looting of the queen's army and the actions of Lord Scales, ensured that London welcomed their new king 'joyously'.[7] On 3 March, Cecily witnessed a delegation of the Great Council arrive at Baynard's Castle, to formally invite Edward to take the throne, in line with the Act of Accord made for his father the previous December. The following day, Cecily attended a service in St Paul's with Edward and possibly her younger children. Shortly afterwards, Edward went to Westminster and, after swearing an oath in the Great Hall, was declared king. Then he took his seat on the marble bench and the sceptre was placed in his hand. It must have been a bittersweet moment for his mother, witnessing the fulfilment of her long-cherished ambitions, albeit through her son rather than her husband. But it was not yet over. The Lancastrian threat had to be destroyed.

That March, amid the driving snow, the bloodiest of all the battles of the fifteenth century was fought. It was Palm Sunday, usually devoted to fasting and religious observance. Cecily was probably still in London, as a letter by the Bishop of Elphin claims he was 'in the house of the Duchess of York'. As she made her devotions, with the snow falling thickly and quietly across the city, she must have offered prayers for her eldest son. Despite Edward's military successes at Northampton and Mortimer's Cross, victory was by no means guaranteed. His mother knew his strength and capabilities but, mindful of the loss of her second son, she also knew he was a mere mortal, capable of defeat and death, and still comparatively young and inexperienced beside his many enemies.

Early that morning, Edward had drawn up his battle lines in opposition to the forces of Henry Beaufort, the young Duke of Somerset. With the memories of his rapturous reception in London still fresh in his mind, he knew this was the battle that would prove the most decisive of all if he was to keep a hold on the throne and his life. Yet the conditions were favourable. His army had the wind behind them and their bodkin arrowheads were capable of piercing chain metal. The weather remained atrocious throughout, with terrible blizzard conditions driving snow and ice into the faces of the Lancastrian troops, whose arrows were beaten back by the wind. Through the morning the struggle continued, with bodies piling up on the frozen fields. *The Great Chronicle of London* described it as 'a sore and long and unkindly fight, for there was the son against the father, brother against brother, the nephew against nephew'. Croyland related how the blood 'of the slain mingled with the snow which at this time covered the whole surface of the earth'.

Then, the arrival of troops led by the Duke of Norfolk swung the day in favour of the Yorkists, who pursued their fleeing enemies down through the valley to the river, where many were drowned. Croyland related that it was a 'most severe conflict [with] fighting hand to hand, with sword and spear, there was no small slaughter on either side'. The Yorkists pursued their enemies, 'cutting down the fugitives with their swords, just like so many sheep for the slaughter'.[8] Among them were the Earl of Northumberland, Lord Clifford, who had killed Edmund, and Anthony Trollope, who had deserted York at Ludford Bridge. Contemporary chroniclers estimated that as many as 35,000 men were killed on that day, or in its aftermath. Gregory claims that forty-two Lancastrian knights were captured and put to death when the fighting had finished. Henry VI, Margaret and Prince Edward fled to Scotland, leaving the way clear, at last, for the first Yorkist king. Croyland includes the details of the aftermath, with the burial of bodies 'piled up in pits and in trenches'. It must have been a long and gruelling task.

A celebratory poem, 'The Battle of Towton', written that year, named Edward as the 'Rose of Rone', or Rouen, now the rightful King of England. There was no mention of the circumstances of his birth, no rumours about his conception, though these would surface again soon; he was not the illegitimate son of an archer but England's saviour, the Rose of Rouen.

> Now is the Rose of Rone growen to a gret honoure
> Therefore syng we everychone 'I-blessid be that floure!'
> I warne you everychone, for you shuld understonde
> There sprange a rose in rone and sprade in englonde.[9]

Equally, the poem 'A Political Retrospect', written in 1462, made mention of Edward's birthplace in gratitude:

> Wherfore all trewe englyssh people, pray yn fere
> ffor kyng Edward of Rouen, oure comfortoure,
> That he kepe Iustice and make wedis clere
> Avoydyng the black cloudys of langoure ...
> he it is that schal wynne castell, tounc and toure;
> Alle Rebellyous undyr he shal hem brynge.[10]

Cecily and Margaret were still at Baynard's Castle. They learned of the victory five days later. A letter from William Paston to his brother John captures the moment, on the evening of 4 April 1461, when Cecily received news of her son's great victory:

> Please you yo knowe and wete of suche tydyngs as my Lady of York hath by a lettre of credends, under the signe manuel of oure Soverayn Lord King Edward, which letter cam un to oure sayd Lady this same day, Esterne Evyn, at xi clok, and was sene and red by me William Paston ... Fyrst, oure Soverayn Lord hath wonne the feld and upon the Munday next after Palmesunday, he was ressevved in to York with gret

solempnyte and processyons ... Item, Kyng Harry, the Qwen, the Prince, Duke of Somerset, Duke of Exeter ... be fledde in to Scotteland.[11]

Cecily's first response would have been to offer prayers of thanks for the victory and survival of her eldest son. The Bishop of Elphin was with her at the moment she received the news, and related, in a letter to the papal legate, how they returned to the chapel with two chaplains and had *Te Deums* sung.[12] Then, as Elphin went to write his letter, Cecily's mind would have turned to more practical matters. A new regime was about to begin and she had a coronation to attend. The news broke through London on the following day, 5 April, 'Easter-Eve', and 'great joy was made', as related by *Hearne's Fragment*.[13] Edward, though, did not hurry back. According to Gregory, he 'tarried in the North a great while and made enquiries of the rebellions against his father'.[14] He also visited York and removed from Micklegate Bar the heads of those killed at Wakefield. He went to Durham and Newcastle, and was at Middleham on 6 May. In his absence, he appointed Cecily as his representative in the city, before the burghers of London. Although York had never ruled, she was now as good as queen dowager, the king's mother, with the reins of the country in her hands. The victory came too late to be shared with her husband, but it was the culmination of everything they had hoped for.

The date of the coronation was set. Pageants were prepared and robes sewn, verses penned, meat baked and subtleties carved out of marzipan. Cecily recalled George and Richard from their exile in Utrecht and they sailed at once for England. However, there was concern over the ongoing siege of Carlisle, as related in a letter by Thomas Playter to John Paston that May, so Edward 'changed his day of Coronacion to be upon the Sunday nexst after Seynte John Baptyste, so the'ntent to spede hym northward in all hast'. Then good news arrived. Warwick's brother, Lord Montagu, 'hath broken the sege and slayn of Scotts 6000'. After 'setting all things in good order' in the North, Edward rode to his manor at Sheen, and remained there until June. It is likely that Cecily travelled there too, to be at her son's side during the important preparations. Sheen, or Shene, had yet to develop into the magical palace that Henry VII would rename Richmond. Built by Edward III, it contained glazed windows, chambers with large fireplaces and a roasting house in which to cook meat, as well as tiled courtyards, fish ponds and gardens. Its lands extended over the present-day Kew and Richmond, forming an important royal hunting park. The first few weeks of Edward's reign, between his return to London and the coronation, were spent here. Cecily was now the first lady of the land, and, according to the papal legate, Coppini, could 'rule the king as she pleases'. That April, Coppini was urged by his doctor to write and congratulate Edward and others, 'not forgetting on any account, to write to the Duchess of York'. For Cecily, these summer days must have been euphoric.

Edward made a triumphal entry to London on 26 June. According to *Hearne's Fragment*, he travelled along the south bank from Sheen and was met by the mayor and aldermen in scarlet and 400 commoners dressed in green. They accompanied him over London Bridge, the traditional site of pageantry, and to his lodgings in the Tower. He created thirty-two Knights of the Garter, including the eleven-year-old George, now Duke of Clarence, and eight-year-old Richard, soon to be Duke of Gloucester. Dressed in their gowns, with white silk on the shoulder, they accompanied him the following afternoon from the Tower to Westminster. He was crowned in the abbey on Sunday 28 June, St Peter's Day. Unusually, the processions and pageantry took place the following day.[15] A surviving account in the Cottonian Manuscript Vitellius A xvi relates that 'upon the morn, Sunday, which was St Peter's Even … [Edward] was crowned at Westminster with great solemnity of bishops and other temporal lords. And upon the morn after, the King went crowned again in Westminster Abbey, in the worship of God and St Peter.' The following day, he was crowned again in St Paul's, 'and there the angel came down and censed him. At which time there was as great a multitude of people in Paul's as ever was seen afore in any days.'[16]

Without doubt, there would have been at least one magnificent feast held at Westminster. John Russell's *Boke of Nurture*, written around 1460, provides a good reminder that such occasions were highly formal and ceremonial, with strict rules regarding the behaviour and activities of those serving the tables, as well as the codes of conduct for seating and dining. As Russell outlines, the sovereign was always given new bread, while others received one-day-old bread, while trencher bread, used as plates and for mopping up, was four days old. The important salt, a sign of status, had to be 'sutile, whyte, fayre and drye' and the lid of the salt cellar, or ceremonial nef, must not touch the salt itself.[17] John Fastolf's inventory listed a silver-gilt salt cellar shaped like a little tower decorated with roses, which weighed 77 ounces. The guests would have had their wine topped up from gilt ewers like Fastolf's silver one, engraved with flowers and branches and perhaps would have added spices from silver dishes.[18] Also very important was the napery, or table linen, taken from the Old French word nappe, or cloth. Russell recommended that it was sweet and clean, with brightly polished knives, 'seemly in sight to sene'.[19] Fastolf's 'bottre' or buttery contained two carving knives and three knives whose handles were decorated with gilt nails.[20] Russell advised his readers regarding the best fruit to be served, with plums, damsons, grapes and cherries offered as an 'amuse bouche' and pears, nuts, strawberries and hard cheeses to follow meat. After the meal, baked apples, pears and 'blaunche powder', a mixture of ginger, cinnamon and nutmeg were offered, to aid digestion.[21] The main dishes would have been symbols of opulence and elegance, with roasted meats, tarts and stews flavoured with exotic spices and coloured brightly. Each course would be prefaced with verses and a subtlety carved in the shape of a mythological creature or historical or biblical figure. It is not recorded for certain that Cecily attended the feasting; although it might seem an obvious celebration for the family, sometimes social rules excluded the presence of close family members such as spouses or parents. Edward would not attend the coronation feast of his own queen in 1465. George and Richard had arrived in England in time to attend the coronation, and Cecily would later prepare to attend that of her grandson, so, given the circumstances, she may have been present in some capacity even if she declined a ceremonial role.

Once the feasting was concluded, there was business to attend to. High on the list of Edward's priorities was provision for his family. In June 1461 he granted Cecily property worth 5,000 marks per annum from manors all over the country in York's possession, effective from 30 December 1460, 'on which day the said duke died',[22] and in October 1461 'arrears and rents from the tenants and Lordship of Stoke [were] to be collected for the use of Cecily'.[23] As Edward's 'most beloved mother', during his absence she was formally given Baynard's Castle, with an allowance of £1,700, along with the family home at Fotheringhay. In January 1462, the Sheriff of York was ordered to pay Cecily an annuity of £100 annually,[24] and on 23 February she was granted 'all sums of money, issues and rents pertaining to the king from all castles, lordships, manors … specified in the letters patent of her jointure and dower'.[25] Now her substantial lands had been restored, Cecily required assistance to help run them smoothly. She had observed York doing so for decades and participated in this process to an extent, but her circumstances were now very different. As a widow, she had greater power, but as the king's mother, she could anticipate that she would have less time to spend in administration. She needed to put it in the hands of men she could trust.

In 1461, Cecily appointed the loyal York family servant Thomas Aleyn as her auditor, after he had been a clerk in her service for at least a decade. On 26 June, she turned to Richard Quartermains, who had been the Yorks' lawyer and councillor since the late 1440s, and made him supervisor of all her lands.[26] Two of the obvious choices, Edmund Mulso and Sir William Oldhall, had died in 1458 and 1460 respectively. Other loyal servants were rewarded early in the new regime. On 12 February 1464, Cecily was at Baynard's Castle for the 'confirmation of letters patent of the king's mother', being a 'grant for life to Alexander Holt, esquire, sergeant of her pantry and Katharine Holt, his wife' of a tenement in Worcester.[27] The same year, on 8 July, a grant was made for life to a Katherine FitzWilliam 'for her good services to the king's mother the duchess of York'. She was to receive a 'deer called a stagge or an herte' from the king's chase at Hatfield and a tun of red wine a year.[28] Others who had been loyal to York were rewarded with grants of land and properties, like the one dating from early in 1462 from Fotheringhay, allocating a yearly income to John and Margaret Langley for their service.[29] She was also awarded the wardship of James Tyrell, a man who was to become closely associated with the history of her youngest son; in 1462, he was around seven years old and Cecily sold his wardship back to his mother, Margaret Darcy.[30]

Richard and George were not forgotten either. In February 1462, George was appointed as Lieutenant of Ireland, with Roland FitzEustace as his deputy from May, followed the next year by the Earl of Desmond.[31] A grant was also made to Thomas Baryngton of Trim, in recognition of his 'good service to the king's father, the Duke of York'.[32] In September, Richard became Admiral of the Sea, and took possession of a large number of estates in the Midlands; the following month, he was Admiral of England, Ireland and Aquitaine 'with all accustomed profits and powers'. He received the confiscated lands of Henry, Duke of Somerset, in 1463.[33] George also received the lordship of Richmond, as well as a number of possessions that had previously been held by Richard Wydeville and Henry Percy, Earl of Northumberland.[34] In January 1463, he was granted a swathe of new properties in Northumberland, Dorset, Devon, Nottingham, Derby, Surrey, Lincoln, Suffolk, Northamptonshire, York and Norfolk. More estates were handed to him in September 1464 in Somerset, Dorset, Devon and Wiltshire and again that November and the following January, February and July. In 1466, George was pardoned of all debts, accounts, arrears, issues and fines and both brothers were to have their charters, letters and writs in chancery and all courts of the king dropped without charge. Anne Holland was granted the impressive Coldharbour House, on the Thames, which placed her near her mother at Baynard's Castle. She was also awarded her husband Exeter's forfeited lands by a grant of July 1462, allowing her to make use of them and pass them on intact to her daughter and any other future children she might bear from other marriages.[35] The fifteen-year-old Margaret was awarded an annual £40 from the Exchequer in early 1462, as was Elizabeth's husband, John de la Pole.[36]

Edward's surviving enemies knew he would not let the events of Wakefield pass. In a series of extraordinary appointments that year, it appears that Edward was considering placing Henry VI on trial for York's murder. His key instrument in this would be the Earl of Warwick. On 12 March, even before Towton had been won, Edward gave Warwick the commission to receive the submission of Henry's followers or seize the property of those who refused.[37] In November 1461, Edward's first parliament passed an Act of Attainder against thirty-six Lancastrians for their guilt in the murders at Wakefield. This suggests that interpretations of the battle veered more towards the broken Christmas truce, or ambush of the foraging party, rather than a fair fight. That December, in an incredible appointment, Warwick was 'to execute the office of steward of England at the trial of Henry VI and other rebels who murdered the king's father, Richard, Duke of York, at Wakefield'.[38]

The Duke of York and Edmund were also remembered in prayers. This was an essential part of the medieval grieving process; it was believed that the souls of departed loved ones could be eased out of purgatory more quickly by the actions of the living. A number of grants were made for Masses to be said for the royal family, including Cecily and Richard, at the Carthusian convent at Sheen in July 1461; St Stephen's, Westminster, in July; St Mary's, Trim, in September; Syon Abbey, St Michael's Mount, Cornwall, Felstead in Essex, St Nicholas in Spalding and Cosham, Wiltshire, in November; and All Souls, Oxford, and Wilmington, Sussex, in December, among other places. They were also remembered at the church of Westbury, Gloucester, in March 1464, St Gregory and St Martin, Wye, in May 1465 and St Mary Redcliff, Bristol, in May 1466.[39] This sent out a decisive message but there was still a significant amount of Lancastrian support in the North. London and the South were largely loyal to Edward now but, for all Henry VI's inabilities, he had been an anointed king for three decades and his plight elicited some sympathy and support.

Through 1463, the threat of an invasion from Scotland rumbled on. With Henry VI and Margaret of Anjou gathering troops with the backing of James III and the rebellious Percy family, the situation became critical. Early that summer, their army crossed the border and besieged Norham Castle. Edward hurried north to deal with it, but by the time he reached Northampton news came that the Earl of Montagu, Cecily's nephew John Neville, had broken the siege. Defeated for the moment, Percy and Somerset mounted attacks the following spring at Hedgeley Moor and Hexham, where both Lancastrians were killed. In 1465, Henry VI was captured and brought south to imprisonment in the Tower, while Margaret fled abroad with her son. A poem in the Bodleian Library, 'God Amend Wicked Counsel', which was written in 1464, harked back at this time to the role the Duke of York occupied in the 1450s and his betrayal. The metaphor used here is of the narrator clambering up a rotten tree, with all its connotations of family trees, descent and lineage. It may have been composed to help provoke memories of injustice and support his son's current cause:

> Rychard of Yorke, that lord ryal
> He was exiled for yeres three
> Than was I leke to have a falle
> I clamer upon a rotyn tre.

The victories marked the end of a series of losses for Cecily's sister Eleanor. Her story also illustrates how fortunate Cecily was – the intermarriage and large families of the nobility meant that the Wars of the Roses truly were fought between cousins. Born around 1397, Eleanor was old enough to have been the mother of her youngest sister. She was already married and widowed by the time Cecily arrived and, after remarrying, gave birth to her first son when her sister was three. She went on to bear nine more children and, with the onset of civil war, was widowed again when her husband, Henry Percy, was killed fighting for the Lancastrians at St Albans in 1455. After that, her sons, Cecily's nephews, died in a succession of battles against York or his supporters. Thomas died at Northampton, while Henry, Richard and Ralph lost their lives at Towton, all taking a stand against their cousin Edward. For Cecily, it meant that extended family ties were lost or strained by the warfare, as she had experienced already with her sister Anne, Countess of Buckingham. Anne would lose her second son Henry, husband of Margaret Beaufort, after he sustained terrible injuries in 1471. It is difficult to know just how far the sisters were able to maintain any sort of personal relationship given these experiences. The losses of their husbands and children could equally have united or divided them. Once they became wives and mothers, their loyalties may well have lain primarily with their direct line rather than with their siblings. Soon enough, one of Cecily's own children would make a rash decision that would open a powerful Yorkist rift.

By 1464, Edward had reigned for three years. At twenty-two, he was still the handsome young king, with a proven military record and the good looks that had earned him an early reputation for womanising, according to some chroniclers. It was essential for him to marry a foreign princess and provide a string of Yorkist heirs to guarantee the continuance of the dynasty that the family had fought so hard to establish. Several possible candidates were put forward, including Margaret, sister of the King of Scots, and Isabella of Castile, but both were considered too young, being nine and thirteen respectively. Warwick may even have suggested the Scottish regent, Mary of Guelders, who was reputed to have been the lover of the Duke of Somerset, although this may have been more of a diplomatic gesture than a real possibility. As early as October 1461, a niece of Philip of Burgundy, a Mademoiselle de Bourbon, was suggested as a possible wife. This may have been Margaret, Catharine or Joanna, all of whom were unmarried at the time and of suitable age. However, Philip proved unwilling to commit to a dynasty still in its infancy, so a future English queen was sought elsewhere.

Cecily had not forgotten the French match that York had tried to negotiate for Edward in the mid-1440s, but the political scene had changed since then. Charles VII had died soon after Edward's succession, to be replaced by his son Louis XI. Charles's infant daughters, once proposed as Yorkist wives, had grown up and were no longer on the marriage market. Joan had already been the wife of the Duke of Bourbon since 1447 and Edward had missed out on his original intended, Madeleine, as she had been married to a Prince of Navarre on 7 March, midway between Mortimer's Cross and Towton. Perhaps Cecily now lent her voice to the quest for a new French princess. If a match had been considered back in 1445, it was eminently more suitable now that Edward was actually king. However, there was a problem of supply. The new king, Louis, had only two surviving daughters: Anne, born in 1461 and Joan, born in 1464. He did, however, have a suitable sister-in-law. Bona of Savoy was fifteen in 1464 and, although she was connected to the throne of France through marriage, not blood, her age and connections made her the most likely candidate.

Edward seemed pleased with the choice. He sent Warwick to the French court, where Bona was then staying, in order to make the necessary negotiations. There seems little reason to doubt that Cecily encouraged the match, given her previous hopes in that direction. Negotiations for peace with France had been ongoing since 1463, with Warwick and Lord Wenlock given a commission in March to bring about a truce with France. As late as 12 April 1464 Wenlock was asked to cross the Channel, and by early summer he had been introduced to Bona in person.[40] Louis was expecting Warwick to arrive in October 1464, to further the treaty for a marriage that would unite France and England, but events would render the trip unnecessary. The king's marriage had been on the cards since the summer of 1461, yet Edward was a young man of sensual appetite, 'prompted by the ardour of youth',[41] whom many feared 'had not been chaste in his living'.[42] Those fears proved well founded. In the interim, the king had fallen in love. That September, when Parliament sat at Reading, the question of a queen was raised again. As *Gregory's Chronicle* records, the lords 'would have sent into some strange land to enquire for a queen of good birth, according to his dignity'.[43] But then Edward made a shocking announcement. He was already married. He had been married for about five months, from early May, even before Wenlock's visit to Louis' court.

It is not clear whether Cecily had any warning that the news was coming. Edward might have hinted his intention or openly confessed or, perhaps, left her to learn of it following his announcement at the Reading parliament. The only accounts that refer to the secret marriage suggest that Cecily was devastated. On a personal level, it represented a considerable betrayal; that her eldest son had not confided his intentions and had chosen a wife without consulting her. In dynastic terms, Cecily and York had arranged all their other children's marriages, but their recent changes in status, with her as a widow and Edward as a king, may provide one reason for his actions. Politically and nationally, it denied the country an opportunity to make a lucrative foreign alliance but, given the recent role taken by Margaret of Anjou, a French bride may not have proved popular. Additionally, a peace treaty had been concluded on 23 April, rendering Bona superfluous.[44] Then, there was the choice of bride. Edward's new wife came from a family Cecily had known for over three decades.

Edward's new wife was none other than the eldest daughter of Jacquetta, Duchess of Bedford, and Richard Wydeville, Earl Rivers. Since their shared days in Rouen, around the time their children were born, the political drama had cast Cecily and Jacquetta on opposing sides, with Wydeville fighting for the Lancastrians and Jacquetta as a lady in Margaret of Anjou's retinue. This culminated in their humiliating capture by Edward in Sandwich. Elizabeth was about five years older than Edward and had already been married to Sir John Grey of Groby, bearing him two sons before he was killed at the Second Battle of St Albans. Edward would have known Elizabeth for a considerable time before being reunited, when, as legend has it, she waited under an oak tree in Whittlesbury Forest to petition him over the return of her sons' inheritance.

The secret marriage took place sometime in the spring of 1464. Tradition places it around 1 May, at the bride's family home of Grafton Regis, in Northamptonshire. According to Fabyan, the ceremony was witnessed by Jacquetta, two gentlewomen, a singing boy and a priest.[45] Many informal matches of the era were made this way, with few people present to mark the occasion, but this was hardly suitable for the King of England. After consummating the union, which made it legal, Edward returned to his court and explained his absence as a hunting trip. The details and legality of this match have given rise to centuries of speculation, mainly for the significance they would later have for the couple's children. It is also interesting to consider Edward's intentions; whether this was simply a ruse in order to bed a woman who had otherwise refused him, or a genuine love match that he intended to formalise. It was an odd way for a woman to become queen. Edward may have acted as he did simply because he knew Parliament was not likely to approve if he were to propose the match. Presented to them as a *fait accompli*, there was little anyone could do, no matter how unsuitable a Lancastrian widow with a large family was considered to be. It was the rash act of a young man in love. As a king, Edward had been impulsive and irresponsible. As a son, he had been insensitive and ungrateful. Yet neither Edward nor Elizabeth, nor anyone else in 1464, could have predicted the impact it would have on the course of English history.

Warkworth's Chronicles describe that Warwick was 'greatly displeased' with the match, after which 'rose great dissension ever more and more between the king and him'. Croyland related the 'great disagreement' that arose, which the 'nobility and chief men of the kingdom took amiss, seeing that he had with such immoderate haste promoted a person sprung from a comparatively humble lineage to share the throne with him'.[46] Waurin confirmed she was 'not his match ... nor a woman of the kind who ought to belong to such a prince',[47] which Vergil later explained as being caused by 'blind affection and not by rule of reason'.[48] Newsletters written at the time to recipients in the city of Bruges confirm that the marriage 'greatly offended the people of England' and that the nobility were 'holding great consultations in the town of Reading, where the king is ... for the sake of finding the means to annul it'.[49] It seems fairly straightforward to deduce that, if Warwick and the English nobility objected to the match on a number of grounds, then Edward's mother did too. When exactly did she learn that it had taken place? Perhaps the king broke the news to his family before Parliament met that September; if she learned about it as a result of his announcement, she would be understandably insulted. It was Dominic Mancini, though, an Italian visitor to England in 1482–83, who first included Cecily's reactions in his commentary. Writing twenty years after the event, he gives a hint of the illegitimacy rumours that historical fiction would fester into fact over the ensuing centuries:

He [Edward] also offended most bitterly the members of his own house. Even his mother fell into such a frenzy that she offered to submit to a public enquiry and asserted that Edward was not the offspring of her husband the Duke of York but was conceived in adultery and therefore in no way worthy of the honour of kingship.[50]

It is unclear exactly how Mancini got hold of this information, unless it was the version that resurfaced in 1483, with the very different context of that occasion. He clearly places the origin of the rumour with Cecily. What rings true in his account is the depth of her anger, her 'frenzy' and its resulting strike back at her son as 'in no way worthy of the honour of kingship'. After the lengths that York had gone to in order to secure his royal claim, and the losses Cecily had suffered, it is entirely within character for her to be incensed by Edward's marriage, to the extent of considering it an insult to the throne. Cecily did not consider that she and York had worked for years to achieve Edward's status, only for him to marry so far beneath him and cast their lineage into disrepute. In the heat of her anger, she may well have cast about for any weapon she could find, even if it hurt her in the process. She was prepared to make any sacrifice for her family, even that of her own reputation, if the Yorks were impugned.

Like her son's marriage, it was a rash act. Assuming that she did say such a thing, the implications for Edward, if it had been believed in 1464, could have been far reaching. His right to rule would have been questioned and there may, possibly, have been calls for him to step aside.

At the very least, it would have given ammunition to the Lancastrian cause. Surely Cecily did not wish to see Edward challenged as king? Not unless she was prepared to offer her next son, the fifteen-year-old George, as a potential monarch, with the divisions within the family that this would cause.

Interestingly, a poem preserved in a manuscript at Trinity College Dublin, hitherto overlooked by historians, contains a telling detail. In 1461, on Edward's succession, the anonymous acrostic verses 'Twelve Letters Save England' made reference to his legitimate conception in order to stress his descent from Richard, Duke of York. In 1461 there was no doubt about Edward's paternity, suggesting that the rumours were a political tool that was later employed at times of need.

> Y is for York that is manly and mightful
> That be grace of God and great revelation
> Reynyng with rules resonable and right-full
> The which for our sakes hath suffered vexation
>
> E is for Edward whos fame the earth shal spred
> Be-cause of his wisdom named prudence
> Shal save all Enland by his manly hede
> Wherfore we owe to do hym reverence
>
> M is for Marche, trewe in every tryall
> Drawn by discrecion that worthy and wise is
> Conseived in wedlock and comyn of blode ryall
> Joynyng unto vertu, excluding all vyces.[51]

Similar verses written in 1461, such as the Lambeth Palace manuscript 'Edward, Dei Gracia', also stress Edward's pure lineage, describing him as a 'springing flower, a rose so white'. The 1462 'A Political Retrospect' used the common literary metaphor of likening England to an overgrown garden, into which came Edward of Rouen to clear away the weeds. It seems that Edward was legitimate when he was required to be and a bastard when it suited his opponents.[52]

Then there was the issue that Edward had won the throne by right of conquest and could not be so easily removed. It may have been a mark of Cecily's belief in the solidity of her son's position by 1464 that she was prepared to make such a statement in the belief that he would not actually be challenged. In which case, why did she make it? She may have hoped that it would deter Elizabeth Wydeville and her family, who might then be bought off, or persuaded to agree to an annulment or divorce. More likely, it has the feel of an emotional truth; a betrayed mother lashing out to try to hurt her son in the only way she could. By saying Edward was not worthy of being his father's son, his heir, inheritor of his title, Cecily could not have caused him more pain if she tried. That appears to have been the point.

Of course, there is also the possibility that she said no such thing. She probably did object to the marriage, but her dislike may have been moulded into certain emotive phrases by writers over the ages. This was certainly the case with Sir Thomas More's quasi-historical fiction of 1513, which includes a long account of the conversation between Edward and Cecily regarding his choice of wife. It is an invention of More's, designed to lend colour and emotional impact to the narrative but, while not an accurate representation of a real event, it does capture many of the potential objections Cecily may have felt. More has Cecily 'sore moved' by the match and trying to persuade her son that it was 'his honour, profit and surety also, to marry in a noble progeny out of his realm'. She tells him 'it was not princely to marry his own subject ... but only as it were a rich man who would marry his maid only for a little wanton dotage upon her person, in which marriage, many more commend the maiden's fortune than the master's wisdom'. Into Cecily's mouth, More put the words that marriage to a widow of Elizabeth's station was 'an unfitting thing, and a very blemish and high disparagement to the sacred majesty of a prince, who ought as nigh to approach priesthood in cleanness as he doth in dignity, to be befouled in bigamy in his first marriage'.[53]

Edward's possible bigamy is another question entirely. More may have intended Cecily to refer to the fact that Elizabeth had previously been another man's wife, when English custom tended to prefer the marriage of a king to a maiden. However, by the time he was writing, in the second decade of the sixteenth century, the controversies surrounding Edward's early love affairs were well known. The issue had also been given more attention in recent years, with the examination of the claims that surfaced in 1483 that Edward had been pre-contracted to an Eleanor Butler, née Talbot. If this was the case, Cecily is unlikely to have heard about it, although she could have been well aware that Edward was not living the pious and chaste life her religious convictions would have led her to prefer. More gives Edward an unusual answer to his mother. He defines marriage as a man, rather than a king, as 'a spiritual thing [which] ought rather to be made for the respect of God where his grace inclineth the parties to love together ... than for the regard of any temporal advantage'.[54] This ideal of the York–Wydeville marriage taking place for love would have been popular in the reign of their grandchildren, with Henry VIII's fixation on chivalry and courtly love. It was hardly an answer that would satisfy Cecily in 1464. If she had snapped and lashed out at her son with allegations of illegitimacy, it was a moment of anger that would come back to haunt her.

12

A Family at Love and War
1465–1471

What kingdom werreth hym-self with-ynne
Distroyeth him-self and no mo.
With-oute, here enemys begynne
On eche a syde assayle hem so.
The comons, they will rob and slo
Make fyere and kyndel stress.
Whan ryches and manhode is wastede and go
Then drede dryeth to trete pes.[1]

Greenwich Palace sat on the south bank of the River Thames, about 6 miles to the east of Westminster. It was an idyllic retreat, where the boats sailed steadily past swathes of green fields, and twists of smoke rose from tall red chimneys. The palace was built of brick and timber around two courtyards, with the queen's range including a great chamber, parlour and gallery overlooking the private, hedged gardens. Built by Humphrey, Duke of Gloucester, it had been shaped by his refined European tastes, and boasted an important library of which forty-six manuscripts survive today, including works by Gower, Boccaccio, William of Ockham, and works of Arthurian legends and the Italian humanists.[2] Its spacious rooms were served by a sophisticated system of water carrying, using a new aqueduct and underground conduits. An extensive deer park was enclosed and the grounds stretched upwards to Shooter's Hill and Humphrey's Tower. It was a country residence fit for royalty.

After the duke's fall, the palace quickly became a favourite residence of Margaret of Anjou. She employed Robert Kettlewell between 1447 and 1452 to develop it for her use, and retreated there with her husband and young son when political conflicts had raged in Westminster. Renaming it the Palace of Pleasaunce or Placentia, she ordered the place to be filled with carved stone daisies, or marguerites, as a pun on her name. The windows were glazed and the reed floor mats replaced with monogrammed tiles. There was a vestry for the Crown Jewels, and a pier for embarkation on the river; the garden was developed, with arbours and a gallery.[3] Yet none of these ornamentations, this crystallisation of her identity in stone, could prevent her world from unravelling. At Greenwich, she had tried to encourage Henry VI to recover his wits during the dark days of 1453 and 1454 but, as the years progressed and the tide of popular opinion moved in favour of York, she had preferred to make her home in the North, leaving the halls and corridors of her pleasure palace quiet.

After Edward's succession in 1461, Greenwich provided a new retreat for Cecily's family. Margaret, George and Richard were quickly established there and, although Cecily retained Baynard's Castle, she would have attended frequently, representing the Yorkist line during the visits of ambassadors, ceremonial occasions and family events. George, Duke of Clarence, now in his early teens, had his own household established at Greenwich, where he began the process of chivalric training that was essential for a young aristocrat. In 1465, Richard would undertake similar supervision under the eye of the Earl of Warwick at Middleham Castle. In October 1466, the palace was the venue for the marriage of Cecily's eldest granddaughter, Anne. The only child of Anne of York and Henry Holland, Duke of Exeter, young Anne was now eleven years old. Her union with Thomas Grey, the queen's son by her first marriage, transferred her considerable inheritance back into the control of the royal family. A couple of years her senior, Thomas had lost his father at the Second Battle of St Albans, before witnessing the dramatic transformation of his mother's fortunes. Queen Elizabeth clearly valued the bride greatly, because she paid Anne of York 4,000 marks for this marriage, as Anne had previously been betrothed to Warwick's nephew, George Neville.[4] In these early years, Greenwich, along with Sheen, formed the new heart of York family life. Baynard's Castle had powerful associations with Richard, Duke of York, but these new locations were symbolic of the future, of the success and status they had achieved. It must have been an unpleasant surprise, then, when Edward granted these properties to his new wife, Elizabeth. Given the other indicators of her dislike of the marriage, it is likely that this provoked Cecily to retreat to Baynard's. It may have been for this reason that the Royal Wardrobe, further along from Thames Street, at the junction of Puddle Dock and

Carter Lane, was refurbished for the use of the royal family and their guests.

In 1463, Edward's parliament had passed a series of sumptuary laws designed to reinforce the difference in status between the ranks of the nobility. Cecily had always been conscious of her duty in maintaining her position through the outward show of ceremony. As the Duchess of York, in England, France and Ireland, part of her weaponry lay in her wardrobe and, now, as the king's mother, she was entitled to express her social standing in exclusive material ways. According to Parliament, these rules had been breached too many times, with men and women wearing 'excessive and inordinate arrays, to the great displeasure of God'. No knights below the title of lord, or their family, were now permitted to wear 'eny manere cloth of gold, or any manere corses wrought with gold, or eny furre of sables' on pain of a £20 fine.[5] Nor were they allowed to wear 'cloth of velvett uppon velvet' or 'eny manere cloth of silke being of the Coleur of Purpull' or 'saten sugary or eny Furre of Ermyn ... damask or sateyn ... or girdles harnessed with gold or silver'. Nor were men under the estate of lord permitted to wear shoes or boots that had toes 'passing the length of eleven inches'.[6] It is little wonder that Cecily's wardrobe, as outlined in 1495, should mostly comprise all these high-status items; clothing then was determined by rank rather than personal inclination or taste and in Cecily's eyes there had been a serious breach of rank in the family. It was at this time that she started using the title of 'My Lady the King's Mother' and retreated into the royal apartments whenever she was at court.[7] It may be true, as Michael Jones suggests, that this, as well as her appellation of 'Queen by rights', was a case of 'one-upmanship' calculated to display her dislike of the Wydeville family.

In May 1465, Queen Elizabeth was crowned at Westminster Abbey. Whatever Cecily's feelings about her new daughter-in-law, there was now little she could do to reverse the hasty match or prevent the young woman from stepping into the very shoes she herself had long coveted. At Edward's side, at the heart of government, Elizabeth would have a far greater personal and political influence than the king's mother. Cecily's name does not feature in the lists of those attending the ceremonies, although her sister and some of her children did. Her sister and former jailer, Anne Stafford, Duchess of Buckingham, bore Elizabeth's train, while George, Duke of Clarence, led the procession. Cecily's daughters Elizabeth and Margaret were among the party that followed. It is difficult to resist drawing the conclusion from this that Cecily did not attend the coronation. She may have chosen not to, or else been asked to stay away, given her earlier outspoken hostility to the match. It is not impossible, though, that she did attend but simply declined a ceremonial role. As the new queen's mother-in-law, senior to Elizabeth Wydeville by virtue of her age and Edward being her son, her situation was a complex one. She may have watched from a dignified distance, or from behind a screen, a device often employed by royalty. Margaret Beaufort would observe the coronation of her daughter-in-law from behind such a screen.

Cecily was also absent from another important family occasion that took place in September of the same year. The inauguration feast of her nephew, George Neville, as Archbishop of York, provided a benchmark in Yorkist extravagance, with its – now notorious – thousands of creatures slaughtered to feed the 2,500 guests in style. The antiquarian Leland recorded that something in the region of 4,000 pigeons, 2,000 chickens, 400 swans, 104 peacocks, 1,000 sheep, 2,000 pigs, 1,000 capons, 4,000 mallard ducks, 1,000 egrets, 5,500 pies, 4,000 dishes of jelly, 4,000 baked tarts and 2,000 custards were consumed at Cawood Castle that day. The seating arrangements listed by Leland include Richard, Duke of Gloucester, on the same table as his sister Elizabeth, Duchess of Suffolk; Cecily's half sister-in-law, the new Countess Westmorland; Cecily's sister Eleanor, Countess of Northumberland; and Warwick's daughters, Isabel and Anne. Elizabeth's mother-in-law, the 'elder Duchess of Suffolk' sat in the second chamber, in company with Warwick's countess, the Countess of Oxford and ladies Hastings and FitzHugh. Other ladies were mentioned in the arrangements but Cecily herself was absent, as were Edward and Elizabeth. However, as the guests were listed under the headings of 'estates' and 'officers'[8] there, it may simply be that the record of the presence of the king, queen and king's mother was excluded, as they were automatically placed on a raised dais, rather than included in the seating plan. Equally, Edward may not have attended, as he would have outranked George Neville, the guest of honour, but Cecily's absence may have been down to any number of factors.[9]

The same year, Cecily's elder sister Katherine made a controversial marriage. Born around 1400, she had already been widowed three times, having conducted illustrious marriages with the 2nd Duke of Norfolk, Thomas Strangeways and Viscount Beaumont, and borne three children. In 1465, she was a wealthy widow of sixty-five but this did not prevent the new queen from considering her a suitable bride for her own nineteen-year-old son John. The pair went through with the wedding that year, and, although their private feelings on the matter are unknown, it forged another royal connection for Catherine and provided the young groom with a considerable fortune. However, the union, for which the bride would go down in history as the 'diabolical duchess', was not fated to last. Surprisingly, though, it was Catherine who outlived her husband; she became a widow for the fourth time when John was executed by Warwick after the Battle of Edgecote in 1469.

That autumn Elizabeth Wydeville's pregnancy with her first child by Edward would have become apparent. Early the following February, she went into confinement in her apartments at Westminster, where she would have been attended by her waiting women, many of whom were the leading ladies of the land. Childbirth was an exclusively female experience, a time of uncertainty and danger when a mother and child hovered between life and death. Something of the rates of infant mortality from the era can be deduced from studying family trees and the records of those who died in childbed, but it is impossible to know exactly how many were lost during the process. Depositions made in the Church courts concerning illegitimacy refer to the delirium of mothers in their vulnerable state, relying on prayer and the support of experienced women in the absence of any pain killers stronger than herbal recipes. It is unsurprising that mothers gathered round them, those experienced women from their circle whose personal knowledge would encompass a range of circumstances. For Elizabeth, custom dictated that, besides her midwife, only high-ranking women were permitted to witness her delivery or help her physically, such as to support her as she rose from her bed. While it appears that Elizabeth's own mother, Jacquetta, assisted in at least one of her lyings-in, Cecily's role is less clear. As the other grandmother of a potential new monarch, she may have remained on hand in London, or fulfilled one of the roles assigned to the queen's 'gossips' or supporters, such as visiting her during confinement, offering advice or company, or bringing her various delicacies or medicines. The Duchess of Warwick, wife of Cecily's nephew, was known to attend women in labour in her area. Cecily's attendance at the child's christening suggested that she was on hand in February 1466.

Elizabeth's daughter, Elizabeth of York, arrived on 11 February. According to tradition, the christening took place a few days later, with Cecily, Jacquetta and the Earl of Warwick acting as godparents. The elaborately formal occasion was recorded by German traveller Gabriel Tetzel, who wrote that eight duchesses and thirty countesses stood in silence in the queen's presence. Cecily's daughter Margaret also played a key role, as a central figure at Elizabeth's court. Given her dislike of Edward's marriage, and the deference she was required to show to a woman of lower status, this may not have been an easy occasion for Cecily. However, she was intelligent and shrewd enough to realise that this new child represented the continuity of her dynastic line and helped guarantee its security on the throne. She had spent decades in submission to the Lancastrian court; at least the birth and christening represented her own bloodline. That bloodline was further advanced during the 1460s by the births of children to her daughter Elizabeth, Duchess of Suffolk. By the end of the decade, she had produced three sons and a daughter, and would go on to bear seven more.

Opportunities now opened up for the marital future of Cecily's final daughter, Margaret. She had entered Elizabeth's court as a lady-in-waiting but, as the sister of the king, she was now a valuable commodity on the European market, in a way that her elder sisters never had been. By 1465, Margaret of York was nineteen, a fairly advanced age for an aristocratic woman to remain unwed. That year, she was awarded an income of 400 marks a year 'until the King shall provide her with a suitable marriage'.[10] In 1466, she was betrothed to Peter, Constable of Portugal, but he died in June that same year, forcing Edward to look elsewhere. With his increasing interest in forging even stronger alliances with Burgundy in order to defeat their common enemy in France, the king invited Duke Philip, 'the good', to send ambassadors to negotiate a union with his widowed son, Charles. To the annoyance of the Earl of Warwick, the negotiations were largely entrusted to the Wydeville family, who played a prominent role in the Smithfield tournament of 1467. Cecily would have witnessed this extraordinary event, when the 'Bastard of Burgundy' famously jousted against Sir Anthony Wydeville, and the marriage seemed so certain that John Paston put a bet of 80 shillings on it taking place. The celebrations were broken up when news arrived, in London that June, of the death of Duke Philip. By February 1468, though, the marriage contract was officially signed and preparations for the bride's departure began.

An account of Margaret's pre-marriage ceremonials, written by one of her heralds, is preserved in the Cottonian manuscript Nero, c ix. The pageantry must have greatly pleased Cecily, as she witnessed the most illustrious of all her children's nuptials, as well as being hopeful for her daughter's future on a personal level. On Saturday 18 June, Margaret left the Great Wardrobe, where she had been staying, and rode to St Paul's, where she made offerings 'with great devocioun'. From there, she was accompanied by Warwick and the Duchess of Norfolk and other ladies and gentlewomen to Stratford Abbey. She passed the night there, with the king and queen. The following day she headed to Canterbury and then to Margate, where she set sail. Where did Cecily say goodbye to her daughter? She is not listed among the family party who waved Margaret off at Margate: 'the Kyng, the Duc of Clarence, the Duc of Gloucester, the Erle of Warrewick' with the queen's father and brother, Richard and Anthony Wydeville, accompanying her on the voyage.[11] The bridal party left English shores on 23 June 1468.

With the departure of Margaret, Cecily's world was about to change once more. The focus fell next upon her income and residences. In July 1468, she was granted £400 yearly from the customs of wool exports from Kingston upon Hull and London, and the right to export sacks of wool from Sandwich and Southampton.[12] England was particularly successful in the rearing of sheep, as its wet climate allowed them to graze longer on high-quality grass, producing a better quality of fleece. By 1500, 85 per cent of exports of cloth and fine wool were shipped from London, and they represented a sizeable part of national trade. This would have provided Cecily with a valuable source of revenue. As a thirteenth-century poet wrote, 'I praise God and ever shall, it is the sheep hath paid for all.'[13] The following March, Queen Elizabeth bore her third child by Edward, a daughter whom they named Cecily. The Duchess of York probably acted as her godmother, attending the christening at Westminster. If this was a gesture of goodwill or reconciliation from the royal couple, it may have been too little, too late. Later that year, Cecily's relationship with Edward would be put to the test.

In 1469, Cecily finally left the castle at Fotheringhay, which had been one of her favourite family homes, and moved to Berkhamsted Castle. According to the grant made at Westminster in March, she had surrendered the manor of Fotheringhay and all her estate by means of a letter to Edward the previous month. In lieu of this, she was given Berkhamsted in Hertfordshire and Kings Langley in Herefordshire, 'to hold for life' with all the fees that arose from 'knight's fees, advowsons, wards, marriages, reliefs, courts leet, woods, parks, warrens, chases, stews, fisheries, fairs, markets, customs' and other local sources. If she was ever to be moved again, she would 'be fairly recompensed'. She was moving to an estate run by Sir John Pilkington, constable of the castle and parker of its grounds.[14] This move presents something of a puzzle. Cecily appears to have been devoted to the place and was responsible for a large programme of reglazing in St Mary's church, cloister and college hall in the 1460s. This incorporated the images and stories of saints with special significance for the York family as well as heraldic devices, which suggests she had no intention of leaving and was expecting to live out the rest of her life there. Instead she was uprooted and sent to an inferior residence.

Berkhamsted was a Norman building, with a traditional motte and an oblong bailey, surrounded by a flint curtain wall and double ditch. Built by a half-brother of William the Conqueror, it was developed greatly by Thomas Becket during his tenure as Lord Chancellor, had been owned by the Black Prince, and had undergone extension and repairs in the fourteenth century. An English Heritage report based on excavations undertaken in 1962 and 1967 described it as a 'high-status residence' with a deer park and the administrative centre for extensive estates.[15] By the time Cecily arrived, though, its heyday had passed and it was in a state of disrepair, being abandoned on her death in 1495 and described by Leland as in 'muche ruine' and unsuitable for royal use. In 1580, the masonry was robbed out to aid the construction of Berkhamsted Place, which was described as having been constructed from flint and Tatternell stone, in the fashionable and expensive chequerboard-pattern style.

– Although ruined today, it appears from the surviving stonework at Berkhamsted Castle that the hall, chapel and living quarters were located along the western side. It would have been an extensive but quiet residence for Cecily who, as a widow living alone, no longer required such a large and important manor as Fotheringhay. It may be the case that she chose to leave, or was gently encouraged to go by Edward, over a period of months or years, but she must have left many happy memories behind at her former favourite home. She may have embraced the move as the final phase of her life, as a place of retirement and religious devotion. There is the chance, though, that this was a deliberate slight. There is no question that she was leaving the property most associated with the House of York, defined by its moat, which had been cut in the shape of the Mortimer falcon and fetterlock. Houses were as much a part of the external manifestation of status and wealth as clothing, and this relocation to an inferior home may have been intended to humble the duchess. Perhaps it was a punishment for her attitude towards the queen, or else she may have transgressed in some other way, refusing to accept that her son and his wife wielded joint authority over the 'queen by rights'. Between 1461 and 1464, Cecily had been the first lady, the dowager queen, with Edward in the palm of her hand; small wonder that she objected to being supplanted by a Lancastrian widow. If the move did happen against her will, her ejection would have been a dramatic step, designed to distance her from the reputation of the dynasty and, to an extent, from the memory and deeds of her husband. If there was some sort of family breach leading up to her move, the subject may have been very close to home. The York family was beginning to fragment.

Cecily's nephew, Richard, Earl of Warwick, had objected to the Burgundian match, hoping that Edward would take the chance to cement the French alliance he had lost in 1464. His increasing dissatisfaction was marked by several contemporaries, with the Milanese papers recording, in 1467, that he had 'met with many opponents to his plan'[16] and Croyland relating that he was 'deeply offended'.[17] Jean de Waurin suggests that, in the lead up to Margaret's marriage, Edward had been actively avoiding the French ambassadors, sending his brother George to meet them instead and then retiring to Windsor for six weeks while they remained in London 'chiefly because the king did not wish to communicate with the French'.[18] It was around this time, according to Waurin, that Warwick lost patience with Edward and began to drive a wedge between him and his brother George:

> Then they spoke of the circle round the king, saying that he had scarcely any of the blood royal at court, and that Lord Rivers and his family dominated everything. And when they had discussed this matter, the duke asked the earl how they could remedy this. Then the Earl of Warwick replied that if the duke would trust him, he would make him King of England, or governor of the whole realm. When the Duke of Clarence, who was young and trusting, heard the earl promise so much to him, together with the hand of the earl's daughter in marriage, he agreed, on these promises that the earl made him, to take her as his wife ...[19]

George, Duke of Clarence, had turned nineteen in October 1468 and was still unmarried. He had participated in the celebrations for his sister's Burgundian match, waving her off from Margate, and could now reasonably expect to make a powerful European alliance of his own. However, as Edward's next surviving brother, he was heir to the throne until such time as Queen Elizabeth produced a son. Both the successful pregnancies she underwent after the birth of Princess Elizabeth had produced girls and, if anything should befall Edward in the meantime, the crown would pass to George. This made the matter of his marriage more complex than that of Margaret, whose real importance had lain in the alliance she cemented outside the realm. Any wife of George could, potentially, become a Queen of England. As early as 1466, the

Burgundians had rejected a bold proposal for Clarence to wed Margaret's stepdaughter, the fabulously wealthy Mary of Burgundy, who would go on to become the wife of Maximilian I, Holy Roman Emperor. The question of George's marriage was left hanging, with Cecily now having little input in its conclusion. Yet she knew her son was ambitious. If he could marry Warwick's eldest daughter Isabel, and father a son, he stood a good chance of supplanting his brother with the earl's help. It was an attractive idea but it was dangerous.

As a mother, Cecily may have had some inkling that one of her sons was turning against the other. Knowing her dissatisfaction with Edward's match, it is not impossible that George spoke to her about his plans, perhaps not so far as to suggest open rebellion, but to gain her support for his marriage to Isabel. However, Edward rejected the idea, giving rise to 'secret displeasure between the king and the Earl of Warwick'.[20] Cecily may have joined Edward and Elizabeth to pass the Christmas of 1467 at Coventry Abbey, where 'for six days the Duke of Clarence behaved in a friendly way'.[21] The following summer, George was still acting as the king's judicial representative, hearing cases of treason at Westminster[22] and receiving grants of land and property of, among other places, Queensborough Castle on the Isle of Sheppey, an important port for the wool trade. In spite of Edward forbidding the Warwick–Clarence union, the earl went ahead and secured the papal dispensation that, the Worcester Chronicle states, Edward had tried to block. Secret plans were put in place. By the summer of 1469, Cecily certainly knew about them. When George, Warwick and his party travelled down to Canterbury and then on to Sandwich, in order to take a ship to Calais for the clandestine wedding, Cecily was with them.[23]

Had Cecily really turned against her eldest son, her king? Historian Michael Jones suggests that she sided with George in retaliation against Edward's relocation of her from Fotheringhay to Berkhamsted. It is possible that she saw part of the danger but not all, hoping that Edward would eventually accept the match and her sons would be reconciled. Given the role that she would play later, in attempting to make peace between them, it seems unlikely that she anticipated just how far the breach would widen. There is also the possibility that she travelled to Sandwich in an attempt to talk George out of going through with the potentially dangerous union. She must have been aware of his prospects on the European marriage market and his position as Yorkist heir, so may have not wanted to see him take a wife from among the English nobility, even from among her own family, as Isabel was her great-niece and god-daughter. Whatever her role, she returned to Berkhamsted to await news. When it came, in mid-July, it was to confirm that the pair had been married at Calais, in an elaborate public ceremony intended to highlight the contrast with the king's marriage.

Warwick and George now planned their return. Cecily's involvement is also suggested by the resurfacing of the allegations of Edward's illegitimacy, which may have been suggested as a strategy before they left England. The implication is that this had acted as the trigger to rebel; did Cecily tell George the story in order to convince him of his right? It forms part of Warwick's manifesto, as it suggested that George was in fact the rightful king, and justified invading and imprisoning Edward. As a woman and a widow, Cecily had few weapons to use against those in the political arena, even her own family. It is not beyond the realms of possibility that, in 1464, she concocted the illegitimacy story to discredit Edward and again, in 1469, she used them against the son she considered had humbled her and ejected her from her rightful home. If so, the rumours could only reflect badly on her; given her pride, it was really a case of cutting off her nose to spite her face. She may have felt powerless and frustrated, and resorted to the only means of defence within her power. If this were the case, she must have been aware of the damage she was causing.

With Edward distracted by uprisings in the North, Warwick and George were able to return and take him by surprise. That July, a significant turning point was reached when they faced the king's army at Edgecote Moor. Queen Elizabeth's father, Lord Rivers, and her brother John had been specifically named in the manifesto as being the cause of mischievous rule, opinion and assent, which 'have caused [our] sovereign lord and his realm to fall into great poverty and misery'.[24] After the battle they were beheaded at Coventry and their heads placed on spikes in the city. Edward was not present but was captured by Warwick and imprisoned at Warwick Castle soon afterwards. When the news reached Cecily, she may have been surprised and dismayed at the sudden escalation of violence that had pitted her nephew and sons against each other. The executions were powerful reminders of the fate that had befallen York and Edmund at Wakefield. Did this soften Cecily's resolve towards the new queen and her old friend Jacquetta? Or did she see it as a justified attack on a family she now considered to be her enemies? Sadly, it is not possible to know.

A strange period of waiting ensued. Edward was transferred to Warwick's home of Middleham Castle, 'in case his faithful subjects in the south might be about to revenge the great insult inflicted upon the king'.[25]

Cecily must have wondered, like everyone else, exactly what Warwick's intentions were. With her son a prisoner of her nephew, she may have held out hope that they would reach a reconciliation; after all, they had been on the same side for years. At Berkhamsted, she could only wait and see how the situation would resolve itself. Then an uprising in the North forced Warwick's hand. Unable to muster enough support to defeat the threat in his own name, he had to release Edward so that the king could appear in York as a free man, which 'scattered' the enemy. Edward then returned to London. Cecily may have travelled to the capital to see him that winter, taking her place at court for the Christmas celebrations, as she was certainly back there by the spring.

The following March, Cecily invited Edward and George to Baynard's Castle in an attempt to reconcile them. She may have had apologies of her own to make, depending upon what role she had played in recent events. If she had previously attempted to undermine her eldest son in favour of George, she now had to humble herself sufficiently in order to ask for his forgiveness. For a woman of her status and pride, it seems unlikely that she would wish to see her sons in direct combat, as she knew all too well the personal, political and material losses she may suffer as a result. She now acted within her interests and those of the two men, to try to bring about a peace. It is not difficult to imagine her in her great hall, with the fire ablaze and servants bringing in dishes, using her powers of persuasion and diplomacy to smooth over the bruised feelings of each of her sons. But whatever passed under the roof of Baynard's Castle that month did not have far-reaching effects. Within weeks, George and Warwick had embarked upon another attempt to oust Edward from power. This time, though, forgiveness would be harder to attain.

The same month, at York, Edward issued commissions of array against the 'rebels'. Warwick and Clarence had refused to obey his summons to declare themselves innocent of the rumours that they were plotting against him. On 12 March, at Empingham in Rutland, Edward easily defeated the troops of Lord Welles, who were fighting in the name of Warwick but fled from the scene in the face of the royal army. The *Chronicle of the Rebellion in Lincolnshire* described how Wells 'acknowledged and confessed the duke and earl to be [his] partners and chief provokers of all [his] treasons'.[26] According to his confession, printed in the chronicle, George's servants urged him and his men to 'call upon my lord of Clarence to be king, and to destroy the king who was thus about to destroy them all'.[27] The rebels then fled to France and, in April, Edward issued commissions for men to raise the 'armed force with which the king is preparing to resist George, Duke of Clarence and Richard, Earl of Warwick'.[28] A day later, further instructions were issued for the seizure of their lands and properties.[29] In France, Warwick made an unlikely alliance with the exiled Margaret of Anjou and betrothed his second daughter, Anne, to her son, Edward of Westminster. This effectively circumvented George's claim to the throne and combined the earl's forces with those who had been responsible for the death of the Duke of York. Cecily must have been horrified to learn of this development. Yet it did not deter George, who sailed back to England with Warwick and a sizeable force that took Edward by surprise.

In October, the news arrived at Berkhamsted. Edward and his younger brother Richard had fled across the North Sea to the Netherlands, leaving a heavily pregnant Queen Elizabeth to flee into sanctuary. Warwick had released Henry VI from the Tower and reinstated him as king. In a proclamation made that September, Cecily would have heard George refer to his elder brother as a 'usurper, oppressor and destroyer of our sovereign lord [Henry VI] and of the noble blood of the realm ... by his mischievous and inordinate new-found laws and profitless ordinances'.[30] It then presented George and his allies as having 'come into this realm for the reformation thereof and in especial for the common weal of all the realm [and to] deliver our sovereign lord out of his great captivity'. All men between the ages of sixteen and sixty were to be ready, 'defensible in their best array, to attend and wait upon the duke and earls and assist them'.[31] This rhetoric was reminiscent of the attempts York had made to rid Henry VI of councillors like Suffolk and Somerset back in the 1450s. Edward had won the day at Towton but it was York who had asserted his right to rule in the autumn of 1460, so this proclamation aligned the rebels with the Lancastrian stance of the time of Wakefield, against the late duke's attempt to take the throne. Surely this was a step too far for Cecily. Even if the words of the proclamation never reached her, the alliance of her nephew and son with Margaret of Anjou must have been a shocking betrayal. The autumn of 1470 must have passed in seclusion and confusion for her. She may have learned that Elizabeth Wydeville had successfully borne her a grandson in confinement that November, and her former adversary may have suddenly seemed more like her friend than her own family.

Yet the wheel of fortune had not finished turning. Edward was temporarily beaten but he was not defeated and, in March 1471, Cecily learned that he had returned to England and landed in the North. Days passed and the news from France was worrying: Queen Margaret was returning with her son Edward, newly married to Warwick's younger daughter, Anne Neville. With the Lancastrians reunited, and Margaret once again the driving force behind the throne, it signalled a return to the problems of the 1450s. Prince Edward would succeed his father and the old conflicts would be resumed by the next generation. However, on 11 April, Maundy Thursday, Cecily's son Edward was 'very joyfully received' in London[32] and reunited with his wife, daughters and newborn son. It is an interesting mark of Cecily's developing relationship with Edward and Elizabeth that he removed his family from sanctuary to the safety of his mother at Baynard's Castle. Richard was there too, now aged eighteen, having arrived safely back from exile. Soon, the prodigal also returned.

Until Good Friday, George had still been at St Albans, plotting with Warwick, Exeter and the Earl of Oxford. The *Great Chronicle of London* relates that Clarence stole away at night – 'contrary to his honour and oath before made, departed secretly from the Earl of Warwick and the other lords … to King Edward his brother'.[33] With the assistance of Cecily and her daughters Margaret and Elizabeth, George was reconciled with his mother and brothers. According to Croyland, 'the former, from outside the kingdom, had been encouraging the King, and the latter, from within, the duke, to make peace'.[34] This may have happened at Baynard's Castle before the departure north[35] or as late as the night before the battle.[36] They must have passed an uncomfortable few hours, as there was much to discuss and bridges to be rebuilt. Eventually, the explanations and recriminations must have given way to apologies and acceptance, before moving on to planning and preparation. On Good Friday, Edward moved his family to the Tower. Cecily's sons had to unite to prevent the country from returning to the Lancastrian regime that would push Edward out into the cold, in the same way that his father had been. Cecily must have had a vision of England in the future being plunged back into the trials of the past; did she stay up with them at Baynard's, reminding them of the past and urging them to act in accordance with their father's wishes? Edward marched out of the capital and, on Easter Day, his army met the Earl of Warwick at Barnet, north of London.

Now Cecily's sons faced her nephew. From having been allies in the Yorkist cause, united by their shared grief after Wakefield, the family had been rent by ambition and dissatisfaction. Her daughter Anne's husband, Henry, Duke of Exeter, was also fighting against them in the Lancastrian cause, as was her other nephew, John, Marquess of Montagu. The duchess retreated into her chapel to pray for the best possible outcome but it must have seemed inevitable that she would soon lose another loved one.

Warkworth's Chronicles describe the terrible mist that descended across the southern counties on the morning of 14 April, plunging Warwick and the Earl of Oxford into confusion. The armies fought from before first light, from four until ten. John Paston took part; his brother wrote to describe how he was 'in no peril of death' but was 'hurt with an arrow on his right arm beneath the elbow'. John had 'sent him a surgeon, who has dressed him, and tells me that he trusts he shall be all whole within a right short time'.[37] Others were less fortunate. The battle left Warwick and his brother Montagu dead. Cecily must have thought of her brother Salisbury, executed at Pontefract after having bravely fought beside the Duke of York. Now two of his sons lay dead, killed by her own boys.

The Croyland Chronicler relates the York brothers' show of unity that afternoon: 'Edward returned in triumph to London, accompanied by his two brothers, the Dukes of Clarence and Gloucester.' As they marched back into the capital, Cecily's relief to see them still alive may have masked a deeper sense of the futility of the losses, of cousin turning against cousin, those who had once stood shoulder to shoulder in battle. There was little time for the victors to catch their breath, as word had reached London by 18 April[38] that Queen Margaret, Prince Edward and Princess Anne had landed in the west. Once again, there were goodbyes and prayers to be said. Once again, Cecily's sons marched off to battle and left her to await the outcome. On 4 May, Edward led the Yorkist forces including George, Richard and Lord Hastings against the Lancastrians under Prince Edward, the Duke of Somerset, Baron Wenlock and the Earl of Devon. Ten years had passed since the decisive battle at Towton. Edward was now twenty-eight, with greater experience and a decade as king behind him. The encounter at Tewkesbury Abbey that May proved to be just as decisive as Towton, but it was more strategically important in furthering the cause of the House of York. The teenage prince, hope of the Lancastrians, was executed on the battlefield and his allies slain. Somerset killed Wenlock before seeking sanctuary in the abbey. He was later removed and executed. After two years of conflict, Edward needed to ensure there were no enemies left to mount future challenges to his throne. The brothers returned to London on 21 May. That night, King Henry VI died in the Tower. In the words of Henry's biographer R. A. Griffiths, 'there can be no reasonable doubt that he died violently'.[39] To Cecily, who had attended the unfortunate king's coronation feast as a new wife, over forty years before, it was the end of an era.

13

The King's Mother
1472–1483

Was never mother had so dear a loss!
Alas, I am the mother of these moans[1]

In November 1472, visiting Italian Pietro Aliprando was not impressed by the English. He wrote to the Duke of Milan that 'in the morning they are devout as angels but after dinner they are like devils … The king is indeed a most handsome, worthy and royal prince, the country is good, the people bad and perverse.' Aliprando had been unfortunate. Mistaken for an envoy of the Pope, he was arrested for supposedly working on behalf of George Neville, Archbishop of York, one of Warwick's surviving brothers. This unfortunate event indicates the family tensions that still ran deep after the victories of Barnet and Tewkesbury. Cecily's nephew had experienced a hiatus in what had appeared to be a promising career. His inauguration as archbishop, at Cawood Castle in 1465, has been remembered by history as a showpiece for Yorkist extravagant consumption and ceremony but, after a brief reconciliation with Edward, he had been arrested on a charge of treason and imprisoned in France. While Edward's defeat of the joint Warwick–Lancastrian threat had been a success, there would be still more consequences of the events of 1471 for Cecily's family.

The death of Henry VI's son, Prince Edward of Westminster, left the fourteen-year-old Anne Neville a widow. The younger of Warwick's two daughters, she had accompanied him into exile in France in 1470, and soon became an integral part of his plans for the Lancastrian restoration. With the help of King Louis, the earl had made an unexpected alliance with his old enemy, Margaret of Anjou. Anne and Edward were betrothed in

July that year and married in December. This made her Princess of Wales and, with her young husband, a viable alternative to the unsuccessful union of Henry VI and Margaret. In time, she may have become Queen of England. The bloodshed at Tewkesbury put an end to those hopes and, like Cecily after Wakefield, Anne was released into the custody of her sister Isabel, Duchess of Clarence. It was under George's roof at Coldharbour House that she and Richard, Duke of Gloucester, formed the plan to be married. She had already written to Jacquetta, Duchess of Bedford, and to Queen Elizabeth asking for assistance; perhaps she also appealed to her great-aunt Cecily to help her out of a predicament. The union was advantageous for both parties, as it gave Anne the security and status she lacked as a widow while bringing Richard half of the Warwick legacy, which was then entirely in George's hands. King Edward approved of the match, so it is likely that Cecily was also aware of it and did not object. However, George did not want to relinquish Anne's inheritance, and this led to the development of a bitter quarrel.

As the Croyland Chronicler related, 'this proposal did not suit the plans of his brother the Duke of Clarence who therefore caused the girl to be concealed … since he feared a division of the earl's inheritance'.[2] This writer was also the source of the story that Anne was dressed as a kitchen maid and hidden in the kitchens, a romantic idea that is not corroborated by any other primary source. The exact details of Richard and Anne's elopement are unclear, beyond the date of her departure from the Clarence household. On 16 February 1472, she left Coldharbour House and fled into sanctuary at the London church of St Martin-le-Grand. She and Richard were married that spring or summer in a ceremony that has left no historical record. As this was done with the support of the king, it may have been attended by Cecily and her daughters, or even taken place in the private chapel at one of their homes. St Martin's may have provided the location, or Baynard's Castle, or even Middleham, where the couple quickly established their permanent residence. For Cecily, it meant that the Neville wealth remained in the family, although the subsequent four years of legal wrangling set two of her sons against each other again.

The year of 1472 also saw Edward remember those who had sheltered him during his recent exile. That autumn he invited Louis de Gruuthuse of Bruges to visit England and accept the gift of the earldom of Winchester. An account written by a Bluemantle Pursuivant, a junior officer of arms, depicts Edward's splendid court and Cecily's family in an informal moment. Queen Elizabeth was playing *morteaulx* (a game like bowls) with her ladies, while others played with nine pins of ivory, 'divers other games' and danced. They heard matins together in the morning, before Edward and his guest heard Our Lady's Mass 'melodiously sung' in the king's own chapel. Cecily may have been present at the 'great banquet' that the queen threw in de Gruuthuse's honour, in her own chambers. Perhaps Cecily brought him a gift and offered her thanks for the role he had played in aiding her son's return. Edward presented de Gruuthuse with a 'cuppe of golde garnished with perle' with a sapphire cover, set with a piece of 'unicorn' horn, which was thought to be a prevention against drunkenness.[3] De Gruuthuse was lodged in splendid, carpeted chambers hung with white silk and linen, with a bed covered in gold counterpane and canopy of shining gold cloth. He also had access to a bath, covered in tents of white cloth, and a couch of feather beds inside a tent of netting. After bathing, 'as long as was their pleasure', they had 'green ginger, divers syrups and comfits, and then they went to bed'.[4] It was the influence of the Burgundian that initiated Edward's restructuring of his household and the introduction of new codes of conduct, architecture, dress and literature that would mark the second half of Edward's reign as culturally innovative.

There was still business to be conducted, even by the king's mother. In 1472, the manors of Southfrith, Tong and Swanscombe in Kent, which had been confiscated from York, were returned to Cecily by Sir George Brown.[5] That November she was granted the patronage of the hospital of St John the Baptist by the bridge of Lechlade in Gloucestershire. She was given a licence to convert the house into a chantry in the name of St Mary, where three priests would celebrate divine service and offer prayers in the names of the royal family, Cecily and the Duke of York.[6] Cecily was clearly still mobile enough to travel around the country. In 1472, she was at her property in Kennington, south of the Thames, to arrange for the building of a new chapel. On 10 May 1475, she was back at Kennington, from where she granted a property in Essex to a John Serle and his son. On the official documentation, she is described as 'late wife to Richard, rightful King of England and France and lord of Ireland'.[7] As she passed her sixtieth birthday, York was clearly still in Cecily's thoughts. On 1 June 1475, her steward at Berkhamsted, Sir John Pilkington, obtained a grant to found a chantry chapel for perpetual prayer in the church of All Saints, Wakefield, with one chaplain, for the annual rent of 9 marks.[8] The Pilkington chapel is referred to in a book of 1866, as being hung with a wooden tablet dated 20 December 1475.[9] James Smethurst was appointed as the first chaplain, with successors appointed by the Abbot of Kirkstall.[10]

A couple of surviving letters indicate that Cecily was still actively managing her estates. In 1474, some of her servants clashed with those of her son Richard, over a land dispute. The duke was ready to send in men-at-arms to resolve the situation but, once he understood that it was his mother's retainers, the matter was resolved between them, in Cecily's favour, through a series of letters. In 1476, she endorsed the lease of a wharf in London to a William Boureman and informed the Justices of the Peace in Essex that she and her son Richard had appointed John Prynce and Thomas Wethiale to act for them regarding the 'land called Gregories'.[11] The life of a duchess was still a busy one, even that of a widow, perhaps even more so. During York's lifetime she had managed his household in his absence and this continued. As a widow, though, Cecily was more likely to have delegated administrative tasks and relied on her tenants to maintain her properties and land under the supervision of her deputies. This developed relationships, between a widow and her staff, of considerable trust. By spending the majority of her time based at Berkhamsted, she would have had the chance to establish close connections with men like her estate manager Sir John Pilkington, her auditor Thomas Aleyn and the supervisor of her lands, Richard Quartermains.

During 1473, King Edward was occupied by an attempted uprising led by John de Vere, 13th Earl of Oxford. His father, the 12th Earl, had been well known to Cecily during the 1440s, sailing to France with her and York in 1441 and being a member of York's council during the first protectorate. In Normandy, Countess Elizabeth would have been among Cecily's circle of friends and was expecting the arrival of her son John, when Cecily had given birth to Edward. However, in 1459, Oxford had finally broken with York and united with Margaret of Anjou. He fought for the Lancastrians at Northampton but ill health led him to retire during the events of 1460–61. In 1462, he had been arrested and convicted of treason. His son John had been pardoned by Edward and, at Elizabeth's coronation, had been created a Knight of the Bath and took the role of Lord Great Chamberlain. However, he had sided with Warwick and Clarence and fled to Scotland after the Battle of Barnet. He was not attainted but his lands were confiscated. In May 1473 he besieged St Michael's Mount in Cornwall and was forced to surrender after having been wounded in the face by an arrow. He was imprisoned at Hammes Castle, near Calais, and the threat was temporarily contained again.

Although such tensions in the kingdom kept Edward busy, he was still a regular visitor to his mother's new home. A letter which Cecily wrote in 1474 suggests that her son Richard was there less often, although he would have been equally welcome:

> Son, we trusted you should have been at Berkhamsted with my lord my son [Edward] at his last being there with us, and if it had pleased you to come at that time, you should have been right heartily welcome. And so you shall be whensoever you shall do the same.[12]

Richard's absence may have been due to his increasing residence in the North, being primarily based at Middleham Castle with Anne and his young son, Edward, who arrived at some point between 1473 and 1476. George also fathered two children who were born at this time: Margaret, who was born in Somerset in 1473, and Edward, who entered the world at Warwick Castle in 1475. Queen Elizabeth continued to provide Cecily with new grandchildren, bearing some familiar names. The short-lived Margaret arrived in April 1472, followed by Richard of Shrewsbury in August 1473, Anne in November 1475 and George in March 1477. Cecily's relationship with Edward was still close, and a meeting between them was recorded by Elizabeth Stonor in a letter of October 1476. Stonor had been in attendance upon Elizabeth, Duchess of Suffolk, and travelled with her and Cecily to Greenwich where she 'saw the meeting between the king and my lady his Mother. And truly me thought it was a very good sight.'[13] Elizabeth also bore five more children during the 1470s, adding to Cecily's increasing brood of grandchildren.

In 1475, Edward declared war on France. His expedition was fairly short-lived and bloodless, concluding in a beneficial treaty by which Louis XI was obliged to pay him an income, and his eldest daughter, Elizabeth, was betrothed to the dauphin. Perhaps the most violent event of the whole episode occurred on the voyage home, when the Duke of Exeter fell, or was pushed, overboard and drowned. Cecily may not have regretted the loss of the man whom she and York had welcomed into the family, as their ward and son-in-law, who then fought against them with the Lancastrians. By this point, he and Anne had been divorced for three years and Anne was pregnant with the child of her second husband, Thomas St Leger. A clever arrangement made in the 1460s meant that this baby, conceived in April, would inherit all of Exeter's lands. Perhaps when he learned of the news, he was inclined to object. Anne did not outlive her ex-husband long, though. In January 1476, she went into labour and delivered a healthy child but died from complications following the birth. She was buried in St George's Chapel, Windsor. Her daughter Anne inherited the Exeter wealth on the same day.

In 1476, Cecily's sons organised the reinterment of Richard, Duke of York, and Edmund, Earl of Rutland, in Fotheringhay church. Tradition did not usually favour the attendance of spouses at funeral services and none of his family had been present at his first burial in Pontefract, immediately after his defeat at Wakefield. The bodies were exhumed in July and placed in coffins in the choir of the church at Pontefract Priory, which seems a likely location for their original burial. The hearses were large, three-dimensional structures, ornate with heraldic and dynastic symbols including the sun and the fetterlock, flags, pennants and candles. York's coffin was draped with cloth of gold and topped with a life-sized effigy of him, as was the custom with the burial of royalty. It was dressed in dark blue, the colour of mourning, with an ermine trim; its hands were clasped in prayer and its eyes open toward heaven. It wore a purple cap furred with ermine and, above its carved wax head, an angel held a white crown, to symbolise Richard's rightful position as an uncrowned king. The hearse would have been hung with epitaphs or verses about his deeds in life, and various personal 'achievements', such as his clothing, helmet or sword may have been displayed too. The following morning, led by Richard, Duke of Gloucester, the procession began its journey, travelling in solemn pomp through Doncaster, Blyth, Newark, Grantham and Stamford, before reaching Fotheringhay on 29 July.[14]

King Edward and George, Duke of Clarence, were waiting at the church door, along with other loyal supporters of the House of York. Inside, the queen and her daughters were waiting in the company of other family members. Richard's coffin was draped in cloth of gold in the shape of a cross, and guarded overnight. The service was held the following day, with Masses and sermons, followed by the ritual offering of pieces of gold cloth. York's black warhorse, still alive sixteen years after his death, was ridden into the church by Lord Ferrers, who carried an axe in his hands, with the blade facing down. Then the mourners paid their respects and offered pennies, before the coffins were lowered into the ground. York was buried in the choir, where Cecily would be laid beside him almost twenty years later, while Rutland was interred in the lady chapel.[15] A huge feast followed, when up to 20,000 people may have been fed, according to one source. A large percentage of these were fed in temporary tents, while alms were distributed to others. Cooks and ingredients were brought up from London, and thousands of pots and bowls were needed in order to feed all those in attendance.[16] It appears that Cecily was not present, even though Charles Ross[17] describes the occasion as taking place 'in the presence of the whole royal family'. As her relatives are specifically named, it would seem odd for Cecily's presence to have been overlooked. Perhaps this was in line with late medieval protocol or it was sufficient for her that the honour was being paid to her dead husband.

An illustration in the Luton Guild Book may depict Cecily at around this time. Manuscript images of her are few and far between, uncertainly attributed, and possibly generic. The frontispiece of the Guild Book, though, shows the most likely image of the duchess, on her knees with her hands clasped in prayer. She wears royal robes furred with ermine and bearing the arms of England and France, as well as a distinct plain black headdress, far more suitable for a pious widow that the elaborate 'hennin' she was depicted wearing as a girl in the Neville book of hours. Her face is simply drawn, with the standard regular features of contemporary portraits, although she does have the hooded eyes and high forehead that were considered beautiful. This is the best surviving likeness of Cecily, combining her beauty, regality and piety and projecting the image of restraint and contemplation she would have perfected as a lady of her rank. However, these years saw less restraint being practised by her sons.

The quarrel between George and Richard over their wives' inheritances had rumbled on until 1476. The Paston Letters record their discontent and Edward's attempts to reconcile them; no doubt, given her earlier efforts, Cecily also interceded to try to resolve their dispute. In 1472, John Paston recorded how 'the king entreats my lord of Clarence for my lord of Gloucester' but 'what will result I cannot say'.[18] In 1473, he captured what was clearly a difficult situation:

The world seems queasy here ... it is said for certain that the Duke of Clarence makes him big in that he can, showing that he would but deal with the Duke of Gloucester. But the king intercedes, eschewing all inconvenience, to be as big as both, and a stifler between them.[19]

Late in 1476, this estrangement entered a new phase. That December, George's wife Isabel Neville died two months after childbirth. The cause is likely to have been some delayed effect of the delivery or a long-term illness, but Clarence believed she had been poisoned. Acting in haste, he arrested, tried and had executed Ankarette Twynyho, one of her ladies-in-waiting. This appears to have been the beginning of George experiencing some sort of severe breakdown. As Croyland relates, George was 'more and more withdrawing from the king's presence, hardly uttering a word in council, not eating or drinking in the king's residence'. The reason given for this was George's loss of certain titles and estates but it was probably a resurgence of the ambition and entitlement he had previously felt, which had provoked his first rebellion in 1469. In 1477, he proposed that he should marry Mary, the stepdaughter of Margaret of Burgundy, and was angered when Edward considered this to be an inappropriate match for him. When several members of George's household were convicted and executed for necromancy, Clarence snapped. Again, Cecily's family was turning against itself. Perhaps, like the Croyland commentator, she thought her sons could be their own worst enemies:

> Indeed, these three brothers, the king and the dukes, possessed such outstanding talents that, if they had been able to avoid discord, such a triple bond could only have been broken by the utmost difficulty.

Storming into the council chamber at Westminster, George read out a declaration of the innocence of his men before the astonished peers. Edward was then at Windsor but, on hearing the news, summoned his brother to appear before him. George's track record of disloyalty must have been an influential factor, as Edward became convinced that he was, once again, aspiring to the throne. For Cecily, this would have been the latest in a line of fraternal conflicts, a further disruption to family harmony. But what happened next must have shocked her. At the Westminster parliament, Edward rebuked the duke before the assembly, accused him of treason and ordered his arrest and immediate removal to the Tower. His younger brother had pushed him too far, too often.

Surely, if Cecily did not leave Berkhamsted to plead with Edward in person late in 1477, she must at least have written him letters that no longer survive. If so, her words had little effect. Early in 1478, George was put on trial. An Act of Attainder was passed against him and he was sentenced to death. The surviving document starts with a reminder of the past:

> The Kyng, our Sovereign Lord, hath called to his Remembraunce the manifold grete Conspiraucies, malicious and heinous Tresons that ... have been made here within this his Royaulme for entent and purpose to have destroyed his moost Roiall person.[20]

He had forgiven much, but it had lately come to his attention that against himself, his queen and children

> hath been conspired, compassed and purposed a moch higher, moch more malicious, more unaturall and lothely Treason, than ate eny tyme heretoforn hath been compassed, purposed and conspired from the Kings first Reigne ... for that not oonly it hath proceded of the moost extreme malice ... but also for that it hath been contrived, imagined and conspired, by the persone that of all erthely creatures, beside the dutie of liegaunce, by nature, by benefeite, by gratitude and by geftes and grants of Goodes and Possessions, hath been moost bounden and beholden to have dradde, loved, honoured and evere thanked the Kyng ... all this had been entendeth by his Brother, George Duke of Clarence.[21]

Delivering the accusation alone, Edward reminded his brother that he had 'evere loved and cherished hym as tenderly and as kynderly, as eny creature myght',[22] even in spite of George's past conduct. Clearly he believed he was burdened by an ungrateful brother. However, the trigger appears to have been George's recent reopening of the rumours regarding Edward's paternity. Now he

> falsely and traitorously intended and purposed the destruction and disinheriting of the king and his issue ... fully intending to exalt himself and his heirs to the regality and crown of England [has] falsely and untruly noised, published and said that the king our sovereign lord was a bastard and not born to reign over us ...[23]

Once again, the Rouen rumours had resurfaced. If these had been previously instigated by Cecily in anger, this latest manifestation must have cut her to the quick. There is a slim chance that George believed the claim, but it is more likely that it was a convenient slur which it suited him to employ again. This time, though, Edward was not inclined to be merciful.

> The king, by the advice and assent of his Lords spiritual and temporal, and the Commons, in this present Parliament assembled, and by the authority of the same, ordains, enacts and establishes that the said George, Duke of Clarence, be convicted and attained of high treason.[24]

There is also the chance that George had heard whisper of another family rumour. This new skeleton in the closet would have had the potential to topple Edward's reign entirely, and cast aspersions on his marriage and the inheritance of his children, leaving the way clear for Clarence to become king. He appears to have shared part of his punishment with Robert Stillington, Bishop of Bath and Wells, who was disgraced at the same time, likely as a result of his association with the duke. Stillington would later emerge as the origin of the story that Edward had been pre-contracted in marriage to another woman before going through with his secret ceremony with Elizabeth Wydeville in 1464. If the bishop was certain of this, as he later claimed, having officially tied the knot between Edward and Lady Eleanor Butler, *née* Talbot, he was in possession of information far more damaging to the House of York than Cecily's reputed adultery. This might have been the tipping point in George's case. He certainly resurrected the slurs against his mother but, if he questioned the legitimacy of his royal nephew, the future Edward V, there is no question why the king moved so decisively against him. The evidence for Edward's bigamy is circumstantial. Whether or not George believed it, or whether it was true, is almost immaterial. Once it was made public, it could be exploited by those who wished to challenge the king and his heirs. It made Clarence dangerous. It sealed his fate.

Amid this uneasy situation, the royal family gathered to celebrate a wedding. On 15 January 1478, with Clarence still languishing inside the Tower, Cecily attended the marriage of her four-year-old grandson, Richard of York, to the Norfolk heiress Anne de Mowbray. The ceremony took place in St Stephen's Chapel, Westminster, and was followed by jousting. Did Cecily take this opportunity to speak to Edward about his brother's fate? No matter how much George had offended, she is likely to have made an attempt to save his life by appealing to Edward as her king and her son.

But Edward was implacable. Cecily was probably back at Berkhamsted when Clarence was executed on 18 February. The traditional story, that he was permitted to choose his method of death, favouring drowning in a butt of malmsey wine, is not confirmed in contemporary records. It was Mancini, writing five years later, who mentioned that 'the mode of execution preferred in this case was that he should die by being plunged into a jar of sweet wine'.[25] One later historian has suggested that this detail was included as a coded reference to the queen, whose favourite wine was malmsey, and Mancini would firmly implicate Elizabeth in the process. However, the iconography in the portrait of his daughter Margaret Pole, who wears a tiny barrel attached to her wrist, may provide a visual clue to her father's ignominious death. No doubt the news was a terrible blow to his mother, in the knowledge that it had been his own fault, as well as the fact that the instrument of justice had been his brother the king. It has also been suggested that it was Cecily's pleading that gave George the choice of method by which he would meet his end but, while this sounds possible, it has no contemporary confirmation. Later suggestions that George was his mother's favourite child have stemmed from this possibility, coupled with her presence with him in Sandwich before his first rebellion.

In 1479–80, a terrible outbreak of pestilence, or bubonic plague, spread through the country. On such occasions, it was wisest to leave the capital and Edward retreated to Sheen and his new palace at Eltham. To the medieval mind, plague was a sign of divine displeasure, a punishment for earthly sins. Various medieval tracts blamed the corruption of the clergy, sexual vices and the development of new, immodest fashions! However, medical men did believe that infection could be passed in the air and that seclusion was the best form of escape. Edward also obtained a papal dispensation in order to break the strict rules of Lent, in an attempt to manage his health through the diet of balanced humours his doctors would recommend. Cecily remained shut in at Berkhamsted, safe from the danger, but, sadly, it did cost the life of her youngest grandson, George, who was aged around two. He was buried in St George's Chapel at Windsor Castle. Queen Elizabeth was four months pregnant at the time and delivered another daughter, Catherine, at Eltham that August. She would bear one more child, Bridget, in November 1480, also at Eltham. At the age of seventy five, Cecily made the journey to north Kent to be present at her christening the next day, as the new baby's godmother. Her daughter Elizabeth also bore her final child in this year, a boy called Richard de la Pole, who would later bear the nickname of the 'White Rose'. Cecily would also suffer the loss of another of her granddaughters, the fourteen-year-old Mary of York, who passed away at Greenwich in May 1482.

Increasingly, Cecily stayed away from court, at Berkhamsted, Baynard's or Merton Priory. She was still conducting official business, issuing licences and joining petitions, but these were mostly in support of religious establishments. However, there was one important occasion that would draw her out of her seclusion. In 1480, her daughter Margaret, Duchess of Burgundy, visited England for the first time since her marriage. Margaret had sailed from Margate twelve years before as a young woman of twenty-two and now returned as a childless widow. Edward chose his brother-in-law, Sir Edward Wydeville, to accompany Margaret on her journey. They arrived at Gravesend in Kent and reached London in a royal barge in the Yorkist livery of murrey and blue embroidered with white roses.[26] Margaret was lodged at Coldharbour House, near Baynard's, and at Greenwich Palace. All the family reassembled; Edward and his queen and children gave Margaret a formal welcome and Richard travelled south despite being occupied by the increasing threats from the Scots. Elizabeth, Duchess of Suffolk, also attended and Cecily travelled from Berkhamsted to Greenwich, to be reunited with her family. There, Edward made a gesture of unity and deference by hosting a state banquet in his mother's honour. As pious as her mother, Margaret visited the shrine of Thomas Becket at Canterbury Cathedral before sailing from Dover.

The next few years saw Cecily's sons increasingly occupied with foreign policy. Edward had reached an alliance with Burgundy in the summer of 1480 but the fragile peace had broken down with Scotland. While Burgundy pushed for English involvement in an invasion of France, Edward sent Richard north to deal with the threat at Berwick. Having repelled a number of attacks and marched into Edinburgh, peace was concluded in the North, as well as in the South, with Edward coming to an agreement with Louis of France, who then also came to terms with Burgundy. By the Christmas of 1482, it seemed that the major questions of foreign policy had temporarily been resolved. This was timely, as the serious danger to the kingdom that would arise in the new year would come from within. Specifically, it came from within Cecily's own family and, perhaps, as a result of her actions.

14

Slanders
1483–1485

My life was lent
Me to one intent
It is not spent
Welcome Fortune[1]

As the dramatic events of 1483 approached, Cecily was passing her days in quiet contemplation in the Hertfordshire countryside. The ordinances[2] that outline her daily life show long hours spent in prayer, religious readings and quiet contemplation. After the hiatus of the late 1470s, it must have seemed that a semblance of peace and stability had returned to her family. However, this was only an illusion. The dramatic sequence of events that followed would turn the brief national peace on its head.

While it is fairly straightforward to describe what happened in England in the spring and summer of 1483, it is far more difficult to explain the motivations and intentions of those involved. A lack of contemporary primary sources further complicates the interpretation and understanding of these events and can only produce theories rather than certainties. As a result, the extent of Cecily's involvement is debatable; some historians have allocated her a distant role of observer and this is a fairly understandable position given her age and the lack of evidence to confirm her reactions. Yet the strong, proud Cecily we glimpse in reaction to Edward's marriage, or riding to meet York on his return from exile, or in dealing with Richard in a land dispute, paints a picture of an influential and powerful matriarch, unwilling to take passive role. Her engagement with the events that tore her family apart may well have been more direct. Richard was the primary mover in these developments but Cecily may have played a significant part by acting as his advisor. There is even a possibility that she helped him initiate them.

At Easter 1483, King Edward fell ill. In spite of comments from Croyland that he had lived a life of overindulgence – 'vanities, debauchery, extravagance and sensual enjoyments'[3] – he had been fairly active until that point, summoning Parliament on 20 January and negotiating a Scottish treaty. In spring he was at Windsor Castle, travelling back to Westminster by Lady Day, 25 March. At some point between then and 2 April, he became ill, possibly as the result of taking a trip on the Thames, as suggested by Mancini. The French chronicler Thomas Basin gave a different cause, stating that the king had upset his digestive system by eating a surfeit of fruits and vegetables. Commines suggests he suffered a stroke, Vergil described the illness as an 'unknown disease' and Dr John Rae, in 1913, suggested pneumonia because contemporaries say that Edward lay on his left side.[4] There appears to have been some warning that he was dying, lasting as long as several days, as false reports of his demise reached York on 6 April. In the following days, Edward attempted to reconcile the Wydevilles with his friend William Hastings. There would have been enough time for Cecily to travel to Westminster, if she had wished to do so, before he died on 9 April. She may have attended his funeral at St George's Chapel, Windsor, ten days later, where Edward was 'interred with all honour in due ecclesiastical form'.[5]

Richard was in the North at the time. He had only left London a couple of weeks before, having fulfilled his parliamentary duties. At Middleham Castle, around the middle of April, he received a letter from William, Lord Hastings, summoning him to London with a large force. This was the first indication of the coming hostilities. It is interesting to consider whether Cecily also may have written to her son at this time. Little of her correspondence survives but her interactions with Richard that date from the 1470s suggest a relationship of warmth and respect. It would seem a fairly logical supposition that she would have contacted her other children on the death of their sibling and king, if only in condolence. In the second half of April, with Edward IV already laid to rest, the future path of the York line still seemed relatively clear. Cecily's grandson, the twelve-year-old Edward V, would automatically assume the throne, by the terms of his father's will, and his direct inheritance. Having received the news at Ludlow on 14 April, the boy made his way to London under the guidance of his uncle and tutor, Anthony Wydeville. Different sources estimated the size of his escort at between 500 and 2,000 men but the numbers were downplayed. His mother had made a request to

Parliament for a large force but this had been disregarded as creating too much suspicion. Queen Elizabeth understood this point and, according to Croyland, wrote to the boy 'to extinguish every spark of murmuring or disturbance'.[6] If one concerned royal mother wrote to her son during these weeks, would Cecily not also have done so? Richard travelled south to intercept his nephew and accompany him to London. The boy's coronation had been set for 4 May and, in theory, it should have been a relatively smooth transition of power from father to son. At this point, in late April, Cecily was probably making preparations to travel to Baynard's Castle, to be in position for the day, where there would be family celebrations for the anointing of a new Yorkist king. However, before Richard or Edward could reach the capital, something happened which totally disrupted these plans and derailed the course of their lives.

As she waited at Baynard's at the end of April, reports reached Cecily about Richard's actions at Stony Stratford. Having met with Edward's party and his ally, the Duke of Buckingham, he had taken command of the young king and arrested Wydeville, along with Sir Richard Grey, the king's half-brother, and Sir Thomas Vaughan. This development has continued to puzzle historians, with some identifying it as the first step in a planned assault on the throne and others casting it as a precautionary measure, in response to some real or perceived threat. Even if Cecily had not been in touch directly with her son, she may have had some understanding of his decision, which could have been born out of the unresolved ill feeling resulting from Edward's marriage into the Wydeville family. She is less likely to have been in the dark than Wydeville himself, for whom the arrest came as a surprise, after having passed an apparently straightforward evening dining with the duke. Richard's explanation to his nephew was that the Wydevilles intended to remove him from power and kill him,[7] a claim he would repeat in the summer.

Whatever Richard's motives in late April, the course of events that followed was by no means guaranteed. However, reactions at court to the arrests only escalated the mistrust and lack of communication that followed. The dowager queen, Elizabeth Wydeville, fled into sanctuary with her children, which demonstrated the degree of danger that she felt she and her family were facing. By the time Richard arrived in London, parading wagons that he claimed were full of Wydeville weapons,[8] there was a mood of increasing uncertainty. This only got worse through the following weeks, with the appointment of Richard as Lord Protector on 27 May, the sudden execution of Lord Hastings on 13 June, and the postponement of the coronation. One letter, written early that month, stated that 'there is a great business against the coronation which shall be this day fortnight'.[9] By mid-June, merchant George Cely was writing about 'great rumour in the realm'[10] and Simon Stallworth wrote to Sir William Stoner that it was better to be 'out of the press, for with us is much trouble and every man doubts another'. He added that 20,000 of Richard and Buckingham's men had arrived 'to what intent I know not, but to keep the peace'.[11] This number is probably vastly exaggerated but helps reflect the degree of uncertainty that seized the city at the time, contributing to the escalating scale of fear. At the end of June, Sir Ralph Shaa or Shaw preached a sermon at St Paul's, stating that Edward IV's marriage to Elizabeth Wydeville had been invalid and his children were illegitimate. This meant the throne would pass directly to Richard, as the next adult representative of the House of York. So what actually happened, and how much did Cecily know?

The evidence suggests that she may have been directly involved. On 7 May, a meeting of the executors of Edward IV's will had convened at Cecily's London home, Baynard's Castle. Among those present were Richard and Buckingham, Lord Hastings, Lord Stanley and Bishop Morton of Ely. The original will, written in 1475, was rejected, and Edward's seals and jewels were confiscated. This may have been a prudent measure designed to incorporate Edward's last-minute deathbed wishes or a means of buying more time. There may have been another reason, though, which would explain the location of this event. Why did Richard call this meeting at his mother's house? If this business was all above board, it could have been conducted at Westminster or, if Richard perceived dangers there, he may have relocated to his own property, Crosby House. In fact, the majority of his meetings during May and June did take place in this town house. Baynard's Castle was to prove an instrumental location on two significant occasions: the meeting of the executors on 7 May, and the offering of the crown to Richard at the end of June. Why would he deliberately choose his mother's house as the theatre for these dramas, unless Cecily herself was complicit in them?

The removal of Edward V from the throne, and the accession of Richard III, turned on two rumours. On 22 June, the day that had been fixed for the delayed coronation, the sermon preached at St Paul's Cross resurrected the old story about Edward's paternity. The closest commentator to these events was Mancini, an Italian diplomat on a short visit to England. While there are some problems with his evidence, in the words of Professor Charles Ross, 'unless the modern historian is to take an unjustifiably benevolent view of Richard's character, he [sic] must, of necessity, pay some credence to these primary authorities'.[12] So, according to the closest source,

> Edward said they, was conceived in adultery and in every way was unlike the late Duke of York, whose son he was falsely said to be, but Richard, Duke of Gloucester, who altogether resembled his father, was to come to the throne as his legitimate successor.[13]

Tudor writers interpreted this as an attack upon Cecily and assumed she must have resented it. Vergil's account includes the detail that she complained bitterly 'in sundry places to many right noble men'. He gives the impression of having spoken to these witnesses, by adding 'whereof some yet live'. However, Mancini does not take this line. In relation to the accusations of 1464, he states that Cecily 'offered to submit to a public enquiry and asserted that Edward was not the offspring of her husband, the Duke of York, but was conceived in adultery'.[14] So was Cecily really the passive victim here, slandered by her son? As this rumour had already been in circulation, used as a political weapon by herself in 1464, by her nephew Warwick in the late 1460s and son George in 1477–78, perhaps she may have seen it as causing her little additional personal harm if it could be deployed to place Richard on the throne. Earlier that month, he had already made an appeal to her family for help.

On 11 June, Richard had written to Cecily's nephew Ralph, Lord Neville of Raby, requesting that he sent troops to London to assist in his defence against the queen who, in his own words 'intended and daily doeth intend, to murder and utterly destroy us … and the old royal blood of this realm'.[15] Such a sentiment makes complete sense regarding Cecily's involvement. Richard's biographer, Charles Ross, claims there is little evidence for this but, even if no evidence survives, Cecily and her son may have believed there was a plot in hand to deprive them of their influence. Mindful of the many past attempts to assail the Duke of York's position, they were particularly sensitive to their dynastic right and perhaps more readily inclined to pre-empt any perceived attacks that might replace their bloodline with one that was less royal. This explanation requires Cecily and Richard to have believed in the pre-contract story or, at the least, for Richard to have used it as a cover for other, more damaging truths. If Richard believed the repeated rumours that his mother had been unfaithful and conceived his brother in adultery, he may have used the pre-contract story to protect her. However, the illegitimacy story was quickly dropped after 22 June. Did Cecily object in strong terms? Did it simply seem less plausible than the likelihood that Edward had committed bigamy? It is more likely that, in collusion, Cecily and Richard acted to protect the inheritance of the 'pure' bloodline of the House of York, rather than allow the accession of a boy who may have been conceived in unlawful wedlock.

Yet that boy was Cecily's grandson and Richard's nephew. To a modern reader, it may appear intolerable or impossible for Cecily to have played favourites, to have chosen to support one of her close blood relatives against another, especially given Edward V's youth. It goes against modern sensibilities to believe that she deliberately sided with Richard to the exclusion of her grandson. Yet this was not a time troubled by modern sensibilities. In June 1483, she cannot have known that, by assisting in the removal of the twelve-year-old Edward, she may also have been signing his death warrant. The bigamy story was apparently leaked by Robert Stillington, Bishop of Bath and Wells, who claimed that, prior to 1464, Edward had gone through some form of pre-contract with a lady named Eleanor Talbot, née Butler. The lady in question was now deceased but the circumstances of Edward's secret marriage to the queen, as well as his reputation for womanising, made this a more plausible story. Richard and Cecily may have agreed to use these two rumours as weapons and remained with the one that proved to be a better fit.

A number of possibilities emerge. Either Cecily was slandered by Richard, in his rise to the throne, as Vergil claims, or Edward was in fact illegitimate as she suggested. If so, had she colluded in Richard's rise, as argued by historian Michael Jones? There is a third alternative. Given her understanding of the importance of dynasty, it is likely that Edward was legitimate but that Cecily knowingly allowed a false rumour regarding his birth to be used to help Richard to the throne. Richard may or may not have believed it. When that failed, they resorted to their second defence, which was Edward's pre-contract. The question of whether or not they believed in this is almost redundant; it was sufficient that the report had the desired effect. It does indicate, though, that the breach caused by Edward's marriage had been festering for two decades. This is not a hostile interpretation of Cecily, although it sits uncomfortably with modern sentiment. It is a realistic possibility that a medieval matriarch was prepared to use the only weapons available to her in order to promote her true bloodline. Far worse atrocities were committed on the battlefields of the day, but women did not have that recourse.

On 25 June, Rivers, Grey and Vaughan were executed at Pontefract and the princes were withdrawn into the inner sanctum of the Tower, while their previous attendants, including Mancini's main source, Dr Argentine, were dismissed. On 25 June, an assembly of lords, either voluntarily or under duress, gathered at Baynard's Castle to offer Richard the crown. Initially, he refused. Whatever conversations passed that night, under his mother's roof, proved decisive. Was this what he and Cecily had planned? Did she persuade him, or did he persuade her, that this was the right course of action? Did they celebrate this turn of events, or spend the hours in earnest discussion, solemn contemplation or prayer? The following morning the lords returned, and this time Richard accepted their offer. He was crowned as Richard III on 6 July. The official records suggest his mother was not present, but this appears to be the trend with Cecily on ceremonial occasions, rather than the exception.

The implications for Cecily's grandsons may have been beyond her comprehension in the summer of 1483. Once Edward V had been deposed, the problem remained of what to do with him and his brother, Richard of York, who had joined him in the Tower on 16 June, ostensibly to await the coronation. The boys' ultimate fate is uncertain. The final sightings of them, playing in the Tower grounds, were made in July, and at the end of that month an attempt was made to free them.[16] Richard was on progress in the North while the ringleaders were captured and executed. Some historians have seen this as the trigger which resulted in the boys' murder, either by direct order, or on the initiative of one of Richard's servants. It is important to remember that no actual evidence exists to prove that they were killed, not even the bones that were excavated from the Tower in 1674 and are currently stored in a sealed urn in Westminster Abbey. Excluding the later theories about pretenders to the Tudor throne, there is no evidence to indicate their existence after the summer of 1483. Many of their contemporaries believed they had been killed, as the shift in focus of anti-Ricardian rebels that autumn toward Henry Tudor reveals.

What did Cecily believe had happened to her grandsons? Did she and Richard have a conversation about their futures, once the decisive step had been taken to declare them illegitimate? It seems unpalatable to suggest that she was aware of their possible deaths, but it is no more so than the possibility that they were killed by their uncle. Viewed as the product of a bigamous connection with the Wydeville family, they presented a danger to the Yorkist inheritance, which Cecily supported unfailingly. It all turns on whether she believed in the story of Edward's pre-contract. During the summer and autumn of 1483, she must have searched her conscience. At one extreme, she may have supported Richard and turned a blind eye to their fate, at the other, she could well have pleaded for them to have been saved; perhaps it was her intervention that ensured their survival thus far, although she could do little to prevent any uprising that took place in July. No matter how much she disliked their mother, the boys were her own flesh and blood, named emotively after her own sons. Whatever the legalities of the succession, she must have grieved for them on a personal level.

The autumn of 1483 saw fresh challenges to Richard's rule. An attempted coup was uncovered in October,[17] with the involvement of the king's former ally, the Duke of Buckingham. His execution for treason took place that November. Also among the rebels was the second husband of Cecily's daughter Anne, Thomas St Leger, who had survived his wife by seven years. A loyal supporter of Edward IV, he had initially been welcomed at Richard's coronation and court, before finding himself deprived of his positions and required to hand over his daughter to the Duke of Buckingham, as a possible bride for the duke's eldest son. Even after Buckingham had been caught and killed, St Leger went on fighting against his brother-in-law but was captured and executed at Exeter on 13 November. This was just another example for Cecily of how the struggles around the throne split the various branches of her family apart and set them against each other. It was a reminder that another powerful breach still festered at Westminster.

In March, Richard reached an agreement with Elizabeth Wydeville, who left sanctuary with her daughters after he swore a public oath to protect them and find them suitable husbands. The dowager queen's action has been read unsympathetically by many historians since then, as an admission of her belief that her sons were dead and as a compact with her enemy. In reality, Elizabeth had little choice. She did not have the benefit of hindsight and, for all she knew, Richard might rule for another three decades or more. She could not keep her daughters hidden away forever, nor could she do anything further to assist the sons she had lost; so she emerged from Westminster on 1 March. Cecily would have approved of her daughter-in-law's decision to come to terms with Richard, with the opportunity it offered to present a united public front even though, realistically, the personal hostilities were irreconcilable.

The following April, Cecily's dynasty suffered a further blow. While Richard was visiting Nottingham, sad news reached her mother in London. His only legitimate son, Edward of Middleham, had died in his northern home, aged around ten. The cause of his death is unknown, but Croyland relates that he was 'seized by an illness of short duration'. Richard's grief, and that of his wife Anne, was described by the chronicler as 'bordering on madness'. Perhaps this loss moved Cecily to a comparison between the boy's fate and that of his cousins in the Tower. Her piety may have led her to view young Edward's death as a divine punishment for the princes' deposition and fate. Richard's grief was deep but his position required him to overcome this and think in practical terms; he later named his nephew, John de la Pole, Earl of Lincoln, as his heir. A few months later, the closeness between Richard and his mother was apparent in a letter he wrote her from Pontefract:

Madam, I recommend me to you as heartily as is to me possible. Beseeching you in my most humble and effectuous wise of your daily blessing, to my singular comfort and defence in my need. And such news as be here my servant Thomas Bryan, this bearer, shall show you, to whom please it you to give credence unto. And, madam, I beseech you to be a good and gracious lady to my lord my Chamberlain, to be your officer in Wiltshire in such as Colyngbourne had. I trust he shall therein do you service. And that it please you that by this bearer I may understand your pleasure in this behalf. And I pray God to send you the accomplishment of your noble desires. Written at Pountfreit, the iii day of June, with the hand of your most humble son, Richard Rex.[18]

The Colyngbourne mentioned in the letter had previously been Cecily's steward at a property she owned in Wiltshire. He had recently been removed from his office and replaced by Francis, Lord Lovell, which had occasioned Richard's letter. Colyngbourne got his revenge six weeks later, on 18 July, when he pinned a series of infamous satirical verses to the door of St Paul's Cathedral, defaming Richard, his rise to power and his allies Catesby, Ratcliffe and Lovell:

> The Cat, the Rat and Lovell our Dog
> Doe rule all England under a Hog.
> The crooke-backt Boar the way hath found
> To root our Roses from our ground.
> Both flower and bud he will confound
> Till King of Beasts the swine be crown'd.
> And then, the Dog, the Cat and Rat
> Shall in his trough feed and be fat.[19]

Worse still, Colyngbourne was found to have been in communication with the Lancastrian Henry Tudor, son of Henry VI's half-brother Edmund.

Tudor was also descended directly from the same Beaufort line, fathered by John of Gaunt, as Cecily's mother. His grandfather John had been Joan Beaufort's brother. Tudor had fled England in the aftermath of the Battle of Tewkesbury in 1471 and remained in exile in Brittany, then in France. In the autumn of 1483, he had attempted to join Buckingham's rebellion but his fleet had been beaten back by storms. That Christmas, he swore an oath to invade England and marry Cecily's granddaughter Elizabeth of York, who had now left sanctuary. Colyngbourne died a traitor's death but the threat of Tudor had not receded. In the autumn of 1484, rumours circulated regarding his planned invasion the following spring, and a number of Lancastrians and supporters of the Wydevilles had chosen to join him in exile. That December, Richard issued a proclamation against his enemy, painting him as a pretentious usurper whose reign would lead to national chaos. It sent out a decisive message but the threat still remained.

There is nothing to suggest that Cecily was at court during Christmas and New Year 1484. The descriptions of the festivities made by the Croyland Chronicler have marked out those days as filled with unexplained and unspecific controversies, giving fuel to another of the most debated issues of Richard's reign. Given the pious life she had adopted, or would soon adopt, Cecily is unlikely to have participated in the uneasy mixture of raucous celebration and the increasing suffering of Queen Anne, who was, by then, fatally ill. Cecily's granddaughters had entered Anne's household, where they had been received with 'courtesies and gracious caresses, and especially the Lady Elizabeth, whom she used with so much familiarity and kindness as if she had been her own sister'.[20] Croyland disapproved of the amount of time given to 'dancing and gaiety' and the 'vain exchanges of clothing' between the queen and princess, which caused people to 'murmur' and 'wonder thereat'.[21] Worse still, rumours circulated that, in the event of Anne's death, Richard would contemplate a marriage with his own niece, Elizabeth of York.

What did Cecily make of this report? Such marriages did occur, when the requisite papal dispensations had been attained, but it was unusual and did incite contemporary censure on a moral level. Richard's loyal adherents Lovell and Ratcliffe advised strongly against it as the match would be resented by the people, would call Elizabeth's illegitimacy into question and would prevent the king from making a lucrative foreign alliance, much in the way that Edward IV had failed to do. In the early months of 1485, as the queen's health worsened, a suitable international princess was already being sought. Perhaps Cecily added her voice to that of her steward Lovell and others by attempting to persuade her son of a less scandalous course of action, if indeed he ever intended to marry his niece at all. When Queen Anne died on 16 March, a plan was already in place for a dual marriage for Richard and Elizabeth with Joana of Castile and Manuel, Duke of Beja. As Anne was laid to rest in Westminster Abbey, the ambassadors were already on their way to Portugal.

The long-awaited invasion came in August. The news arrived that Henry Tudor had sailed from France on 1 August, bringing with it the certainty that a confrontation was imminent, and activating all the preparations Richard had made in establishing a naval and espionage network, gathering troops and arms. Before he travelled to Bosworth to confront his foe, Richard went to stay at Berkhamsted with his mother.[22] He was Cecily's only surviving son and her youngest surviving child. Together, on bended knee in the chapel at Cecily's home, they prayed for his delivery and safe return. No doubt they discussed the challenge ahead, and she would have given him her blessing and encouragement. After all, it was a battle they believed Richard should win. He was an anointed King of England, a son of York, an experienced and intelligent strategist and military commander, repelling an invader with a weak personal claim who had never been tested on the battlefield. Richard had the advantage of location – England was his country and its men were his subjects. To oppose him was treason. He would arrive in Leicestershire with a firm belief in his own right, marching before his troops with a large cross to demonstrate that God was on his side. Cecily bade her son farewell, in the hope of soon hearing of his victory, and retreated to her prayers. She would never see him again.

On 22 August 1485, Richard was killed at the Battle of Bosworth Field. His last moments, recaptured by the forensic analysis undertaken by Leicester University in 2012/13, reinforced the contemporary accounts that he made a brave charge at his enemy, which ended when his horse floundered in a marsh. The wounds on his body indicate a sustained attack, by several different weapons, from a number of angles. His crown was found under a hawthorn bush and passed to Henry Tudor. His body was carried back into Leicester and buried in the choir of the Grey Friars' church. A few days later, the devastating news arrived at Berkhamsted.

15

Old Age
1485–1495

A book of hours, too, must be mine,
Where subtle workmanship will shine,
Of gold and azure, rich and smart,
Arranged and painted with great art,
Covered with fine brocade of gold;
And there must be, so as to hold,
The pages closed, two golden clasps.[1]

An extraordinary document survives from the end of the fifteenth century which gives a vivid glimpse of Cecily at the end of her life. The ordinances of her household were composed at her instigation between 1485 and 1495, when she was living at Berkhamsted almost as a vowess, in accordance with having entered a strict religious regime. The first line states that it was 'requisite to understand the order of her own person concerning God and the world', which might imply it was some sort of attempt to impose routine and regulation following years of a turbulent and unpredictable existence. Although the document is actually undated, it refers to Cecily as the mother of the late King Edward, while making no mention of Richard at all, placing it firmly under the reign of Henry VII, her granddaughter's husband. It is remarkable for its insights into her piety, her reading and the household regime established by this very elusive but highly important woman.

Cecily rose at seven in the morning. Her chaplain was waiting to say matins while she dressed and, when she was ready, he administered the Mass. This would be followed by a visit to the castle chapel to hear divine service, followed by two more low Masses. She then went to dinner and, while she ate, listened to religious readings, usually from the Lives of the saints or reflective, contemplative texts. A few are mentioned specifically, including the Lives of St Maude, St Bridget and St Katherine, as well as other hagiographical collections and the works of Nicholas Love and Walter Hilton.

Hilton's *The Scale of Perfection* would have reinforced Cecily's chosen mode of life; in chapter seventeen, 'Of the Means That Bring a Soul to Contemplation', he advocates the reading of Holy Scripture and good books, spiritual meditation and diligent prayer with devotion. Hilton advocated that the devout put all their faith in Christ, and use these methods to wipe away sin and cleanse their hearts, the better to ultimately achieve grace.[2] Love's translation of the *Mirror of the Blessed Life of Jesus Christ* had been composed around 1400 and approved by the Archbishop of Canterbury for circulation. It proved to be one of the most popular new works of the times, and the advent of printing under Edward IV saw an explosion in the facilities necessary to circulate it among a wide audience. In the century following 1485, it was republished ten times. Likewise, the thirteenth-century *The Golden Legend* was one of the first texts to run off William Caxton's printing press, which was based in the precincts of Westminster Abbey, in 1483.

Dinner was taken at eleven o'clock or twelve on fast days. On Sundays, Tuesdays and Thursdays, Cecily's household dined on boiled beef, mutton and one roast dish, while on Monday and Wednesday they had just the beef and mutton. On fast days, which were regular throughout the pre-Reformation calendar, two dishes of fresh fish and one of salt fish were served. Berkhamsted may have had its own fish ponds, which were expensive to maintain, or fish may have been caught from the River Bulborne, flowing beside the castle, or transported from merchant ships in London, or from popular suppliers in Essex or Kent. On Saturdays the diet was supplemented with butter and eggs.

After dining, Cecily allowed an hour for business. In the great hall at Berkhamsted, she gave 'audyence to all such as hath any matter to shewe unto her'.[3] She then slept for a frugal quarter of an hour before rising to devote herself to further prayer until the first peal of the bells for evensong. Depending on the season, this could vary between three and five in the afternoon. It was the sign for Cecily to 'drynketh wyne or ale at her pleasure'[4] before reaching the chapel by the last peal of the bell. From there she went to supper and, while eating, she recited to her household the text of the sermon she had heard earlier at dinner. After the meal, she pursued 'honest mirth' by being 'famyliare with her gentilwomen',[5] then, an hour before bedtime, she drank a glass of wine and retired to her private closet, making her final prayers. She was in bed by eight.

Her household ran along very regular lines, especially for those who served her at Berkhamsted. Friday was payment day for the supplies of fresh produce to the castle; otherwise, bills were settled at the end of each month. The exceptions were those employed in the chapel, who received their dues each quarter, the biannual household wages and the yearly wardrobe accounts. Four times a year, a proclamation about the castle was made in the marketplace at Berkhamsted, to call in outstanding payments and debts and to state that certain sums owing had been settled. Cecily's servants were also provided for, but not particularly lavishly. Her head officers, if they were present at Berkhamsted rather than 'lying within the town', were assigned bread, ale, fire and candles; this was extended to waiting women, so long as they were married. The sick were given 'a lybertye to have all such things as may be to their ease' and if a servant was incapacitated or 'fell impotent' they would still receive the same wages.[6]

The world outside the closed walls of Berkhamsted underwent significant changes in the final decade of Cecily's life. In January 1486, her granddaughter Elizabeth of York was married to Henry VII at Westminster, and the duchess's feelings about her union with the man who had killed her son Richard in battle cannot have been straightforward. Perhaps this was the trigger that spurred her to lead a more retired life. After all, there was little she could do about it other than accept the situation and withdraw into her religion. In September 1486, Elizabeth gave birth to her first son, Arthur, a great-grandson for Cecily, who was to be the heir to the Tudor dynasty. There is no record of the duchess's attendance at his christening, which was held near to the place of his birth in Winchester. Her granddaughter and namesake, Cecily of York, carried baby Arthur into the church of St Swithin, accompanied by her grandson John de la Pole, Earl of Lincoln. Dowager Queen Elizabeth Wydeville was his godmother; it may have been distance that prevented Cecily from attending.

In February 1486, Cecily was awarded a licence for life to export wool from the ports of Sandwich, London and Southampton through the 'straits of Marrok', round the tip of Gibraltar and into the Mediterranean Sea.[7] This was a continuance of previous grants made to her by Edward IV in 1468 and would have provided her with a useful income, which served as a continuation of York's activities. During the 1450s, the duke had been issued with a similar licence to export wool to the customs value of 10,000 marks,[8] some of which may have been drawn from his extensive lands and prepared by his tenants. That June, she was granted 'certain farms in recompense of her dower', which may well have contributed to the production of sheep and wool.[9]

As early as 1486, Cecily was considering how to bestow her many properties after her death. This highlights the responsibility she had to her many tenants, who lived and worked on her lands, to find them a suitable and sympathetic replacement lord. To this end, in November, she appointed John, Earl of Oxford, as the steward and keeper of the park and manor of Hunden, Suffolk, 'after the death of the said duchess'.[10] In January 1489, she granted the stewardship, keeping of the parks and honour of Berkhamsted and King's Langley to Ralph Verney, possibly son of the Ralph Verney who had been Lord Mayor of London.[11] That spring she granted property in Gloucestershire to Thomas Poyntz and in Hertford and Kent to Roger Cotton. Thaxted in Essex went to Sir Thomas Grey and Marshwood in Dorset to 'the King's servant John Knollys, yeoman for the King's own mouth in the king's pantry'.[12] Stoke Clare went to a Sir William Hastings, who may have been the son or grandson of her son Edward's close friend. In February 1492, a lengthy document recorded in the Patent Rolls divided up the majority of her remaining lands.[13] As she advanced through her seventies, possibly beset by illness, having seen many of her relatives die young, she would have been aware that any illness might signal the end.

Cecily's life was drawing to a close. However, the House of York was not completely defeated. Henry Tudor may have won a decisive victory at Bosworth and claimed the throne of England as a result, but there were still members of the York family to claim the titles and claims of Richard, Duke of York. The most notable of these were the sons of Cecily's daughter Elizabeth, the eldest of whom, John de la Pole, had been *de facto* heir to Richard III from 1484. Now in his mid-twenties, he briefly resolved to live under the Tudor regime, as his role at Arthur's christening showed, but he was soon drawn into a plot to replace it with his own line. An amenable priest introduced him to a boy named Lambert Simnel, who bore a striking resemblance to Edward, Earl of Warwick, son of George, Duke of Clarence. This ten-year-old could provide the chance the House of York needed. Lincoln travelled to Burgundy to visit his aunt Margaret and ask for her support against the regime that had replaced her brother. She offered 2,000 mercenaries, perhaps because, as Vergil later described, she 'pursued Henry with an insatiable hatred and with fiery wrath never desisted from employing every scheme which might harm him as a representative of a hostile faction'. Her mother may have felt the same way but she was now Henry's subject and had to tread carefully.

Lincoln also recruited Richard III's loyal friend Francis, Lord Lovell, leading a similar number. The boy was crowned in Dublin Cathedral as Edward VI, and an Irish–Burgundian army landed on the west coast of England led by Lincoln. At Berkhamsted, Cecily must have been torn. On one side, her grandson was leading a rebellion in the Yorkist name, but it was against her granddaughter and the claim of her newly established line, embodied in her granddaughter's young son, Arthur. In her retirement, Cecily was fortunate that she did not have the option to actively take sides. What her private hopes and wishes were cannot be guessed at; she may have simply stepped back and awaited the result.

The armies clashed at the Battle of Stoke on 16 June 1487. It was clear, by that point, that the young boy Simnel was an imposter, as Henry had taken the precaution of temporarily releasing the real Edward, Earl of Warwick, from the Tower and parading him through the streets of London. Still, Lincoln urged the confrontation onwards, perhaps having used the boy as a screen to further his own claim. The encounter is often relegated to an afterthought, a brief rebellion after the impact of Bosworth, but no line was drawn in the historical sand in 1485. For those Yorkists lined up on the top of Rampire Hill, facing the royalist army led by Henry Tudor, his uncle Jasper and the Earl of Oxford, as well as for those like Cecily waiting at home for news, the battle had the potential to swing power away from the Tudors again. With the hiatus of 1470–71 in mind, as well as Bosworth, all those involved knew that short-lived kings could be displaced and sudden change could sweep through the political world, with all the resulting personal implications. If the outcome of Bosworth had been determined by a series of misfortunes for Richard, luck could equally turn against Tudor and his men. Cecily may have been expecting to hear that her grandson was returning to the capital as John II.

However, luck favoured Henry Tudor that day. While Lincoln's trained mercenaries initially beat back Tudor's forces, the following three hours saw them roundly defeated and the majority of their leaders were killed. Lincoln died in the field, and only Lovell escaped to an uncertain future. No doubt Cecily would have learned the result by letter a few days after the event and offered up her prayers for yet another grandson lost to the conflicts of the age.

The future looked more secure for the Tudor dynasty with the arrival of more children. Elizabeth of York bore a daughter, Margaret, in 1489 and another son, Henry, in 1491. As one regime was getting established, the final members of the old one were gradually dying away. In early June 1492, Cecily would have heard news of the death of her one-time daughter-in-law, Elizabeth Wydeville, the woman whose marriage she had so bitterly opposed. Elizabeth had spent five years at Bermondsey Abbey, and her will revealed few bequests of value for the mother of a queen. She was buried without fuss on Whit Sunday beside Edward at Windsor, accompanied on her final journey by her husband's illegitimate daughter Grace. She may also have been aware of an upsurge in the posthumous reputation of Henry VI, with the composition of the poem 'A Remembrance of Henry VI' by James Ryman in 1492 and the attempts made by her son-in-law to advance his acceptance as a saint. The thoughts of Henry VII would also turn to the resting place of his predecessor, Richard III. In 1495, he would pay for the construction of an alabaster tomb to lay over his resting place in the Grey Friars at Leicester.

In November 1494, Cecily may have heard of the celebrations to invest Prince Henry as Duke of York. After a month of preparations, during which the three-year-old was invested as a Knight of the Bath, he was created duke on All Hallows' Day, standing on the dais in the parliamentary chamber at Westminster, dressed in royal estate. He was presented with the symbols of office before celebrating High Mass in St Stephen's Chapel. He then witnessed the jousting at Westminster Hall, with his parents and elder sister. Perhaps someone, mindful of the significance of the title, wrote to Cecily to describe her great-grandson's excitement at seeing the challengers dressed in the tawny-and-blue Yorkist livery.

The last years of Cecily's life saw a second, more serious, threat rise against Henry VII. In 1491, another pretender emerged, claiming to be one of her grandsons, lost after entering the Tower in 1483. The young man, Perkin Warbeck, bore a striking resemblance to Edward IV and soon enlisted the support of Margaret in Burgundy to mount a challenge to the throne under the identity of Richard, Duke of York. His true identity has never been satisfactorily resolved, although it has been suggested that he may have been an illegitimate son of Edward's, conceived during his exile in the Netherlands in 1470–71. He was proclaimed as King Richard IV on attending the funeral of Emperor Frederick III in 1493, and planned to invade England with a foreign army via Ireland, much as Simnel and Lincoln had attempted. The appointment of Henry as Duke of York had been a significant move to present a legitimate bearer of that title, to which the pretender now laid claim. It was during Cecily's final weeks, in the late spring of 1495, that Warbeck gathered his armies. As she dictated her will, he was setting sail across the North Sea. Perhaps she heard that he was on his way. Margaret may even have written to her mother, explaining her belief in the young man's chances and provenance. However, by the time Warbeck's ill-fated ships appeared off the coast of Kent, the woman he claimed was his grandmother had passed away.

Cecily began dictating her will on 4 April 1495.[14] She was approaching her eightieth birthday but of 'hole mynd and body'. She followed the traditional Catholic convention of surrendering her soul into the hands of God and her body to be buried beside that of her husband Richard at Fotheringhay church. Then she began the lengthy process of dividing up and bequeathing her worldly goods. To the best of her knowledge, she was 'not muche in dett' but, if her coffers were found wanting in the execution of her will, she assigned parcels of plate, to help pay the necessary costs. To King Henry VII, she left all customs money owing to her still and two gold cups. Her granddaughter, Queen Elizabeth, received a small diamond cross, a psalter with silver clasps covered in green cloth of gold and a pyx, a little box made of wood or metal, which contained the flesh of St Christopher. To Henry's mother, Margaret Beaufort, she left a service book covered with black cloth of gold, with gold clasps. To her great-grandson, Prince Arthur, she left an arras hanging for a bed, a tester and counterpane embroidered with the image of the Wheel of Fortune and another arras 'with the pope'. To his younger brother, Henry, Duke of York, she left three arras hangings, depicting St John the Baptist, Mary Magdalene and the final one with the 'Passion of our Lord and St George'.

She left a number of religious items to the church at Fotheringhay, many for use in services: a canopy of crimson cloth, two altar cloths of crimson cloth of gold, two altar cloths of embroidered crimson damask, three Mass books, three grails and seven processioners. By way of priests' clothing, she bequeathed them two copes of crimson cloth of gold and three of embroidered blue velvet, chasubles and tunicles, for celebrating the Mass. Similar items were left to the college at Stoke Clare in Suffolk and to Syon Abbey. Her granddaughter Bridget, a fourteen-year-old nun at Dartford Priory, received Cecily's copy of *The Golden Legend* in vellum, a book of the life of St Katherine of Siena and one of Saint Matilda. Her granddaughter Cecily was the recipient of a purple velvet service book with clasps of silver and gilt as well as another 'without note'.

Other grandchildren received more practical items. Edward IV's daughter Anne, then unmarried but betrothed, was left a large bed of 'bawdekyn', a rich silk brocade, with matching counterpoint and other items, while her sister Catherine, who married that year, received a blue satin curtain or hanging. To her daughter Elizabeth, Duchess of Suffolk, Cecily left her travelling chair with its coverings, cushions, horses and harness, as well as all her palfreys. Elizabeth's de la Pole sons were also beneficiaries; Edmund received a cloth of estate and three cushions in purple damask cloth of gold, while Humphrey, who had entered holy orders, was given two altar cloths of embroidered blue damask and a vestment of crimson satin. To William de la Pole she left a curtain of white sarcenet, two beds made of down and two bolsters, while his sister Anne, Prioress of Syon Abbey, was bequeathed a jointly bound book of *Bonaventure de infancia* and Hilton's *Epistle on Mixed Life*[15] in English, as well as copy of the Revelations of St Bridget. Numerous items were left to parish churches with which Cecily had had some connection during her lifetime.

She left various gifts to her household and servants. Richard Lessy was given all the money owing to Cecily in debts, and others received items such as religious artefacts, books and clothing, also feather beds, bolsters and cushions. A John Walter received a large bequest, including a range of ceremonial objects used in the celebration of the Mass, as well as two curtains of fringed blue sarcenet, a long lantern and two little coffers. Sir John Verney and his wife Margaret were given a cross of silver, gilt and beryl, a piece of the holy cross and other 'divers relics'. Cecily also had an inn to bestow. She gave the George at Grantham to another widow, Dame Jane Pesemershe, for the term of her life, after which it would revert to the ownership of the Fotheringhay College. The George was a medieval hospital, in the sense of hosting travellers rather than a medical centre, and had been granted to Cecily by Edward IV in 1461. It remained standing until 1780. Another bequest of two religious books and an altar cover went to a John More, who may well have been a London lawyer and the father of Thomas, who would write his own version of the life of Richard III, well after Cecily's death. To a John Brown, she left 'all such stuf as belongith to the kechyn in his keeping at my place at Baynardscastell in London'. She did not forget her servants, all received something – 'all other gentilman that be daily waiting in my household … every grome … every page … every yoman'.

The will gives a wonderful insight into the lifestyle of a late medieval duchess, and reads rather like opening her coffers and rifling through her wardrobe. Richard Boyvile and his wife, Griseld, were given Cecily's chariot and horses, a purple satin gown with a train furred with ermine, a short purple gown lined with civet cat fur, a white damask kirtle, a gold spoon, a girdle decorated with a diamond, sapphire, amethyst and pearls, a little gold box with a diamond on top and a gold 'pomeamber' or pomander. Richard and Jane Brocas received more clothing, two gold-encased *Angus Dei*, which were wax talismans made from Easter candles, a string of white amber beads, another string of gold and coral, a coffer and a goblet. Nicholas and Jane Talbot were given a number of treasures: a gold spoon set with a 'sharp diamond', a variety of girdles made of gold or blue tissue, one set with columbines and diamonds, one with a buckle and pendant, also a gold hook with three roses, a 'pomeamber', of gold garnished with a diamond, six rubies and six pearls. As well as gowns, Anne Pinchbecke was left some cooking utensils: a little pot for malmsey wine and a 'possettnett' with a silver cover. Other friends received similar gowns, girdles, pendants and jewels, while Cecily left all her rings to John and Alice Metcalfe.

As her executors the duchess named a number of men with strong connections to her past and present life. There was Oliver King, Bishop of Bath and Wells, who had been clerk of the signet and then king's secretary under Edward IV. Sir Reginald Bray is a surprising inclusion, as he had been a strong Lancastrian supporter, acting as the steward of Margaret Beaufort's household and, traditionally, being the person to hand Richard III's crown to Tudor at Bosworth Field. By 1495 he had been greatly advanced by Henry VII, rising to chancellor of the duchy of Lancaster. Also of surprise is Sir Thomas Lovell, who had fought against York at Bosworth and Stoke, serving the Tudors, who had previously been attainted by Richard III. It seems likely that, in all her years of witnessing conflict and the changing fortunes of her family, Cecily had come to recognise and perhaps even value the pragmatism of certain survivors, whom she could still entrust with such a task despite their history. Her other executors were William Pinkenham, Dean of the College of Stoke Clare, William Felde, Master of Fotheringhay College, and Richard Lessy, dean of her chapel. They were to be rewarded by 'such things as shalbe delivered unto theme by my commaundement of the hondes of Sir Henry Haiden, knyght, stieward of my household and Master Richard Lessy'.

Cecily made provision for her funeral by stating that all her plate that remained un-bequeathed should be sold in order to pay 'for carrying of my body from the castell of Barkehampstead unto the colege of

Fodringhey'. She signed her name by hand, her 'signmanual', and added the imprint of her seal on 31 May 1495. She died either that same day or very soon afterwards. She was indeed buried at Fotheringhay, in the tomb that her sons had built for Richard, Duke of York, in 1476, with a papal indulgence around her neck.

Epilogue

ffarewell London, and hafe good day
At the I take my leve thys tyde
ffarewell Grenewyche, for euer and ay
ffarewell fayre place upon temys side!
ffarewell, all welth in world so wyde
I am [re]sygned where I shall be.[1]

What exactly was Cecily's contribution to history? On a purely dynastic level, she bore two kings of England and was grandmother to another. Her granddaughter became Queen of England and established a line that went on to rule in England and Scotland. She was the matriarch of the York family, a fitting partner for Richard, Duke of York, to uphold and fight for his overruled claim to the English throne. Her position was significant and ceremonial too. At York's side for decades, she was the female face of English rule in France and Ireland, following the twists and turns of his turbulent career, and mourning his violent and controversial death. She certainly acted as advisor to her son Edward in the early years of his reign, and probably to George and Richard too, exerting a formidable influence behind the scenes that directly influenced royal policy and certain challenges to it. As a woman, she had little choice but to operate within the confines of medieval society, and her gender determined that she adopt certain courses of action instead of others. Cecily was one of the most powerful ladies in the land; in fact, between 1461 and 1464, as the king's mother, she had no superior. Still, her life illuminates just how greatly she was prey to the whims of fortune and how powerless she often was in real terms. Prohibited from entering the masculine fields of combat or debate, she resorted to the tools of rumour and gossip, yet she was prepared to sacrifice her own good name in the process, if this achieved the desired result. Ultimately, she appears to have valued her regal claim above all, even when it necessitated the transcending of certain family ties. This may have contributed to situations that escalated beyond her control, with devastating consequences. Above all, Cecily was a woman of her times. But she was also far more than a typical woman of her times; she came within a hair's breadth of sitting on the throne, on the verge of realising her long-cherished ambition, before fate cruelly snatched away her opportunity to rule. Most likely she was as ruthless, determined and impulsive as she was regal, beautiful and proud. This would have made her typical of the House of York, her *raison d'être*. It should come as no surprise that she was just as committed to her cause as her husband and sons, the Yorkist answer to the Lancastrian Margaret of Anjou. Cecily was the most formidable queen that England never had.

At the time of Cecily's death in 1495, she was survived by thirteen legitimate grandchildren. Her eldest daughter, Anne, had died in 1476 while giving birth to her second child, a girl named Anne St Leger. She inherited the huge Exeter estates, and Elizabeth Wydeville took an interest in her future, planning a match between her and Thomas Grey, Lord Ferrers of Groby, who had previously been married to her half-sister, who had died before Anne was born. In 1483, an Act of Parliament settled all the Exeter lands on Anne but, following the death of her uncle, Edward IV, Anne's father supported a rebellion against Richard III and was executed. Anne was disinherited and did not marry until around the time of Cecily's death. Her husband was George Manners, Baron de Ros, who was a supporter of Henry VII. She bore him eleven children and died in 1526, being buried in St George's Chapel, Windsor. In the twenty-first century, it was Anne's genealogical line, through her daughter Catherine, that provided the mitochondrial DNA to identify the remains of Richard III.

Five of Cecily's grandchildren from her son Edward outlived her. She had witnessed his eldest daughter, Elizabeth, become queen on her marriage to Henry VII in 1486, and since then she had borne four children, including princes Arthur and Henry, who were remembered in their grandmother's will. After 1495, Elizabeth bore three, possibly four, more children, and died unexpectedly in childbirth in 1503. She was buried in the splendid new Lady Chapel that Henry VII had built for her, and he joined her there in 1509. Their eldest son, Arthur, was eight at the time of Cecily's death, a studious young man whom his father was schooling carefully for kingship. His grandmother would have considered him to be the future king, but she also knew that fate could cheat children of their inheritances and there was no guarantee of succession. It was a devastating blow for Arthur's parents and the country when he died in April 1502, shortly after his marriage to Catherine of Aragon. It left his ebullient young brother Henry to inherit the throne. He became Henry VIII in 1509. His sisters, Margaret and Mary, became queens of Scotland and France.

Edward's second daughter was named after his mother. Cecily of York had already had a turbulent marital history by 1495, having been betrothed as a child to James IV of Scotland, then to his uncle Alexander Stewart, Duke of Albany. At some point after June 1482, Cecily was married to Ralph Scrope of Masham/Upsall, brother of Lord Thomas Scrope, a supporter of her uncle Richard III, whom Vergil referred to as 'an obscure man'. Following the Battle of Bosworth, this match was annulled and she probably entered the household of Margaret Beaufort before being married to Beaufort's half-brother, John, Viscount Welles, in 1487. She played a significant part in court ceremonies at the christening of her nephew Arthur and later bore the train of his wife. She delivered three children before being widowed in 1499. Her third marriage, though, was a quite different matter. Between 1502 and 1504, she became the wife of Thomas Kyme, a Lincolnshire knight, who was considered to be an unworthy match; this appears to have been entered into for love. As a result, she was banished from court and all her lands were confiscated. The intervention of Margaret Beaufort allowed many of these to be restored to her in time but she stayed away from court, living at East Standen on the Isle of Wight. Some sources suggest she bore Kyme two children, Richard and Margaret, before she died in 1507. Her final resting place is uncertain, with the Beaufort family books claiming she died at Hatfield, suggesting a burial local to there, while the chronicler Hall claimed that she lies in Quarr Abbey on the Isle of Wight.

Edward's third surviving daughter was Anne of York. She had been betrothed as a child to Philip, son of Maximilian I, Archduke of Austria, but Edward's death meant this was allowed to lapse. She was betrothed in 1484 to the grandson and namesake of Richard III's supporter Thomas Howard, whom she married in 1495, making her the aunt of two of Henry VIII's wives, Anne Boleyn and Catherine Howard. She also played prominent roles in court ceremonies and bore at least one child. She was granted a number of lands by Henry VIII that had belonged to Richard of York's mother, Anne Mortimer, but died the following year. She was buried first in Thetford Abbey but was later moved to the Howard Mausoleum at Framlingham.

Edward also planned an illustrious future for his daughter Catherine, the ninth of his children. Initially intended for a brother of Catherine of Aragon, she was betrothed to the Duke of Ross, a younger son of James III of Scotland, in a 1487 treaty that also allied her mother with the king. Before Cecily's death, she married William Courtenay, later Earl of Devon, of Tiverton, Devon. She went on to bear three children but the family fell from favour. Having helped repel the threat to the Tudor throne from John de la Pole at Stoke in 1487, Courtenay backed a plot in favour of Pole's younger brother Richard. For this he was attainted and imprisoned in 1504, finally being pardoned by Henry VIII in 1511, shortly before he died. Catherine chose not to remarry. Just weeks after Courtenay's death, she took a vow of chastity and remained a widow until her death in 1527.

Catherine's younger sister Bridget of York entered Dartford Priory as a child in the late 1480s. She became a nun there, taking the Augustinian vows of poverty, chastity and obedience and was in receipt of charity from her sister, the queen. She died around the year 1517 and was laid to rest in the priory.

Cecily's surviving grandchildren from her daughter Elizabeth had far less good fortune. The daughter, Catherine, married Baron Stourton but produced no children, and her brother Humphrey entered the Church. However, the others suffered the consequences of being male heirs to the Yorkist throne and met with violent ends, following the death of their eldest brother, John, Richard III's heir, at Stoke.

On John's death in 1487, his brother Edmund took on the title of leading Yorkist claimant and married Margaret, daughter of Sir Richard Scrope. In 1501, he fled England to seek the assistance of Holy Roman Emperor Maximilian I in overthrowing the Tudor regime. However, he failed to get Maximilian's support and the Emperor's son Philip handed him over to England in 1506, on the promise that Henry VII would not harm him. Edmund was imprisoned on his return and Henry VII kept his word; however, his son, Henry VIII, was bound by no such promise and executed the earl in 1513.

The next de la Pole brother, William, reputedly earned the dubious honour of suffering the longest ever incarceration in the Tower of London. At the time that Edmund fled the country, he was imprisoned and remained there until his death in 1539. His youngest brother, Richard, known as the 'White Rose', fled to exile with Edmund but later moved to a place of greater safety in Hungary. In 1514, he was poised to invade England with an army of German missionaries but a French truce with Henry VIII stripped him of support. In 1523 he again planned an invasion, with the assistance of the Scots and French, but this never came to fruition. He was killed at the Battle of Pavia in 1525.

Edward, the son of George, Duke of Clarence, was equally dangerous to the Tudor regime as a male member of the York family. Cecily was still alive when Edward was imprisoned in the Tower as a boy of ten. In 1490, he was allowed to inherit his maternal grandfather's title of Earl of Warwick, but soon after Cecily's death his lineage got him in trouble. In 1499, the pretender Perkin Warbeck was incarcerated in the Tower following an attempt to escape from close supervision at the court of Henry VII. He was lodged close to Warwick and a plot was alleged to have sprung up between them, if not actively encouraged by their jailers to incriminate them. Warwick pleaded guilty at his trial that November and was executed a week later. His body was buried in the mausoleum of the Neville family at Bisham Priory, in Berkshire, which no longer survives.

Edward's sister Margaret was married in 1487 to Henry VII's cousin, Sir Richard Pole. They served in the short-lived household of Prince Arthur, with Pole acting as his chamberlain and Margaret as a lady-in-waiting to his young wife, Catherine. Margaret bore five children, and re-entered the royal household under Henry VIII. In the late 1530s, her sons rebelled against the king: Reginald fled the country, Geoffrey was pardoned and Henry was executed. Margaret was arrested on fabricated evidence and held in the Tower for over two years before being sent to the block at the age of sixty-seven.

Few of the places Cecily knew in her lifetime would be recognisable to her today. In the City of London, Westminster Palace, Baynard's Castle and Sir John Fastolf's house have long gone. All that remains of her place of retirement, Berkhamsted Castle, are a few thick walls, and there is even less of the castle where she lies buried at Fotheringhay. Ludlow still stands, with its window braces, fireplaces and doorways intact, but in order to find the one place that remains a testament to Cecily's life it is necessary to return to its beginning. Advertised today as 'one of England's finest medieval castles', Raby has remained in continual occupation since Cecily's arrival, its interiors decorated and improved to chart the different centuries. Enthralling to Victorian and modern visitors alike, its 'noble and extensive pile' unites 'great security and great antiquity'. Through the summer months, the castle throws open its gates to welcome twenty-first-century sightseers. Neville enthusiasts can pick out the dynastic badges surrounded by garters on the four-storeyed gateway and watch the sun setting behind the fourteenth-century Joan's Tower.

> Now ys my pore clene [clan] ovrthrown
> Wher I was kynge and bear the belle
> Than was I hye, now am I lowe
> God amend wikked cownsel.
>
> Sum tyme I rode in cloth of gold so redde
> Throrow-oute Ynglond in many a town
> Alas, I dare nowth schewe now my hede
> Thys word ys turnyd clene uppe so down.[2]

Notes

Introduction

1. Halsted, Caroline Amelia, *Richard III as Duke of Gloucester and King of England* (London: Longman, Brown, Green & Longmans, 1844).

Prologue, 1495

1. Paston Letters.
2. Cecily's Will.
3. *Ibid.*
4. Ordinances.
5. Will.
6. *Ibid.*
7. *Ibid.*
8. *Peachum's Compleat Gentleman* (1634).
9. *Ibid.*

1 A Significant Year, 1415

1. From Anon., *The Descyuyng of Mannes Membres* MS Digby 102, quoted in Scattergood, V. J., *Politics and Poetry in the Fifteenth Century* (Blandford Press, 1971). My translation.
2. Calendar of Patent Rolls (CPR) Henry V June 1415.
3. Riley, H. T., *Memorials of London and London Life* (1868) [Online: http://www.british-history.ac.uk/source.aspx?pubid=585, accessed 21 January 2014].

4. The Agincourt Carol.
5. Niles, J. J., *The Ballad Book of John Jacob Niles* (University of Kentucky Press, 1961).
6. Johnes, Thomas (trans.), *The Chronicles of Enguerrand de Monstrelet* (London: William Smith, 1840).
7. Bordin, de Johannes, *Henrici Quinti, Angliae Regis* (London: Sumptibus Societatis, 1850).
8. Gairdner, James (ed.), *Gregory's Chronicle 1461–9* (London, 1876).
9. Monstrelet, Enguerrard, *Chronicles* (France: W. Smith, 1840).
10. Gregory.
11. Whittock, Martyn, *A Brief History of Life in the Middle Ages* (Robinson, 2009).
12. Harding, Vanessa and Laura Wright (eds), *Bridge House Weekly Payments Book, Volume 2, London Bridge, Selected Accounts and Rentals 1381–1538 (1995)* [Online: http://www.british-history. ac.uk/source.aspx?pubid=1273, accessed 21 January 2014].
13. *Ibid.*
14. *Ibid.*
15. *Ibid.*
16. Anon. (previously attributed to Lydgate, John), *London Lickpenny.*
17. Nichols, John Gough (ed.), *London Pageants 1: An Account of Sixty Royal Processions and Entertainments in the city of London, chiefly extracted from contemporary writers* (J. B. Nichols & Son, 1831).
18. *Ibid.*
19. *Ibid.*
20. *Ibid.*
21. Andrews, Allen, *Kings and Queens of England and Scotland* (London: Marshall Cavendish Publications, 1976).
22. Nichols.
23. Bordin.
24. Usk, Adam of, *Chronicon Adae de Usk 1377–1421* (trans. Edward Maunde Thompson) (London: H. Frowde, 1904).
25. Nichols.
26. Usk.
27. Nichols.
28. Gregory.
29. Nichols.

2 'Rose of Raby', 1415–1429

1. Lydgate, John. From 'On Forked Headdresses' in Nicolas, Nicholas Harris, *A Chronicle of London from 1089 to 1483* (1827).
2. F. M. L., *The Visitor's Guide to Raby Castle, Barnard Castle and the neighbourhood.* (London: Whittaker & Co., 1857).
3. *Ibid.*
4. Lewis, Samuel, *A Topographical Dictionary of England* (1840) [Online: http://www.british-history.ac.uk/source.aspx?pubid=445, accessed 21 January 2014].
5. F. M. L.
6. *Ibid.*
7. *Ibid.*
8. http://rootingforancestors.blogspot.co.uk/2009/02/ralph-neville-1st-earl-westmorland-1364.html.
9. http://www.geni.com/people/Gilbert-de-Neville-c-1115/6000000003051190882.
10. http://www.geni.com/people/Gilbert-de-Neville/6000000002302694490.
11. Ibid.
12. Windeatt, B. A. (ed.), *The Book of Margery Kempe* (Penguin, 2000).
13. *Ibid.*
14. Page, William (ed.), *A History of the County of Durham, Volume 2, Victoria County History* (1907) [Online: http://www.british-history.ac.uk/source.aspx?pubid=241, accessed 21 January 2014].
15. http://www.stmarysstaindrop.org.uk/Staindrop/History.html.
16. Twemlow, J. A., *Calendar of Papal Registers relating to Great Britain and Ireland, Volume 7 1417–1431* (1906) [Online: http://www.british-history.ac.uk/source.aspx?pubid=986, accessed 21 January 2014].
17. F. M. L.
18. *Ibid.*
19. *The Regulations and Establishment of the Household of Henry Algernon Percy, the fifth Earl of Northumberland, at his castles of Wresill and Lekinfield in Northumberland in Yorkshire* (London, 1770).
20. F. M. L.
21. Rickert, Edith (ed.), *The Babees' Book or Medieval Manners for the Young* (Chatto & Windus, 1908).

22. *Gregory's Chronicle* for 1421.
23. James I of Scotland, *The Kingis Quair* (ed. Walter Skeat) (Edinburgh: Blackwood & Sons, 1911).

3 Duke of York, 1411–1429

1. 'Antona's Banks' (1797), quoted in Bonney, H. K., *Historical Notices in Reference to Fotheringhay* (2011).
2 Rymer's *Foedera*.
3. *Ibid.*
4. Calendar of Fine Rolls (CFR) Henry V, August 1415.
5. CFR Hen. V April 1416.
6. CFR Hen. V August 1415.
7. As researched by Paul Fairbrass.
8. CFR Hen V August 1415.
9. *Ibid.*
10. Edginton, Brian W., *Charles Waterton: A Biography* (James Clarke & Co., 1996).
11. The Peerage.
12. Scattergood.
13. Johnson, P. A., *Duke Richard of York 1411–1460* (Oxford Historical Monographs, 1988).
14. Calendar of Close Rolls (CCR), Henry VI, Volume 1, membrane dated 1423.
15. CCR Henry VI, November 1426.
16. *Ibid.*
17. CCR Hen. VI August 1431.
18. Griffiths, R. A., *The Reign of King Henry VI* (Ernest Benn, 1981).
19. Paston Letters.
20. Griffiths.
21. Paston Letters.
22. *Ibid.*
23. *A Collection of Ordinances and Regulations for the Governance of the Royal Household, made in divers reigns from King Edward III to King William and Queen Mary* (London: Society of Antiquities, 1790).
24. Bentley, Samuel (ed.), *Excerpta Historica* (1831).
25. *Oxford Dictionary of National Biography.*
26. Thank you to DeAnn Smith for her very helpful discussions with me regarding the location of Westminster marriages.

27. *Gregory's Chronicle.*
28. *Ibid.*
29. *Ibid.*
30. *Ibid.*
31. *Ibid.*
32. *Ibid.*

4 His Young Duchess, 1429–1437

1. 'The Assembly of Ladies', Anonymous medieval poem, ed. Derek Pearsall, University of Rochester online TEAMS texts.
2. Shahar, Shulamith, *The Fourth Estate: A History of Women in the Middle Ages* (Methuen, 1983).
3. Licence, Amy, *In Bed with the Tudors* (Amberley, 2012).
4. Amt, Emilie, *Women's Lives in Medieval Europe: A Sourcebook* (Routledge, 1993).
5. 'The Chronicle of the Grey Friars: Henry VI', *Chronicle of the Grey Friars of London: Camden Society Old Series,* 53 (1852), pp. 15–21.
6. CCR Hen. VI Feb 1430.
7. *Ibid.*
8. Griffiths.
9. *Ibid.*
10. Amt.
11. DNB.
12. CCR Hen. VI May 1432.
13. CCR Hen. VI May 1433.
14. *Ibid.*
15. CCR Hen. VI May 1433.
16. Barbican Research Associates
17. CCR Hen. VI May 1433.
18. *Ibid.*
19. Crawford, Anne, *The Yorkists: The History of a Dynasty* (Hambledon Continuum, 2007).
20. CCR Hen. VI July 1435.
21. Ordinances.
22. http://www.winchelsea.net/visiting/winchelsea_history_pt14.htm.
23. Rymer's *Foedera.*
24. Cook, Sir Theodore Andrea, *The Story of Rouen* (J. M. Dent, 1899).

25. Spear, David S., 'Rouen Médiéval: Medieval Art, Architecture and Archaeology at Rouen', *Persée*, 45 (1995), pp. 460–462.
26. Nicolas, Sir Harris (ed.), *Proceedings and Ordinances of the Privy Council of England* (POPCE), V, 15 Henry IV to 21 Henry VI (PRO, 1835).
27. Johnson, P. A.

5 Becoming a Mother, 1438–1442

1. From 'The Chastity of Wives', John Audelay.
2. Nicolas.
3. *Ibid.*
4. Griffiths.
5. Johnson.
6. POPCE Volume V, Nov 1440, 15 Henry IV to 21 Henry VI.
7. Griffiths.
8. POPCE Volume V, March 1441.
9. *Ibid.*, May 1441.
10. *Ibid.*
11. Gristwood, Sarah, *Blood Sisters* (Harper Press, 2012).
12. *Ibid.*
13. Jones, Michael, *Bosworth 1485* (The History Press, 2003).
14. Wilkinson, Josephine, *Richard III: The Young King to Be* (Amberley, 2009).
15. Scattergood.
16. Chiquart, Maistre, *Du Fait de Cuisine* (trans. Elizabeth Cook).
17. National Archives.
18. Dufferwiel, Martin, *Durham: Over 1,000 Years of History and Legend* (Mainstream, 1996).
19. Philips, Kim M., *Medieval Maidens: Young Women and Gender in England 1270–1540* (Manchester University Press, 2003).
20. See *Gregory's Chronicle* for 1441 and Griffiths, whose footnote 102, p. 477 also cites *Brut* p. 477 and Flenley, R., 'London and Foreign Merchants in the reign of Henry VI', *English Historical Review*, XXV (1910), pp. 644–655.
21. Jones.

6 The Question of Edward, 1442–1445

1. Gregory, Philippa, *The White Queen* (Touchstone, 2009).
2. Griffiths.
3. Stevenson, Joseph (ed.), *Letters and Papers Illustrative of the Wars of the English in France in the Reign of Henry VI, King of England* (Longman Green, 1841).
4. Weightman, Christine, *Margaret of York, Duchess of Burgundy, 1446–1503* (New York: St Martin's Press, 1989).
5. Ross, Charles, *Edward IV* (Yale University Press, 1997).
6. Stevenson.
7. Griffiths.
8. Scattergood.
9. Griffiths.
10. Johnson.

7 Loss of Focus, 1446–1452

1. Scattergood.
2. CPR Hen. VI Oct. 1446.
3. Shahar.
4. CPR Hen. VI July 1447.
5. Crawford, *The Yorkists.*
6. *Ibid.*
7. CPR Hen. VI May 1447.
8. Johnson.
9. Oxford DNB entry 'Mulso family'.
10. Johnson.
11. *Ibid.*
12. Griffiths.
13. Johnson.
14. *Ibid.*
15. Harvey, John H., 'Westminster Abbey: The Infirmarer's Garden', *Journal of Garden History*, 2(2) (1992).
16. CPR Hen. VI May 1449.
17. *Ibid.*, April.
18. *Ibid.*, July.
19. Dufferwiel.
20. Curtis.
21. Dufferwiel.

22. Curtis.
23. Dufferwiel.
24. Irish Chancery Rolls 1449.
25. Dufferwiel.
26. *Ibid.*
27. *Letters & Papers Illustrative.*
28. Paston Letters.
29. *Ibid.*
30. Brewer and Bullen (eds), *The Calendar of Carew*, MSS Book of Howth, cited in Johnson.
31. Maddocks, Sydney, 'Old Ford', *The Copartnership Herald*, 3(31) (1933).
32. Paston Letters.
33. *Excerpta Historica.*
34. Paston Letters.
35. *Ibid.*
36. Giles, John Allen, *The Chronicles of the White Rose of York* (London: James Bohn, 1845).
37. Paston Letters.

8 The Lord Protector's Wife, 1453–1455

1. 'The Lament of Eleanor Cobham' (1446) in R. H. Robbins (ed.), *Historical Poems of the XIVth and XVth centuries* (New York, 1959).
2. Page, William (ed.), *A History of the County of Hertfordshire* (1912) [Online: http://www.british-history.ac.uk/source.aspx?pubid=306, accessed 21 January 2014].
3. Hile, Reginald, *Hitchin Priory* (Carling and Hales, 1918).
4. Translated by Rawcliffe, BIHR (Huntingdon Library, 1987), pp. 237–8. Reproduced in Crawford, Anne, *Letters of Medieval Women* (Sutton, 2002).
5. CPR Hen. VI Dec 1453.
6. Griffiths.
7. Paston Letters, Vol. 2, p. 235.
8. CPR Hen. VI April 1454.
9. *Ibid.*
10. Paston Letters, Vol. 2, p. 235.
11. Halsted.
12. *Ibid.*

13. Johnson.
14. *Ibid.*
15. *Ibid.*
16. Halsted.
17. Ordinances.
18. *Ibid.*
19. Amt.
20. Pollard, Anthony, 'Percies, Nevilles and the Wars of the Roses' *History Today*, 43(9) (1993).
21. Griffiths.
22. Ordinances.
23. Crawford, *Letters.*
24. CPR, Hen. VI March 1455.
25. Griffiths.
26. *Ibid.*
27. *The Chronicles of the White Rose of York.*

9 Fortunes of War, 1455–1459

1. Scattergood.
2. Griffiths.
3. Paston Letters, Vol. 3, p. 285.
4. Scattergood.
5. *Ibid.*
6. Paston Letters, Vol. 3, p. 287.
7. *Ibid.*, p. 322.
8. *Ibid.*
9. *Ibid.*
10. Griffiths.
11. *Ibid.*
12. *Ibid.*
13. Paston Letters, Vol. 3, p. 348.
14. Robbins.
15. Johnson.
16. Clark, Linda (ed.), *Of Mice and Men: Image, Belief and Regulation in Late Medieval England* (Boydell Press, 2005).
17. *Ibid.*
18. *Ibid.*
19. *Ibid.*
20. *Ibid.*

21. *Ibid.*
22. *Ibid.*
23. *Ibid.*
24. *Ibid.*
25. Blatherwick, Simon and Richard Bluer, 'Great Houses, Moats and Mills on the South Bank of the Thames: Medieval and Tudor Southwark and Rotherhithe', *Museum of London Archaeology Monograph 47* (Museum of London Archaeology, 2009), pp. xvii, 246.
26. *Ibid.*
27. Seward, *A Brief History of the Wars of the Roses* (Robinson Publishing, 2007).
28. Scattergood.
29. Gairdner.
30. Griffiths.
31. Clive, Henry Robert, *Documents Relating to the History of Ludlow* (J. Van Vorst, 1841).
32. Davies, J. S. (ed.), *An English Chronicle of the Reigns of Richard II, Henry IV, Henry V and Henry VI* (London: Camden Society, 1856).
33. CPR Hen. VI Oct. 1459.
34. Ross, *Edward IV.*

10 Fickle Fortune, 1459–1460

1. Shakespeare, William, *Henry VI, Part 3.*
2. Rawcliffe.
3. *Ibid.*
4. Wilkinson.
5. *Ibid.*
6. CPR Hen. VI Jan. 1460.
7. *Ibid.*, Feb.
8. *Ibid.*, June.
9. *Ibid.*, Feb.
10. *Ibid.*, March.
11. *Ibid.*
12. *Ibid.*, April.
13. *Ibid.*, June.
14. *Ibid.*
15. Robbins

16. Warkworth.
17. Scattergood.
18. *Ibid.*
19. Halsted.
20. Paston Letters, Vol. 3.
21. Johnson.
22. Gristwood.
23. http://http://www.herefordshire.gov.uk/1172.aspx.
24. Warkworth.
25. Paston Letters, Vol. 3, p. 419.
26. Wyrcester.
27. Griffiths.
28. Bib. Nat. MS Fr. 20136 fo. 6.
29. Seward.
30. Warkworth.
31. *Ibid.*
32. Johnson.
33. *Rotuli Parliamentorum* 39 Henry VI 1460.
34. *Ibid.*
35. *Annales.*
36. Johnson.
37. Dockray, Keith and Richard Knowles, *The Battle of Wakefield* (Wakefield M. D. Council, 1999).
38. CSP Milan 9 Jan. 1461.
39. Hall.
40. Wilkinson.
41. Griffiths.

11 In the Name of the Father, 1461–1464

1. Shakespeare, William, *Richard III.*
2. Crawford, *Letters.*
3. CSP Milan 1461.
4. Croyland.
5. Ross, *Edward IV.*
6. *Ibid.*
7. *Gregory's Chronicle.*
8. Croyland.
9. Robbins.
10. Scattergood.

11. Paston Letters, Vol. 3, p. 450.
12. Gristwood.
13. Dockray.
14. Gregory.
15. Gairdner's introduction to the Paston Letters.
16. Paston Letters, Vol. 3. p. 460, n. 5.
17. Russell, *Boke of Nurture* (1460).
18. Paston Letters, Vol. 3, p. 460.
19. Russell.
20. Paston Letters, Vol. 3, p. 460.
21. Russell.
22. CPR Ed. IV June 1461.
23. *Ibid.*, Oct.
24. *Foedera.*
25. CPR Ed. IV Feb. 1462.
26. Johnson.
27. CPR Ed. IV Feb. 1464.
28. *Ibid.*, July.
29. *Ibid.*, Feb. 1462.
30. BL Western MS Add Ch 16564:1462
31. CPR Ed. IV Feb./May 1462.
32. *Ibid.*
33. *Ibid.*, 1463.
34. *Ibid.*, 1462.
35. *Foedera.*
36. CPR Hen. VI Jan./Feb. 1462.
37. *Foedera.*
38. *Ibid.*
39. CPR Hen. VI 1461.
40. Hicks.
41. Croyland.
42. Gregory.
43. Dockray.
44. CPR Ed. IV 1464.
45. Fabyan.
46. Croyland.
47. Dockray.
48. Vergil.
49. Dockray.
50. Mancini.

51. Robbins.
52. Both poems can be found in Robbins.
53. More.
54. *Ibid.*

12 A Family at Love and War, 1465–1471

1. Anonymous poem, Scattergood.
2. Petrina, Alessandra, *Cultural Politics in Fifteenth Century England* (Netherlands: Brill, 2004).
3. British History Online.
4. Ross, *Edward IV.*
5. *Rotuli Parliamentorum.*
6. *Ibid.*
7. Gristwood.
8. Leland.
9. Thanks to Karen Clark for sharing her thoughts on this with me.
10. *Foedera.*
11. *Excerpta Historica.*
12. CPR Ed. IV.
13. Power, Eileen, *The Wool Trade in English Medieval History* (Ford Lectures, 1941).
14. CPR Ed. IV March 1469.
15. http://www.heritagegateway.org.uk/Gateway/Results_Single.aspx ?uid=MHT39&resourceID=1008.
16. CSP Milan 1467.
17. Croyland.
18. Dockray.
19. *Ibid.*
20. *Annales.*
21. *Ibid.*
22. CPR Ed. IV July 1468.
23. Jones.
24. Warkworth.
25. Croyland.
26. Dockray.
27. *Ibid.*
28. CPR Ed. IV Apr. 1469.
29. *Ibid.*
30. *Chronicle of the White Rose.*

31. *Ibid.*
32. Commines.
33. Dockray.
34. Croyland.
35. Gristwood.
36. *Great Chronicle of London.*
37. Paston Letters.
38. *Ibid.*
39. Griffiths.

13 The King's Mother, 1472–1483

1. Shakespeare, *Richard III.*
2. Croyland.
3. Crawford, *The Yorkists.*
4. Dockray.
5. Sweetinburgh, Sheila (ed.), *Late Medieval Kent 1220–1540* (Boydell & Brewer, 2010).
6. CPR Ed. IV Nov 1472.
7. CPR Ed. IV May 1475.
8. CPR Ed. IV June 1475.
9. Camidge, Charles Edward, *A History of Wakefield and its Industrial and Fine Art Exhibition* (Hamilton, Adams & Co., 1866).
10. Banks, William Stott, *Walks in Yorkshire: Wakefield* (Longmans, 1871).
11. SEAX D/DCe L63.
12. Crawford, *Letters.*
13. *Ibid.*
14. Hammond, P. W., Anne F. Sutton and Livia Visser-Fuchs, *The Reburial of Richard, Duke of York, 21–30 July 1476* (Richard III Society, 1996).
15. *Ibid.*
16. *Ibid.*
17. Ross, Edward IV.
18. Paston Letters.
19. *Ibid.*
20. *Rotuli Parliamentorum.*
21. *Ibid.*
22. *Ibid.*
23. *Ibid.*

24. *Ibid.*
25. Mancini.
26. Weightman.

14 Slanders, 1483–1485

1. Poem reputed to be by Anthony Wydeville, *The Chronicles of the White Rose.*
2. Ordinances, see Chapter 15 for more detail.
3. Croyland.
4. More on this in Licence, A., *Anne Neville.*
5. Croyland.
6. *Ibid.*
7. Dockray.
8. Ross, *Richard III* (1999).
9. Paston Letters.
10. Cely Letters.
11. Paston Letters.
12. Ross, *Richard III.*
13. *Ibid.*
14. *Ibid.*
15. *Ibid.*
16. Jones.
17. *Ibid.*
18. Legge, Alfred Owen, *The Unpopular King: The Life and Times of Richard III* (Ward & Downey, 1885).
19. Petre.
20. Croyland.
21. *Ibid.*
22. Jones.

15 Old Age, 1485–1495

1. Deschamps, Eustace in Coss, Peter, *The Lady in Medieval England 1000–1500* (Sutton, 1998).
2. Hilton, Walter, *The Scale of Perfection* (London: James Philp, 1870).
3. Ordinances.
4. *Ibid.*
5. *Ibid.*

6. *Ibid.*
7. CPR Hen. VII Feb. 1486.
8. Johnson.
9. CPR Hen. VII June 1486.
10. *Ibid.*, Nov.
11. *Ibid.*, Jan. 1489.
12. *Ibid.*
13. *Ibid.*, Feb. 1492.
14. All quotations from Ordinances.
15. Spedding, Alison J., 'At the King's Pleasure: The Testament of Cecily Neville', *Midland History*, 35(2) (2010), pp. 256–272.

Epilogue

1. Anon., 'The Ballad of Eleanor Cobham' in Robbins.
2. Anon., 'God Amend Wikkid Cownsel' in Robbins.

Bibliography

Primary Sources

A Collection of Ordinances and Regulations for the Governance of the Royal Household, made in divers reigns from King Edward III to King William and Queen Mary (London: Society of Antiquities, 1790).

Amt, Emilie (ed.), *Women's Lives in Medieval Europe: A Sourcebook* (Routledge, 1993).

Anon. (previously attributed to Lydgate, John), *London Lickpenny.*

Bentley, Samuel (ed.), *Excerpta Historica* (1831).

Bird, W. H. B and K. H. Ledward (eds), *Calendar of State Papers, Henry VI, Edward IV, Edward V, Richard III* (1953).

Bordin, de Johannes, *Henrici Quinti, Angliae Regis* (London: Sumptibus Societatis, 1850).

Calendar of Close Rolls, Edward IV 1461–1468.

Calendar of Close Rolls, Henry VI 1422–1461 and 1470–1471.

Calendar of Fine Rolls, Henry V 1413–1422.

Calendar of Fine Rolls, Henry VI, 1422–1461.

Calendar of Patent Rolls, Henry VI 1422–1461.

Calendar of State Papers of Milan 1385–1618.

Clive, Henry Robert, *Documents Relating to the History of Ludlow* (J. Van Vorst, 1841).

Davies, J. S. (ed.), *An English Chronicle of the Reigns of Richard II, Henry IV, Henry V and Henry VI* (London: Camden Society, 1856).

Ellis, Henry (ed.), *New Chronicles of England and France in two parts by Robert Fabyan, 1516* (London, 1811).

Ellis, Henry (ed.), *Three Books of Polydore Vergil's English History, comprising the reigns of Henry VI, Edward IV and Richard III* (Camden Society, 1844).

Furnivall, Frederick J., *Early English Meals and Manners* (Oxford University Press, 1868).

Gairdner, James (ed.), *Gregory's Chronicle 1461–9* (London, 1876).

Gairdner, James (ed.), *The Paston Letters* (Alan Sutton, 1986).

Gairdner, James (ed.), *The Paston Letters, 1422–1509* (Edinburgh: John Grant, 1910).

Giles, John Allen, *The Chronicles of the White Rose of York* (London: James Bohn, 1845).

Hali Maidenhad in Amt, Emilie, *Women's Lives in Medieval Europe, A Sourcebook* (Routledge, 1993).

Harding, Vanessa and Laura Wright (eds), *Bridge House Weekly Payments Book, Volume 2, London Bridge, Selected Accounts and Rentals 1381–1538 (1995)* [Online: http://www.british-history.ac.uk/source.aspx?pubid=1273, accessed 21 January 2014].

Hilton, Walter, *The Scale of Perfection* (London: James Philp, 1870).

Irish Chancery Letters, Patent Roll 28 Henry VI 1449–1450.

James I of Scotland, *The Kingis Quair* (ed. Walter Skeat) (Edinburgh: Blackwood & Sons, 1911).

Johnes, Thomas (trans.), *The Chronicles of Enguerrand de Monstrelet* (London: William Smith, 1840).

Monstrelet, Enguerrard, *Chronicles* (France: W. Smith, 1840).

Nichols, John Gough (ed.), *London Pageants 1: An Account of Sixty Royal Processions and Entertainments in the city of London, chiefly extracted from contemporary writers* (J. B. Nichols & Son, 1831).

Nichols, John Gough and John Bruce (eds), *Wills from Doctors' Commons 1495–1693* (Camden Society, 1863).

Nicolas, Sir Harris (ed.), *Proceedings and Ordinances of the Privy Council of England*, V, 15 Henry IV to 21 Henry VI (PRO, 1835).

Rickert, Edith (ed.), *The Babees' Book or Medieval Manners for the Young* (Chatto & Windus, 1908).

Riley, H. T., *Memorials of London and London Life* (1868) [Online: http://www.british-history.ac.uk/source.aspx?pubid=585, accessed 21 January 2014].

Robbins, R. H. (ed.), *Historical Poems of the XIVth and XVth centuries* (New York, 1959).

Rotuli Parliamentorum, Volume 5: 1439–1472.

Rymer, Thomas, *Foedera* (1704–1713).

Scattergood, V. J., *Politics and Poetry in the Fifteenth Century* (Blandford Press, 1971).

Stevenson, Joseph (ed.), *Letters and Papers Illustrative of the Wars of the English in France in the Reign of Henry VI, King of England* (Longman Green, 1841).

'The Chronicle of the Grey Friars: Henry VI', *Chronicle of the Grey Friars of London: Camden Society Old Series*, 53 (1852), pp. 15–21.

The Regulations and Establishment of the Household of Henry Algernon Percy, the fifth Earl of Northumberland, at his castles of Wresill and Lekinfield in Northumberland in Yorkshire (London, 1770).

Twemlow, J. A., *Calendar of Papal Registers relating to Great Britain and Ireland, Volume 7 1417–1431* (1906) [Online: http://www.british-history.ac.uk/source.aspx?pubid=986, accessed 21 January 2014].

Usk, Adam of, *Chronicon Adae de Usk 1377–1421* (trans. Edward Maunde Thompson) (London: H. Frowde, 1904).

Various medieval lyrics, University of Rochester online TEAMS texts [Online: http://d.lib.rochester.edu/teams/text-online, accessed 21 January 2014].

Windeatt, B. A. (ed.), *The Book of Margery Kempe* (Penguin, 2000).

Secondary Sources

Andrews, Allen, *Kings and Queens of England and Scotland* (London: Marshall Cavendish Publications, 1976).

Archer, Rowena E. and Simon Walker (eds), *Rulers and Ruled in Late Medieval England* (Hambledon Press, 1995).

Banks, William Stott, *Walks in Yorkshire: Wakefield* (Longmans, 1871).

Blatherwick, Simon and Richard Bluer, 'Great Houses, Moats and Mills on the South Bank of the Thames: Medieval and Tudor Southwark and Rotherhithe', *Museum of London Archaeology Monograph 47* (Museum of London Archaeology, 2009), pp. xvii, 246.

Camidge, Charles Edward, *A History of Wakefield and its Industrial and Fine Art Exhibition* (Hamilton, Adams & Co., 1866).

Chiquart, Maistre, *Du Fait de Cuisine* (trans. Elizabeth Cook) [Online: http://www.daviddfriedman.com/Medieval/Cookbooks/Du_Fait_de_Cuisine/du_fait_de_c_contents.html, accessed 21 January 2014].

Clark, Linda (ed.), *Of Mice and Men: Image, Belief and Regulation in Late Medieval England* (Boydell Press, 2005).

Cook, Sir Theodore Andrea, *The Story of Rouen* (J. M. Dent, 1899).

Coss, Peter, *The Lady in Medieval England 1000–1500* (Sutton, 1998).

Crawford, Anne, *Letters of Medieval Women* (Sutton, 2002).

Crawford, Anne, *The Yorkists: The History of a Dynasty* (Hambledon Continuum, 2007).

Curtis, Edmund, 'Richard, Duke of York, as Viceroy of Ireland 1447–1460', *The Journal of the Royal Society of Antiquaries of Ireland*, Seventh Series, 2(2) (1932), pp. 158–186.

Dockray, Keith and Richard Knowles, *The Battle of Wakefield* (Wakefield M. D. Council, 1999).

Dufferwiel, Martin, *Durham: Over 1,000 Years of History and Legend* (Mainstream, 1996).

Edginton, Brian W., *Charles Waterton: A Biography* (James Clarke & Co., 1996).

F. M. L., *The Visitor's Guide to Raby Castle, Barnard Castle and the Neighbourhood* (London: Whittaker & Co. London, 1857).

Fritze, Ronald M. and William Robinson, *Historical Dictionary of Late Medieval England 1272–1485* (Greenwood, 2002).

Fryde, E. B., *Studies in Medieval Trade and Finance* (Continuum, 1993).

Gilbert, J. T., *History of the Viceroys of Ireland with Notices of the Castle of Dublin* (J. Duffy, 1865).

Gordon, G. S. (ed.), *Peachum's Compleat Gentleman 1634* (The Clarendon Press, 1906).

Gregory, Philippa, *The White Queen* (Touchstone, 2009).

Gregory, Philippa, David Baldwin and Michael Jones, *The Women of the Cousin's War* (Simon and Schuster, 2011).

Griffiths, R. A., *The Reign of King Henry VI* (Ernest Benn, 1981).

Gristwood, Sarah, *Blood Sisters* (Harper Press, 2012).

Halsted, Caroline Amelia, *Richard III as Duke of Gloucester and King of England* (London: Longman, Brown, Green & Longmans, 1844).

Hammond, P. W., Anne F. Sutton and Livia Visser-Fuchs, *The Reburial of Richard, Duke of York, 21–30 July 1476* (Richard III Society, 1996).

Harvey, John H., 'Westminster Abbey: The Infirmarer's Garden', *Journal of Garden History*, 2(2) (1992).

Hicks, Michael, *Warwick the Kingmaker* (Blackwell, 1998).

Higginbotham, Susan, *The Woodvilles* (The History Press, 2012).

Hile, Reginald, *Hitchin Priory* (Carling & Hales, 1918).

Johnson, P. A., *Duke Richard of York 1411–1460* (Oxford Historical Monographs, 1988).

Laynesmith, J. L., *The Last Medieval Queens: English Queenship 1445–1503* (Oxford University Press, 2004).

Lewis, Samuel, *A Topographical Dictionary of England* (1840) [Online: http://www.british-history.ac.uk/source.aspx?pubid=445, accessed 21 January 2014].

Leyser, Henrietta, *Medieval Women; A Social History of Women in England 450–1500* (Weidenfeld & Nicolson, 1995).

Licence, Amy, *In Bed with the Tudors* (Stroud: Amberley, 2012).

Maddocks, Sydney, 'Old Ford', *The Copartnership Herald*, 3(31) (1933).

Niebrzydowski, Sue (ed.), *Middle-Aged Women in the Middle-Ages* (D. S. Brewer, 2011).

Niles, J. J., *The Ballad Book of John Jacob Niles* (University of Kentucky Press, 1961).

Pearson, Andrea G., *Envisioning Gender in Burgudian Devotional Art 1350–1530* (Ashgate Publishing, 2005).

Petrina, Alessandra, *Cultural Politics in Fifteenth Century England* (Netherlands: Brill, 2004).

Philips, Kim M., *Medieval Maidens: Young Women and Gender in England 1270–1540* (Manchester University Press, 2003).

Pollard, Anthony, 'Percies, Nevilles and the Wars of the Roses', *History Today*, 43(9) (1993).

Power, Eileen, *The Wool Trade in English Medieval History* (Ford Lectures, 1941).

Pugh, T. B., 'Richard, Duke of York, and the Rebellion of Henry Holland, Duke of Exeter, in May 1454', *Historical Research*, 63(152) (1990), pp. 248–262.

Rawcliffe, Carol, *The Staffords: Earls of Stafford and Dukes of Buckingham 1394–1521* (Cambridge University Press, 1978).

Ross, Charles, *Edward IV* (Yale University Press, 1997).

Ross, Charles, *Richard III* (Yale University Press, 1999).

'St Mary's Staindrop Church, Staindrop' [Online: http://www.stmarysstaindrop.org.uk/Staindrop/History.html, accessed 21 January 2014].

Seward, *A Brief History of the Wars of the Roses* (Robinson Publishing, 2007).

Shahar, Shulamith, *The Fourth Estate: A History of Women in the Middle Ages* (Methuen, 1983).

Spear, David S., 'Rouen Médiéval: Medieval Art, Architecture and Archaeology at Rouen', *Persée*, 45 (1995), pp. 460–462.

Spedding, Alison J., 'At the King's Pleasure: The Testament of Cecily Neville', *Midland History*, 35(2) (2010), pp. 256–272.

Spriggs, Gereth M., 'The Nevill Hours and the School of Hermann Scheerre', *Journal of the Warburg and Courtauld Institutes*, 37 (1974), pp. 104–130.

Sweetinburgh, Sheila (ed.), *Late Medieval Kent 1220–1540* (Boydell & Brewer, 2010).

Tytler, Patrick Fraser, *History of Scotland, Volume 3* (Edinburgh: William Tait, 1829).

Weightman, Christine, *Margaret of York, Duchess of Burgundy, 1446–1503* (New York: St Martin's Press, 1989).

Weir, Alison, *Lancaster and York: The Wars of the Roses* (Vintage, 1995).

Weir, Alison, *The Princes in the Tower* (Vintage, 2008).

Whittock, Martyn, *A Brief History of Life in the Middle Ages* (Robinson, 2009).

Wilkinson, Josephine, *Richard III: The Young King to Be* (Amberley, 2009).

List of Illustrations

1. Henry V. Courtesy of Ripon Cathedral.
2. Henry V and Catherine of Valois. Courtesy of Jonathan Reeve, JR1729b90fp85 14001500.
3. Raby Castle, the Neville Gate. Courtesy of Kristie Dean.
4. Raby Castle. Courtesy of Kristie Dean.
5. Rood screen in Staindrop church. Courtesy of Kristie Dean.
6. Effigy of Joan Beaufort. Courtesy of Kristie Dean.
7. Julian of Norwich. Courtesy of Anne Lord.
8. Falcon and Fetterlock. Courtesy of Simon Leach.
9. Falcon and Fetterlock misericord, Ludlow church. Courtesy of Anne Lord.
10. Ruins of Fotheringhay Castle. Courtesy of David Noble.
11. St Mary and All Saints' church, Fotheringhay. Courtesy of Amanda Miller at Amanda's Arcadia.
12. Window, Fotheringhay church. Courtesy of Simon Leach.
13. Richard, Duke of York, in Ludlow church. Courtesy of Anne Lord.
14. Rouen Cathedral. Courtesy of Geoff Licence.
15. Medieval Rouen. Courtesy of Paul Fairbrass.
16. Medieval Rouen. Courtesy of Geoff licence.
17. Rouen's *Gros Horloge*. Courtesy of Geoff Licence.
18. Dublin Castle. Courtesy of Alan Jue Liu.
19. Ludlow Castle. Courtesy of Philip Blayney.
20. Ludlow Castle. Courtesy of Philip Blayney.
21. Ludlow Castle. Samuel Scott, c. 1765–69. Courtesy of the Yale Center for British Art, Paul Mellon Collection.
22. Henry VI. Courtesy of Jonathan Reeve, JR1561folio6

23. Millennium Bridge. Courtesy of Alan Lavish.
24. Edward IV. Bernard Lens, 1732. Courtesy of the Yale Center for British Art.
25. Elizabeth Woodville. Courtesy of Ripon Cathedral.
26. Caister Castle. Michael 'Angelo' Rooker, n.d. Yale Center for British Art, Paul Mellon Collection
27. Tonbridge Castle. Amy Licence.
28. Tonbridge Castle. Amy Licence.
29. Tomb of Joan Neville. Courtesy of Amanda Miller at Amanda's Arcadia.
30. Plaque for the Paston House. Courtesy of Paul Fairbrass.
31. The site of the Paston House. Courtesy of Paul Fairbrass.
32. Sandwich, Kent. Courtesy of Jane Ring.
33. Berkhamsted Castle. Courtesy of Alan Lavish.
34. Berkhamsted Castle well. Courtesy of Alan Lavish.
35. Windsor Castle. Artist unknown, seventeenth century. Courtesy of the Yale Center for British Art, Paul Mellon Collection.
36. Edward V. Courtesy of David Baldwin.
37. Princes in the Tower. William Marshall Craig, *c.* 1820. Courtesy of the Yale Center for British Art.
38. Richard III. Courtesy of Ripon Cathedral.
39. Anne Neville. Courtesy of Jonathan Reeve, JR JR1731b90fp109C 14001500
40. Elizabeth of York. Courtesy of Amanda Miller at Amanda's Arcadia. Thanks also to the Reverend Canon of Leicestershire.
41. Tomb of Thomas Bourchier. Amy Licence.
42. *Richard, Duke of Gloucester, and the Lady Anne* by Edwin Austin Abbey. Courtesy of the Yale University Art Gallery, Edwin Austin Abbey Memorial Collection.
43. Madonna and Child, Fordwich church. Amy Licence.
44. Margaret Beaufort. Courtesy of Elizabeth Norton.
45. Henry VII and Henry VIII by Holbein. Courtesy of Elizabeth Norton.
46. Fotheringhay memorial. Courtesy of Simon Leach.
47. Raby Castle in the 1930s. Courtesy of Keith.

Acknowledgements

Thanks go to the team at Amberley: Jonathan, Nicola, Nicki, Alice, Christian and others for their continuing support and promotion. Thank you also to Derek Bull for confirming my belief that Cecily deserved a book of her own. I have also been particularly lucky to have made some wonderfully helpful and knowledgeable friends online, who have generously shared their thoughts and time with me, in particular the members of my Edward IV discussion group. Thanks also to all my family, to my husband Tom for his love and support; also the Hunts, for Sue's generosity and John's local knowledge and continual supply of interesting and unusual books. Thanks again to Paul Fairbrass for his photographs and support. Most of all, it is for my mother for her invaluable proofreading skills and for my father for his enthusiasm. This is the result of the books they read me, the museums they took me to as a child and the love and imagination with which they encouraged me.

Also available from Amberley Publishing

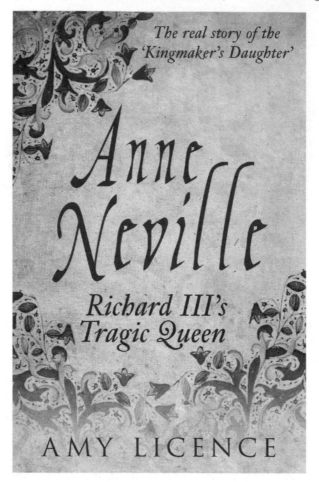

The real story of the 'Kingmaker's Daughter'

Anne Neville

Richard III's Tragic Queen

AMY LICENCE

The real story of the Kingmaker's daughter

Shakespeare's enduring image of Richard III's queen is one of bitterness and sorrow. Anne curses the killer of her husband and father, before succumbing to his marriage proposal, bringing to herself a terrible legacy of grief and suffering an untimely death. Was Anne a passive victim? Did she really jump into bed with the enemy?

This fascinating and elusive woman is shrouded in controversy and unanswered questions. Amy Licence reassesses the long-standing myths about Anne's role, her health and her marriages, to present a new view of the Kingmaker's daughter.

£10.99 Paperback
30 colour illustrations
304 pages
978-1-4456-3312-1

Also available as an ebook
Available from all good bookshops or to order direct
Please call **01453-847-800**
www.amberleybooks.com

Also available from Amberley Publishing

The true story of
the white princess

Elizabeth
of York

Forgotten Tudor
Queen

AMY LICENCE

The true story of the white princess

As Tudors go, Elizabeth of York is relatively unknown. Yet she was the mother of the
dynasty, with her children becoming King of England (Henry VIII) and Queens of
Scotland (Margaret) and France (Mary Rose) and her direct descendants included three
Tudor monarchs, two executed queens and, ultimately, the Stuart royal family.

But was she as placid as history has suggested? In fact, she may have been a deeply cultured
and intelligent survivor who learned to walk a difficult path through the twists and turns of
fortune. Perhaps she was more of a modern woman than historians have given her credit for.

£10.99 Paperback
40 colour illustrations
272 pages
978-1-4456-3314-5

Also available as an ebook
Available from all good bookshops or to order direct
Please call **01453-847-800**
www.amberleybooks.com

Also available from Amberley Publishing

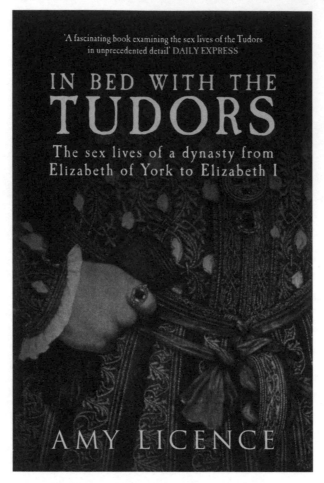

'A fascinating book examining the sex lives of the Tudors in unprecedented detail' DAILY EXPRESS

IN BED WITH THE
TUDORS

The sex lives of a dynasty from
Elizabeth of York to Elizabeth I

AMY LICENCE

Sex and childbirth were quite literally a matter of life or death for the Tudors

'A fascinating book examining the sex lives of the Tudors in unprecedented detail' *THE DAILY EXPRESS*

Amy Licence guides the reader through the births of Henry VII and Elizabeth of York's two sons, Arthur and Henry, Catherine of Aragon's subsequent marriages to both of these men, Henry VIII's other five wives and his mistresses, and the sex lives of his daughters. This book details the experiences of all these women, from fertility, conception and pregnancy through to the delivery chamber, on to maternal and infant mortality. Each woman's story is a blend of specific personal circumstances, set against their historical moment: for some the joys were brief, for others it was a question that ultimately determined their fates.

£9.99 Paperback
35 illustrations
272 pages
978-1-4456-1475-5

Also available as an ebook
Available from all good bookshops or to order direct
Please call **01453-847-800**
www.amberleybooks.com

Also available from Amberley Publishing

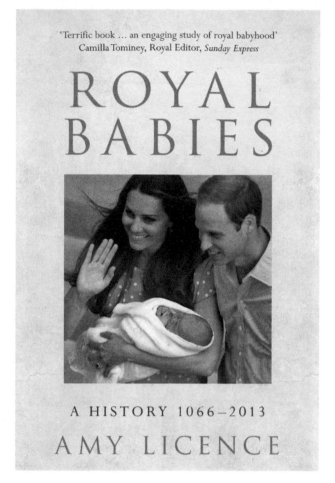

'Terrific book ... an engaging study of royal babyhood'
Camilla Tominey, Royal Editor, *Sunday Express*

ROYAL
BABIES

A HISTORY 1066–2013

AMY LICENCE

*The 25 most important, poignant and downright bizarre royal babies
and births in British history*

Babies are born every day, but only once or twice in a lifetime, a child arrives who will inherit
the throne. This summer, the nation watched as Catherine, Duchess of Cambridge, delivered our
future king. There have been predictions, expectations and a flurry of media attention around
the new parents but apart from the flashing cameras and internet headlines, this is nothing
new. Royal babies have excited interest before their births, for more than a millennium.

£16.99 Hardback
25 illustrations
192 pages
978-1-4456-1762-6

Also available as an ebook
Available from all good bookshops or to order direct
Please call **01453-847-800**
www.amberleybooks.com

Also available from Amberley Publishing

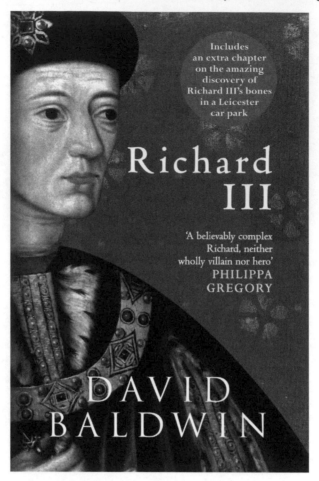

Includes an extra chapter on the amazing discovery of Richard III's bones in a Leicester car park

'A believably complex Richard, neither wholly villain nor hero' PHILIPPA GREGORY

'David Baldwin correctly theorised the final resting place of Richard... 27 years ago' *LEICESTER MERCURY*

Some would argue that a true biography is impossible because the letters and other personal documents required for this purpose are simply not available; but David Baldwin has overcome this by an in-depth study of his dealings with his contemporaries. The fundamental question he has answered is 'what was Richard III *really* like'.

£9.99 Paperback
80 illustrations (60 colour)
296 pages
978-1-4456-1591-2

Also available as an ebook
Available from all good bookshops or to order direct
Please call **01453-847-800**
www.amberleybooks.com

Also available from Amberley Publishing

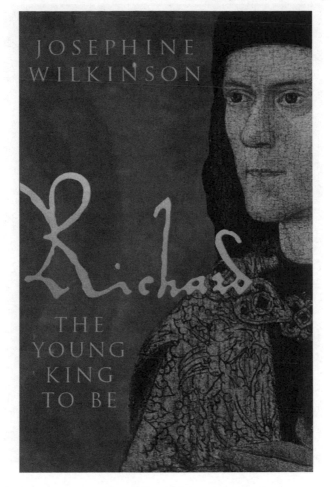

A major new biography of the young Richard III

Richard III is a paradox – the most hated of English kings, yet the most beloved, a deeply pious man, yet materialistic to the point of obsession, puritan, yet the father of at least two illegitimate children. This new biography concentrates on the much neglected early part of Richard's life – from his birth in 1452 as a cadet of the House of York to his marriage to the beautiful Anne Neville – and shows how his experiences as the son of an ambitious duke, a prisoner of war, an exile, his knightly training and awe of his elder brother, King Edward IV, shaped the character of England's most controversial monarch.

£9.99 Paperback
40 illustrations (25 colour)
352 pages
978-1-84868-513-0

Also available as an ebook
Available from all good bookshops or to order direct
Please call **01453-847-800**
www.amberleybooks.com

Also available from Amberley Publishing

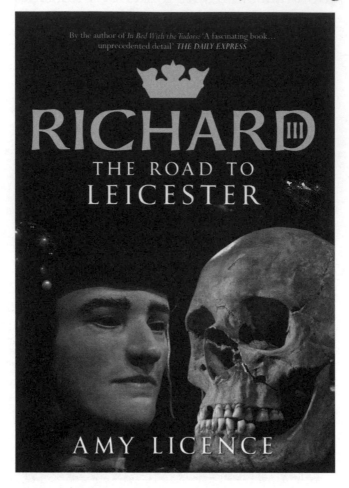

By the author of *In Bed With the Tudors:* 'A fascinating book...
unprecedented detail' THE DAILY EXPRESS

RICHARD III
THE ROAD TO LEICESTER

AMY LICENCE

Following the dramatic announcement that Richard III's body had been discovered, past controversies have been matched by fresh disputes. Why is Richard III England's most controversial king? The question of his reburial has provoked national debate and protest, taking levels of interest in the medieval king to an unprecedented level. While Richard's life remains able to polarise opinion, the truth probably lies somewhere between the maligned saint and the evil hunchback stereotypes. Why did he seize the throne? Did he murder the Princes in the Tower? Why have the location and details of his reburial sparked a parliamentary debate? This book will act as both an introduction to his life and reign and a commemoration to tie in with his reburial.

£9.99 Paperback
75 illustrations
96 pages
978-1-4456-2175-3

Also available as an ebook
Available from all good bookshops or to order direct
Please call **01453-847-800**
www.amberleybooks.com

Index

Agincourt, Battle of 18–19
Anne of York, Countess of Exeter
  birth 67, childhood 74, death
  184, 214, marriage 87, pregnancy
  111, 112, 119, 141, remarriage
  183, sister of the king 154
Anne of York, Duchess of Norfolk
  210, 215

Barnet, Battle of 176–7
Baynard's Castle 20, 112, 138,
  140, 141, 147, 152, 164, 174,
  176, 194, 197
Beauchamp, Richard, Earl of
  Warwick 46, 48, 57, 63, 67
Beaufort, Edmund, 2nd Duke of
  Somerset 88, 90, 93, 95, 96, 97,
  98, 106, 107, 112, 113–14, 115,
  116, 117
Beaufort, Edmund, 4th Duke of
  Somerset 177
Beaufort, Henry, 3rd Duke of
  Somerset 120, 122, 127, 141,
  142, 148, 153, 155
Beaufort, Joan, Countess of
  Westmorland 29, 30, 31–2, 43–

4, 45, 52, 59, 66, 68, 87, 200
Beaufort, Joan, Queen of Scots 35
Beaufort, Margaret 124, 155,
  166, 209
Beaufort, Thomas, Duke of Exeter
  45
Berkhamsted Castle 169, 170, 201
Bohun, Joan de 39
Bona of Savoy 156–7
Bourchier, Thomas, Archbishop of
  Canterbury 113, 117, 138
Bridget of York 189, 209, 216
Butler, Eleanor, also Talbot 161

Cade, Jack 93
Caister Castle 122–4
Catherine of York 189, 210, 216
Cecily of York 205, 215
Charles VI of France 17, 44–5
Charles VII of France 82, 83
Charles the Bold 168
Clifford, Lord 143, 148
Cobham, Eleanor 74–5
Colyngbourne, William 199–200

Dublin 92

Edgecote Moor, Battle of 167
Edmund of Langley 37, 58
Edmund, Earl of Rutland baptism 78, 81, 82, birth 81, childhood 89, 107–8, 110, claim to the throne 139, 140, 141, in exile 132, reinterred 184, remembered 150, 154, youth 126, 127, death 143, 148
Edward III 17, 21, 29, 37
Edward, Earl of March, later Edward IV appearance 80, 146, 156, in battle 134–5, 146, baptism 78, becomes king 147–8, 150, betrothals 82–3, 156, birth 74, 77–8, 81, childhood 89, 99, 107–8, 110, claim to the throne 139, 140, 141, 147, 149, coronation 150–2, court 180–1, death 79, 192, deposed 173, 175, as Earl of March 106, 126, 127, 137, father's reinterment 184, and George 172–5, 186–9, honours father 150, 154, invasion of 1460 133, 134, 135, paternity of 77–81, 82, 149, 159–61, 173, 187, 195, precontract 161, 188, 194, 195–6, return from exile 176, 177, war with France 183, wedding 157–158, will 194
Edward, Earl of Warwick 183, 207, 217
Edward V 110, 175, 188, 192, 193, 196, 197
Edward of Middleham 183, 198
Edward of Norwich, 2nd Duke of York 23–4, 38, 39
Edward of Westminster, Prince of Wales 105, 107, 113, 119, 139, 142, 149, 175, 176, 177, 179
Elizabeth of York, Duchess of Suffolk birth 81, childhood 110, children 168, 183, marriage 124, 141, sister of the king 165, 166, 190, recipient of bequest 210
Elizabeth of York, Queen 66, 167, 183, 200, 205, 208, 209, 214
Empingham, Battle of (Losecoat) 174

Fastolf, Sir John 44, 60, 61, 89, 97, 100, 119, 122–4, 136, 151–2
Fotheringhay Castle 58, 169, 170

Gaunt, John of 20, 29, 68, 87, 200
George, Duke of Clarence attainted 186, birth 92, brother to the king 151, 153–4, 164, 165, 171, 174, 177, childhood 110, 126, 132, 136 141, 145, children 183, claim to throne 160, 171, death 188–9, father's reinterment 184, marriage 171–2, 173, opposes Richard's marriage 180, rebellion 172–4, 175, 186–9, widowed 185
Greenwich Palace 163–4
Grey, John 166–7
Grey, Richard 193, 196
Grey, Thomas 164, 214

Harrington, William, Lord 143
Hastings, William Lord 177, 192, 193, 194

Henry IV 17, 29

Henry V 17–19, 22–24, 41, 55, 60, 63

Henry VI 35, 44–5, 47, 52, 53, 55, 63, 69, 83, 88, 94, 95–96, 98, 105–6, 107, 112, 115, 118, 119, 120, 137, 138–9, 146, 149, 154, 155, 164, 175, 177, 208

Holland, Lady Anne 119, 164

Holland, Henry, Duke of Exeter 87–8, 111, 113, 115, 119, 122, 125, 133, 176, 183

Humphrey, Duke of Gloucester 45, 53, 74, 75, 86–7, 163

James I of Scotland 35, 39, 55

James II of Scotland 120

James III of Scotland 155

Jaquetta of Luxembourg, later Baroness Rivers 60, 61, 73–4, 77, 81, 133, 147, 157–8, 167, 180

Jeanne d'Arc 55

Joan of Navarre 63

Kemp, Margery 29–30

Lancaster, John of, Duke of Bedford 33, 45, 59, 60, 61, 74, 88

Lionel of Antwerp, Duke of Clarence 37, 91

Louis XI of France 183

Loveday, the 124–5

Lovell, Francis, Lord 199, 200, 201, 207

Ludford Bridge, battle of 127

Ludlow Castle 89, 110

Margaret of Anjou 52, 83, 88, 101–6, 113, 118, 119, 125, 139, 140, 146–7, 149, 155, 163, 175–6, 177

Margaret of York, Duchess of Burgundy betrothals 168, birth 85–6, childhood 110, 126, 132, 136, 141, 145, marriage 168–9, sister of the king 154, 165, 167, 168, supports rebellions 206–7, 298, visits England 189–90

Mary of York 189

Methley Hall 40

Moleyns, Adam 88, 90, 93

Montagu/Montacute, Alice, Countess of Salisbury 34, 128–9, 141

Mortimer, Anne 38

Mortimer, Edmund, Earl of March 43, 88, 92

Mortimer's Cross, Battle of 146

Mowbray, Anne de 73, 188

Mowbray, John de, Duke of Norfolk 46

Neville family history 27–29, 31

Neville, Anne, Duchess of Buckingham 31, 46, 52, 115, 119, 128, 131, 132, 133, 135, 136, 147, 155, 165

Neville, Anne, Princess of Wales, Duchess of Gloucester, later Queen 141, 166, 175, 176, 177, 179–80, 183, 198, 200, 201

Neville, Cecily appearance 29, 35, 72–3, 185, at Henry VI's court 43–8, 54, baptism 31–2, betrothal 42, birth 27, 30, burial 15, 212, at Caister Castle 122–4, in 'captivity' 131–6, childhood 44, and her children's ambitions 99, 126, 148, 149, 150, 152, 172–173, 175, 186, 191–197, 213, and her children's marriages 82–83, 124, 141, 156–162, 165–166, 169, 172, 172–3, 180, 183, 193, 200, consummation 52–3, death 212, education 33–4, 44, fertility 52–3, 58, 65, friendship with Margaret of Anjou 83, 101–6, 117, 118, 125, 126, household 14, 58–9, 70–1, 81, 88–9, 91, 108–10, 111, 112, 153, 182, 203–5, infancy 32, in Ireland 91–94, library 111, marital homes 56–8, 61, 69, 78, 86, 89, 96, 102, 108, 110, 112, official role 47–9, 62, 71, 73, 83–4, 85, 89, 108–9, 213, opulence 70–3, piety 61, 66, 72, 87, 191, 199, 203–5, 209, pregnancies 61, 65–7, 68–9, 71, 77–8, 81, 85, 87, 90–1, 92, 94, 97, 99–100, 103, 112, 118, pride 72, 148, properties 152, 169, 181, 182, 206, attempts to reconcile sons 174, 185, 186, 188, 189, reputed infidelity 77–81, 82, 159–61, 173, 187, 195, in Rouen 70–84, reunion with husband (1460) 137, 138, sack of Ludlow 127–9, siblings 31, 155–6, status 27, 56, 71–3, 79–80, 83, 85, 100, 107, 108, 118, 120, 128, 139–140, 150–1, 159–61, 165, 167–8, 170–1, 174, 196, 214, wedding 47, as a widow 152, widowed 143, 145, 147, will 13–15, 111, 209–12, and York's reinterment 185

Neville, Edward, Baron Bergavenny 31

Neville, Eleanor, Countess of Northumberland 31, 46, 52, 155, 166

Neville, Elizabeth, Lady Greystoke 30

Neville, George, Archbishop of York 166, 179

Neville, George, Baron Latimer 31

Neville, Isabel, Duchess of Clarence 141, 166, 172, 180, 185

Neville, John, Marquess of Montagu 150, 155, 176, 177

Neville, Katherine, Duchess of Norfolk 31, 44, 46, 47, 52, 166

Neville, Ralph, 1st Earl of Westmorland 29, 31, 33, 41, 43, 52

Neville, Ralph, 2nd Earl of Westmorland 195

Neville, Richard, Earl of Salisbury 34, 44, 46, 48, 60, 90, 95, 107, 111, 113, 114, 117, 125, 126, 127, 134, 136, 140, 141, 142, 146, 177

Neville, Richard, Earl of Warwick 34, 46, 106, 113, 114, 117, 125, 126, 127, 133, 134, 135, 140, 145, 146, 154, 157, 158, 167, 168, 171, 172, 173–4, 175, 176–7

Neville, Robert, Bishop of
  Salisbury 46
Neville, Thomas 142–3
Neville, William, Lord
  Fauconberg 45, 60
Northampton, Battle of 134–5

Oldhall, Sir William 89, 95, 97,
  99, 153

Paston, John 44, 54, 112, 128,
  133, 136, 168, 177, 185
Paston, Margaret 54, 101
Percy, Henry, Earl of
  Northumberland 46, 52, 148,
  153, 155
Pole, de la, Anne 210
Pole, de la, Catherine 216
Pole, de la, Edmund 210, 216
Pole, de la, Humphrey 210, 216
Pole, de la, John, Duke of Suffolk
  124, 141, 154
Pole, de la, John, Earl of Lincoln
  199, 205, 206
Pole, de la, Richard 189
Pole, de la, William, the 'White
  Rose' 210, 216–7
Pole, de la, William, Duke of
  Suffolk 83, 88, 93
Pole, Margaret 183, 188, 217

Raby Castle 25–27, 32, 217
Richard of Consiburgh, 3rd Earl
  of Cambridge 24, 38
Richard II 17, 29, 37, 39
Richard, Duke of Gloucester, later
  Richard III birth 78, 99–100,
  brother to the king 151, 153,
  164, 166, 177, 190, 192,
  childhood 110, 126, 132, 136,

138, 141, 145, coronation 197,
  death 201, father's reinterment
  184, in exile 175, as king
  198–201, marriage 180, 200,
  201, as Protector 193, and his
  son 183, 198
Richard of Shrewsbury, also Duke
  of York 183, 188, 197
Rouen 55, 60–3, 70–1, 78, 93

St Albans, First Battle of (1455)
  115–6
St Albans, Second Battle of (1461)
  146
St Leger, Anne 184, 214
St Leger, Thomas 183, 198
Scales, Lady 147
Scales, Thomas, Lord 135, 136
Simnel, Lambert 206, 207
Southampton Plot 24
Stafford, Henry 2nd Duke of
  Buckingham 193, 194, 198, 200
Stafford, Humphrey, 1st Duke
  of Buckingham 46, 105, 113,
  115, 119, 131, 133, 135
Stafford, Margaret 29
Stillington, Robert, Bishop of
  Bath and Wells 189, 196
Stoke, Battle of 207
Swynford, Katherine 30, 52, 68

Talbot, Eleanor, also Butler 73,
  188, 196
Talbot, John, Earl of Shrewsbury
  73, 84
Tewkesbury, Battle of 177
Towton, Battle of 148–9
Tudor, Arthur, Prince of Wales
  205, 207, 209, 214–5
Tudor, Edmund 55, 106, 112

Tudor, Jasper 55, 68, 96, 106, 112, 140, 146, 207
Tudor, Margaret 208, 215
Tudor, Mary 215
Tudor Henry, later Henry VII 197, 199, 201, 203, 205, 207, 209
Tudor, Henry, later Henry VIII 208, 209, 214
Tudor, Owen 55, 62, 146
Twynho, Ankarette 185

Valois, Catherine, of, Queen 34, 44, 45, 54, 55, 62
Vaughan, Thomas, Sir 193, 196
Vere, Elizabeth de, Countess of Oxford 74, 81, 166, 182
Vere, John de, 12th Earl of Oxford 74, 177, 182
Vere, John de, 13th Earl of Oxford 182, 206, 207

Wakefield, Battle of 141–3
Warbeck, Perkin 208, 209, 217
Waterton, Cicely 40–1
Waterton, Robert 39–40, 43
Wenlock, Lord 157, 177
Wydeville, Anthony, Earl Rivers 74, 110, 133, 168, 169, 192, 193, 196
Wydeville, Edward 190
Wydeville, Elizabeth, Queen 60, 63, 74, 157–9, 161, 165, 167, 169, 171, 175, 180, 183, 188, 189, 193, 194, 198, 205, 208

Wydeville, John 173
Wydeville, Richard, Baron Rivers 61, 73, 133, 153, 157, 169, 173

York, Richard Plantagenet, Duke of 24, accusations of rebellion 90, 94, 96, 97, 99, 103–4, 114, 121–2, 126, 135, acts of defiance 95, 97–9, 115–7, 126–7, 133, 137, aims at throne 138–40, assassination attempts 111, 117, 123, 124, 125, betrothal 42–3, Blackheath rebellion 98–9, childhood 39–41, comes of age 56, consummation 52–3, death 142, descent 37–8, early career 53–4, 55–6, 59, 62, 67, as a father 78–80, 82, 91, in exile 127, 132, knighted 45, Lieutenancy of Ireland 89–94, Lieutenancy of Normandy 67, 68, 70–3, 79, 83, 84, middle years of his career 85, 86, 88–9, 90, 91, 93, 95, properties 39, 56–8, 59, 69, 86, 96, 102, 108, 137, as Protector 106, 107, 112–3, reforms 112, reinterred 184, remembered 150, 154, 155, 181, return from exile 136, second Protectorate 118–20, titles 43, 56, 92, 100, 106, wardship 39, 41, 44, wedding 47, youth at court 43–8